C. S. LEWIS IN CONTEXT

C. S. LEWIS
IN CONTEXT

~

Doris T. Myers

THE KENT STATE UNIVERSITY PRESS

Kent, Ohio, & London, England

© 1994 by The Kent State University Press, Kent, Ohio 44242
ALL RIGHTS RESERVED
Library of Congress Catalog Card Number 94-7537
ISBN 0-87338-497-0
Manufactured in the United States of America

Extracts from C. S. Lewis's letters and his marginalia in *The Control of Language*
are reproduced by permission of Curtis Brown, London, and
The Marion E. Wade Center, Wheaton College.

Library of Congress Cataloging-in-Publication Data
Myers, Doris T.
    C. S. Lewis in context / Doris T. Myers.
        p.   cm.
    Includes bibliographical references and index.
    ISBN 0-87338-497-0 (cloth : alk. paper) ∞
    1. Lewis, C. S. (Clive Staples), 1898–1963—Criticism and
interpretation.   I. Title.
PR6023.E926Z798 1994
823'.912—dc90   94-7537
                                                                CIP

British Library Cataloging-in-Publication data are available.

CONTENTS

PREFACE ix

ACKNOWLEDGMENTS XV

1. THE CONTEXT OF METAPHOR 1

The Meaning of Meaning and *Poetic Diction* 4
Two Kinds of Metaphor in *The Pilgrim's Regress* 11

2. THE CONTEXT OF LITERARY CRITICISM AND GENRE 27

Out of the Silent Planet 39   *Perelandra* 56

3. THE CONTEXT OF LANGUAGE CONTROL 72

The Control of Language and *The Abolition of Man* 73
That Hideous Strength 84

4. THE CONTEXT OF CHRISTIAN HUMANISM 112

Abolishing the Controllers: The First Three Chronicles 126
Language North and South: The Middle Chronicles 148
Mutability: The Last Two Chronicles 165

5. THE CONTEXT OF MYTH AND HISTORY 182

Till We Have Faces 190

POSTSCRIPT 214

NOTES 218

WORKS CITED 231

INDEX 239

PREFACE

IN TEACHING and writing about medieval and renaissance literature, C. S. Lewis was concerned with reviving the works for modern readers by placing them in the context of their time. He made the works accessible by reconstructing the scientific knowledge, the word meanings, and the unspoken assumptions of these previous eras. In the process, he often pointed out that the early twentieth century would in turn become a "period" like all others. What Lewis foresaw has now happened. Much of what he took for granted has become quaint, old-fashioned, even alien to present-day readers. Many previous critics have discussed his work as an expression of relatively timeless Christian doctrine; others have discussed it as timeless mythmaking. But if Lewis is to speak to the twenty-first century, if the scope of his literary achievement is to be understood, it is time to examine his fiction in the context of its period, to state explicitly what early critics such as R. J. Reilly and Chad Walsh understood implicitly.

Even during his lifetime, his work was the subject of master's and doctoral theses, and since his death in 1963 there has been a flood of articles and books on Lewis. But for most of the earliest critics, the interest was primarily in his defense of Christianity. His religious essays such as *Mere Christianity* were valued more than his fiction, and his fiction was valued more as Christian instruction than as literary art. Also, many of the earliest studies were "more hagiography than scholarship, more paraphrase than analysis" (Edwards 3). Such studies appealed primarily to people interested in Christianity and confirmed the impression of the mainstream literary critics that Lewis was "not literature" and not worthy of serious consideration.

Nevertheless, against all rules that nobody in court should be more than fourteen feet high, interest in Lewis continued to grow. His fiction was called "mythopoeic," and the concepts of archetypal criticism applied to it. Studies of his romanticism and Platonism, more scholarly than hagiographic, began to appear. Finally, the publication of Joe R. Christopher's study of Lewis in Twayne's English Author Series in 1987 seemed to confirm that Lewis belonged in the canon of English authors. Until very recently, however, Lewis's literary reputation was purely an American phenomenon; British literary scholars responded to the enthusiasm of their overseas counterparts with well-bred indifference. John D. Haigh's University of Leeds dissertation in 1962 was careful and perceptive, but it did not set a trend for increased study of Lewis in Great Britain.

Besides the concentration on the Christian and mythopoeic elements in his fiction, another barrier to the serious literary consideration of it has been the interest in Lewis as a person. His theological works were written in an easy conversational tone, so that readers came away from them feeling that they knew him as a friend. His autobiography, *Surprised by Joy,* fostered this feeling. So did his unauthorial willingness to answer letters. The personal interest was nourished by the publication, after his death, of letters selected by his brother, the Green and Hooper biography, and several collections of reminiscences such as Keefe's *C. S. Lewis: Speaker and Teacher.* Recently there has been another cycle of biographies; less hagiographic than the earlier publications, their facts and speculations about Lewis's weaknesses, especially sexual ones, again threaten to overpower interest in his art.

The purpose of this book is to redirect attention to Lewis's fiction as art worthy of serious study. I am less interested in Lewis the *person,* the tobacco-addicted Oxford don, than in the *persona* of Lewis that emerges from his fiction. To follow him as he struggles with the intellectual and moral problems of the early twentieth century is a joy and an awakening.

Lewis lived in a difficult time. He belonged to the generation described by Vera Brittain in *England's Hour:*

> Never, perhaps, has an English generation suffered so much as the one that was born in the closing years of the nineteenth century—a century which, in the unparalleled speed of its material achievements, had lost the spiritual resilience which alone can rescue the race of man from its tendency to self-destruction. (126)

Born in 1898, Lewis served in the First World War and was wounded at the front. He suffered from the postwar malaise. Then came the Second

World War. Lewis lived through the anxieties of the Battle of Britain, when England stood alone against Nazi Germany and it seemed that civilization would be destroyed. Although too old for military duty, he served in the Home Guard, delivered sermons and addresses, and endured the wartime threat of hunger. Where Vera Brittain hoped that a new civilization would arise, one which would make it "expedient that one generation should suffer for posterity" (126), Lewis hoped to preserve the ancient verities of classicism and traditional Christianity.

With all his traditionalism, Lewis was very much a child of his own time. Indeed, the portrait of Lewis as a dinosaur, a surviving specimen, has been much exaggerated. Part of the misconception is due to Lewis's Cambridge Inaugural Address, *"De Descriptione Temporum,"* in which he dramatized his devotion to earlier cultures—a right and proper devotion, since he was accepting a chair in medieval and renaissance literature—by calling himself "Old Western Man." Part is due to John Wain's characterization: "Lewis grew up in the Edwardian age, and his chief allegiances were to that age." Wain adds that Lewis was fighting "a perpetual rearguard action in defense of an army that had long since marched away" (Como 71, 73).

When one examines Lewis's encounter with the language issues of the early twentieth century, Wain's characterization seems eminently unfair. The period between the two world wars was marked by a growing distrust of language, an awareness that language can be used to manipulate behavior in unfair ways, and, on the positive side, a growing subtlety and boldness in the analysis of language. Michael Bell, in his Introduction to *The Context of English Literature: 1900–1930* (1980), makes the following generalization: in the eighteenth century, the machine was the model of the universe; in the nineteenth century, it was organic evolution, and thinkers in every field tried to understand their subject in terms of developmental processes; in the twentieth century, language itself has become the model of the universe (52).

Thus the context I seek to establish is not the private context of Lewis's personal habits or relationships, but the public context of language. The twentieth-century preoccupation with language affected Lewis particularly in the areas of philosophy and literary criticism. At both Oxford and Cambridge, the new philosophers were saying that the primary—perhaps only—duty of philosophy was to determine whether meaningful statements were being made in other branches of learning. Especially at

Cambridge, the new literary critics sought to replace impressionistic, gentlemanly appreciations of literary works with conclusions arrived at by "objective," quasi-scientific methods.

In redirecting attention to Lewis's art of fiction, then, it is necessary to locate his works in the context of early twentieth-century language controversies. Each chapter thus consists of an introductory section discussing an issue related to language and a main section examining one or more works of Lewis in relation to that issue. Chapter 1 introduces the overall problem. After a brief survey of the effect of World War I on the perception of language as an instrument of social control, I compare Ogden and Richards's *The Meaning of Meaning*, a fairly accessible statement of an early attempt to desacralize language, to Owen Barfield's *Poetic Diction*, a brilliant reworking of a largely Platonic view of language, and focus on the handling of metaphor in these contrasting works. Then I analyze Lewis's *Pilgrim's Regress* as both a description of the time between the wars and an artistic structure built on two kinds of metaphor.

Chapter 2 deals with matters of literary criticism and genre. In a contrast between I. A. Richards's *Principles of Literary Criticism* and Lewis's *An Experiment in Criticism*, I discuss how the new philosophy of language was related to the separation of readers into highbrows and lowbrows. I suggest that in writing science fiction Lewis was contributing to the later-twentieth-century acceptance of the genre by serious novelists. A comparison of *Out of the Silent Planet* with its literary prototype, H. G. Wells's *First Men in the Moon*, and of *Perelandra* with *The Time Machine* shows that Lewis both contributed to the development of the genre and refuted what he regarded as misconceptions arising from a low view of the nature of language.

Chapter 3 deals with *That Hideous Strength* in relation to the common fears of early-twentieth-century people that their freedom was being curtailed by language manipulators. I begin with an analysis of Lewis's attack on "the Green Book," as he called *The Control of Language* by King and Ketley, in *The Abolition of Man*. This analysis leads to an understanding that the nature and use of language is a major theme of the novel.

Chapter 4 deals with the Chronicles of Narnia, in my opinion Lewis's best work. Although the Chronicles have sometimes been read as sugar-coated Christian doctrine, their admitted didacticism is not intended as a presentation of cognitive concepts, but rather as a modeling of moral and emotional attitudes. In *The Abolition of Man*, Lewis asserted the importance of training the emotions to make proper moral responses, a kind of education which, despite I. A. Richards's concept of the "adjustment of attitudes" as the major function of literature, was undermined by the new linguistic philosophy. Lewis believed that Spenser's *Faerie Queene* provided such emotional training, so that the Chronicles of Narnia may be best understood as a miniature *Faerie Queene.* The Chronicles can be divided into three groups. The first three—*The Lion, the Witch, and the Wardrobe, Prince Caspian,* and *The Voyage of the Dawn Treader*— deal with the role of Joy in sanctification and the achievement of a balanced way of life. They are less directly related to language issues, but very much related to the strengthening of the Chest discussed in *The Abolition of Man.* The second group, *The Silver Chair* and *The Horse and His Boy,* present Narnia as a place where language is used properly, as opposed to the erroneous language attitudes of the North and South. *The Silver Chair* refutes the new linguistic philosophy, and *The Horse and His Boy* shows how moral character is related to rhetorical practice. The last two stories, *The Magician's Nephew* and *The Last Battle,* together provide a survey of England's struggles in the early twentieth century, from pre–World War I innocence to post–World War II devastation.

Chapter 5 argues that Lewis's last great work, *Till We Have Faces,* represents a departure from the science fiction/fantasy mode into a more realistic kind of fiction. In it Lewis explores the process by which the real experiences of Orual and Istra become the myth of Cupid and Psyche. In doing so he exposes the weaknesses of the empiricism on which the new linguistic philosophy is based and makes an oblique criticism of "the quest for the historical Jesus." When read without archetypal or Christian preconceptions, the book emerges as a stylistic tour de force.

In each chapter, the contextual study with which I begin may be more meaningful after the reader has become familiar with the criticism that emerges from the context. As a person who normally skips from the beginning to the ending of a novel before filling in the middle, I have tried to make this book amenable to skip-reading.

Some explanation of the limitations of the present study seem in order. It does not survey the rise of linguistic philosophy; indeed, it deals with this philosophy only in the semipopular work of Ogden and Richards. It does not trace the later development of Richards's thought. It does not survey the rise of New Criticism, but instead takes Richards as representative of the movement. In treating Lewis's fiction, *The Screwtape Letters* and *The Great Divorce* are omitted; they seem more concerned with right actions than with right thinking, and more concerned with right thinking than its basis in the philosophy of language. For the same reason, I have largely omitted references to his works on Christian doctrine. I have also concentrated on major works published in Lewis's lifetime, although I have occasionally referred to minor works. Without these limitations, the work could not have been completed at all.

In this contextual study I hope to switch the focus from whether one agrees with Lewis's Christianity or is attracted to his mythopoeia and to divert attention from his personal life. It is literary craftsmanship, after all, that will ensure for Lewis a permanent place in the canon. If his books are to continue to be read, they must continue to give pleasure. If this contextual study helps us to recover an appreciation of his craftsmanship and a response to the resonances of his style, it is worth doing.

ACKNOWLEDGMENTS

THIS BOOK began in 1987 with presentations on the Chronicles of Narnia prepared for the annual Valyermo retreat sponsored by the Southern California C. S. Lewis Society. I am grateful for the criticisms and responses I received from the participants at that time. The research and writing of chapters 1 and 5 were done during a sabbatical leave from the University of Northern Colorado. Kathy Earle and Lucy Schweers of UNC's Michener Library were especially helpful. I am also grateful for a University of Northern Colorado faculty research grant to support my explorations in the Marion E. Wade Center of Wheaton College and for the patient and sensible help I received from the librarians there.

I am grateful to the executors of the estate of C. S. Lewis for permission to quote from unpublished materials of Lewis and to the Marion E. Wade Center for permission to publish the quotations.

Paul A. Olson of the University of Nebraska-Lincoln read the whole manuscript, made useful suggestions, and gave generous encouragement. Robert E. Longacre, University of Texas at Arlington, and Msgr. Robert Trupia, then at Catholic University, read and commented on chapter 5. Professor Longacre called my attention to Wilbur Urban and the high and low views of language when I was seeking an Ariadne's clue for my subject. Dorothy Koone read and commented on chapter 1. The two readers for the Kent State University Press made extensive, insightful comments and suggestions. My husband, Thomas M. Myers, read the whole manuscript at least four times, helped me with documents in Latin and German, helped with proofreading and final checkings, located misplaced notes, and encouraged me with lavish praise. I am also grateful for the personal guidance and encouragement of Bill C. Grissom.

As for the errors and shortsightednesses, I can only say with Chaucer that I hope my readers will "arrette it to the defaute of myn unkonnynge and nat to my wyl, that wolde ful fayne have seyd bettre if I hadde had konnynge."

· 1 ·

THE CONTEXT OF METAPHOR

A S PHILOSOPHER Wilbur M. Urban has pointed out, each turning point in Occidental history has been marked by intense concern about the nature of language. Every time such a period occurs, there are what he calls high and low evaluations of language. The high evaluation involves a belief in the reality of universals and connects the word closely with the thing it designates. It identifies reason with the Word, the Logos, and is therefore closely connected with the Greek-Christian tradition. The low evaluation involves some form of nominalism and detaches the word from the thing. It is the characteristic underlying assumption of all periods of empiricism, and Urban calls it the "beginning of skepticism" (21–24).[1] The period after World War I was just such a turning point in human history, and the old battle between the high and low evaluations of language was fought out anew, with new justifications, new combatants, and new applications of abstract theory to real-life issues.

C. S. Lewis was involved in this struggle. In the process of reaching an informed, intellectually based decision to embrace Christianity, he had to decide how to evaluate language. One common criticism of Lewis is that he dealt with the struggles of the twentieth century by ignoring them,[2] but this observation is at best only half true. Once Lewis had made up his mind that many modern assumptions, especially those about language, were wrong, he naturally did not promote them; nevertheless, all his fiction is influenced by, and responds to, twentieth-century issues, especially language issues. Lewis's first work of fiction, *The Pilgrim's Regress*, was, among other things, a response to the modern controversy over the nature of language.

Any discussion of this controversy must of necessity be sketchy and tentative, for there are simply too many subtleties, too many unknowns, too many complex relationships for definitive treatment. Even a limited discussion, however, can provide new insight into *The Pilgrim's Regress,* and indeed all of Lewis's fiction.

Certainly the postwar period was very much dominated by the low evaluation of language, both in intellectual and practical realms. In the intellectual realm it is easy to point to the twentieth-century fruition of nineteenth-century Darwinian naturalism; to the development of twentieth-century linguistics (much influenced by behaviorism) from nineteenth-century philology; to Bertrand Russell's logical atomism, which contributed to twentieth-century logical positivism, and Ludwig Wittgenstein's *Tractatus Logico-Philosophicus* (1918), which led to the whole movement known as linguistic philosophy with its credo "All philosophy is a critique of language."[3] But intellectual movements such as these do not have much effect on literature, or life in general, unless they answer some deeply felt, nonintellectual need.

In postwar society at large this need was reflected in a widespread conviction that people had been duped by language into sacrificing themselves and their well-being in the war. There is no doubt that World War I caused people to look at language in a new way. More than at any previous time in history, World War I was fought with language as well as weaponry. Although the propaganda methods were unsophisticated compared with those used in World War II, the communications media were more pervasive and invasive than they had been in previous wars. There was no radio or television, but the available media—newspapers, posters, books, pamphlets, pictures, maps, songs, and lantern slides (Roetter 33–34; John Williams 26)—were used to the fullest. Horatio Bottomley's weekly newspaper, *John Bull,* was especially effective among the working and lower-middle classes, and citizens on all levels were perhaps more dependent on public information than in previous times. Furthermore, the military need for propaganda, for the mobilization of public opinion, was greater than it had ever been before. Young men had to be persuaded to volunteer for military service, since there was no universal conscription until 1916. Civilians had to be persuaded to replace the fighters in factories and fields, to control their consumption of alcohol, to eat less bread. Young women were urged to promote the war effort by refusing to go out with able-bodied men in civilian dress (John Williams 190, 62–63, 55).

From a post-Vietnam perspective, the wartime idealism and excitement seem almost unimaginable. Religious as well as social sanctions were invoked. When Prime Minister Asquith said "The conflict . . . is not merely a material but a spiritual one," the Church of England backed him up (John Williams 26, 17). H. G. Wells idealistically called the conflict "the war to end war" and became excited enough to lay aside his agnosticism; his *Mr. Britling Sees It Through* was his first (and last) book espousing belief in God. The newspapers whipped up the excitement generated in other quarters. Unreliable as a source of hard news, these papers circulated wild rumors that promoted false optimism and glamorized the fighting (John Williams 127). England was drunk on words, set up for the postwar hangover. C. E. Montague's postwar book, significantly entitled *Disenchantment,* expressed the prevailing mood of the morning after: "The only new thing about deception in war is modern man's more perfect means for its practice."[4] Lewis's often-noted refusal to read newspapers suggests that he shared the postwar disillusionment with language that replaced public idealism and excitement.

Literary language also played a part in leading young men to their deaths. Paul Fussell, in *The Great War and Modern Memory,* demonstrates that the language of the trenches was literary. He notes that World War I occurred at a time when "two 'liberal' forces were powerfully coinciding in England"—the first a conviction of the value of classical and English literature, and the second a rage for popular education and self-improvement (157). Young men were asked to suffer death (poetically called "sacrifice") according to the rhetoric of boys' books, male romances, and pseudo-medieval fiction. Fussell mentions especially George Alfred Henty, Rider Haggard, the poems of Robert Bridges, and Tennyson's *Idylls of the King* (21). Almost every literate man had read William Morris's *The Well at the World's End*—C. S. Lewis was reading it in 1917 just before he went into the army—and saw Mametz Wood, Trones Wood, and High Wood in terms of Morris's Wood Debateable and Wood Perilous (Fussell 135–37).

After the war, many of the survivors concluded that they had been betrayed by noble language. A quotation from Horace, "Dulce et decorum est pro patria mori" (It is sweet and fitting to die for the fatherland), was a focus for their disillusionment. Wilfred Owen's "Dulce et Decorum Est," though written during the war, is the most famous expression of the betrayal. Owen counters the civilian view of the glory of warfare with images of muddy trenches, artillery fire, and poison gas, telling the noncombatant that if he could see the reality of a man drowning in poison gas,

My friend, you would not tell with such high zest
To children ardent for some desperate glory,
The old Lie: Dulce et decorum est
Pro patria mori. (ll. 25–28).

Ezra Pound scathingly quotes the same sentence in "Hugh Selwyn Mauberley":

Died some, pro patria,
                non "dulce" non "et decor" . . .
walked eye-deep in hell
believing in old men's lies, then unbelieving
came home, home to a lie. (Espey 121)

The postwar disillusionment with the traditional language of glory and valor gave strength to the low views of language which would have developed in any case as a response to the intellectual movements of the nineteenth century. The war simply made it more urgent to reevaluate the nature of language, to find out what had made "the old Lie" look so plausible.

The Meaning of Meaning and Poetic Diction

One of the most influential studies of language in this direction was *The Meaning of Meaning* (1923) by C. K. Ogden and I. A. Richards. Like Owen and Pound, Ogden and Richards see World War I as an extreme example of the tyranny of language and concern themselves with building a theory of language that will get rid of traditional philosophic and religious assumptions about it. They hold to a low evaluation of language. For students of C. S. Lewis, *The Meaning of Meaning* is usefully considered in conjunction with Owen Barfield's *Poetic Diction* (1926), which espouses a high evaluation of language. As Barfield explains in the preface to the second edition (1952), he did not originally intend his book to be an answer to Ogden and Richards (15). Nevertheless, the contrast between the two books provides an insight into the intellectual context of Lewis's fiction, for in it Lewis defends a view similar to Barfield's and reacts against the view of Ogden and Richards.[5]

Like others who hold to a low evaluation of language, Ogden and Richards believe that mankind has always been hampered by language superstition, which they define as the erroneous view "that words... always imply things corresponding to them" (31). The seemingly sophisticated philosophy of the ancient Greeks is based on their misconception that language has some necessary relationship to the structure of reality. Out of this misconception they created "the World of Being, in which bogus entities reside" (32). Although language superstition has always been a problem, twentieth-century advances in the technology of communication have made it more dangerous by disseminating more linguistic confusion (29).

In order to combat language superstition and get rid of the bogus entities, Ogden and Richards formulate a theory of meaning in terms of Watson's behaviorism (Wolf 86–87). An external object causes a sensation—the modification of a sense organ; repeated encounters with the object will produce similar sensations, and gradually the connection between "symbol" (word) and "referent" (object) will be established by a process similar to the one by which the dinner bell came to have meaning for Pavlov's dogs (Ogden and Richards 53, 56–57).[6] This behaviorist formulation eliminates "the primitive idea that Words and Things are related by some magic bond" (47), which leads to the use of symbols that have no referent. The empty use of language leads to the creation of bogus entities and what Ogden and Richards refer to as psittacism (the parrot disease), the inability to free oneself from catchphrases (217–18).

Their theory of metaphor is an extension of this behaviorist formulation. They assert that a metaphor arises when a speaker abstracts similarities between something physical and some other thing. An alternate definition is that metaphor occurs when the properties of a referent within one universe of discourse are applied to another universe of discourse.[7] Both of these definitions imply that metaphor is an especially complex kind of abstraction. Indeed, Ogden and Richards state that educated people use metaphor easily while "very simple folk" have small vocabularies based on concrete experience and do not use metaphors (213–14).[8] In a chapter entitled "The Canons of Symbolism" they set up rules for classifying referents and making sure that each symbol stands for only one referent. Since metaphor by definition refers to more than one thing, it belongs only to poetic, emotional, and nonreferential discourse.

This description of how language is or should be used seems counter-intuitive, but with it Ogden and Richards propose to exhibit the sources of linguistic confusion and free mankind from language-based irrationality. They do not explicitly state that their method will replace religion, but they do occasionally use salvation rhetoric, as in the assertion that their approach will "free" us from metaphysicians and bishops and "restore our faith" in physicists (83–84).

Busy with the studies that won honors degrees in philosophy, classics, and English, Lewis may not have read *The Meaning of Meaning* at the time of its first publication in 1923. Indeed, his postwar disillusionment was declining by then. As he recalls in *Surprised by Joy*, when he returned to Oxford in 1919 he worked to become "a realist," assuming what he calls his "New Look." His realism was chiefly characterized by the determination "never . . . to be taken in again" (204). It probably did not involve an explicit abandonment of the high evaluation of language inherent in his classical education; indeed, Ogden and Richards would have regarded his Hegelianism as riddled with bogus entities. Lewis's shaky hold on his New Look was threatened when Owen Barfield, his closest friend, became involved in Rudolf Steiner's anthroposophy. As Lewis remarks in *Surprised by Joy*, "here [in anthroposophy] was everything which the New Look had been designed to exclude" (206). He and Barfield began to engage in an "incessant discussion" of philosophy, "sometimes by letter and sometimes face to face," which they called "the Great War" (207). Lionel Adey, who has examined the surviving documents of "the Great War" in detail, says that Lewis especially objected to the idea that truth could be grasped by the imagination, to the blurring of the distinction between the real and the imagined, and to Steiner's system of exercises for training one's intuition (Adey 30–31, 51).

Although Lewis could never follow Barfield into anthroposophy, "the Great War" was influential in forcing him to "take that look off [his] face" (*Surprised by Joy* 217)—that is, to give up his hard-edged realism. The chronology suggests the extent of the influence. According to Adey, Barfield first became interested in Rudolf Steiner and anthroposophy in 1923 (12–13); meanwhile, Lewis's temporary appointment as a philosophy tutor in 1923–24 forced him to reevaluate his "watered Hegelianism" for tutorial purposes (*Surprised by Joy* 222). Barfield began drafting *Poetic Diction* in 1924–25, and the bulk of the "Great War" letters were written in 1925–27 (Adey 12–13). As can be seen in his mature writings, Lewis ultimately adopted most of Barfield's theory of language while rejecting its basis in anthroposophy. In *Surprised by Joy* he says, "Much of the thought which he [Barfield] put into *Poetic Diction* had already become mine before that important little book appeared" (200).

Barfield's whole theory of language is opposed to that of Ogden and Richards.[9] Instead of viewing the human being as a passive recipient of sensory stimuli, he sees the mind as an active participant in the very nature of the universe. And instead of regarding metaphor as an abstraction, something added on to more precise, more basic expressions, he regards it as the source of both language and knowledge.

As an anthroposophist, Barfield believes that there is a cosmic Intelligence which is gradually becoming visibly incarnate in human intelligence. A person who is thinking is participating in this cosmic Intelligence. Raw sensory data do not constitute knowledge, or even mental activity; "the pure sense-datum" (48) is merely the *percept,* meaningless in itself. In order for cognition to occur, the percept must be synthesized with the *concept,* which Barfield defines as "what I bring to the sense-datum from within" (55). The act of cognition, the synthesis of percept and concept, "creates" the world we experience. His formulation is, of course, reminiscent of Coleridge's primary and secondary imagination, Shelley's understanding of metaphor, the philosophy of the American Transcendentalists, and ultimately Plato.

It is not surprising, then, that instead of beginning with behaviorism or any other psychology, he begins with six texts which exemplify poetic language. His first example, a description of a steamship in Pidgin English, is used to show the relationship between language and knowledge: "Thlee-piecee bamboo, two piecee puff-puff, walk-along inside, no-can-see" (43). For the South Sea Islander, who speaks pidgin, the words are not poetic. They simply express his concept of the steamship in the words available to him. But for the Englishman, who holds a different concept of the steamship, these words act as poetry. By experiencing the Islander's concept as expressed in pidgin, the Englishman sees the steamship "in a new and strange light" and broadens his understanding (48–49). The words bring him to a new state of awareness, give him a "felt change of consciousness" (52). Poetic pleasure arises from this knowledge that one is moving from a previous state of awareness to a new, expanded awareness. Although the pleasure is momentary, the knowledge of the new concept that came through pleasure is permanent (57).

This opening example of *Poetic Diction* implies an evaluation of language that is very high indeed. For Barfield, language is not just the symbolization of referents, but a source of knowledge in itself. He believes that concepts are inseparable from the language in which they are expressed, so that the Englishman who has added the pidgin description of the steamship to his linguistic repertoire has added to his inventory of knowledge. Barfield sees a variety of verbal expressions—synonyms and stylistic flourishes—as eminently valuable because each one provides a different perspective to the referent. (His first book, *History in English Words*, is a fascinating exploration of this view.) Whereas Barfield seeks the enlargement of language, Ogden and Richards seek to control it and narrow its scope. For example, on the basis of the theory of definition set forth in *The Meaning of Meaning*, Ogden reduced the vocabulary of Basic English to a mere 850–1000 words, a number he deemed sufficient to symbolize most referents.[10] In the second edition of *Poetic Diction* (1952), Barfield explicitly criticizes the Ogden-Richards theory, arguing that the distinction between emotive and referential language is fallacious because the very nature of language is metaphorical.

Barfield's position may be stated in this way: in order to know something, a person must recognize it, and to recognize it, he must be able to relate it to other things. Such relationships are concepts, and concepts must be expressed as resemblances and analogies—metaphors. Since Barfield defines knowledge as "the ability to recognize significant resemblances and analogies" (55), it follows that our knowledge of the universe depends on metaphor. And since human intelligence is a participation in the cosmic Intelligence, the knowledge that human beings gain through metaphor corresponds with the way the universe really is. (Ogden and Richards, of course, would dismiss all this as the creation of "bogus entities" through the manipulation of empty verbal shells.)

Philologists before Barfield had discussed the metaphorical basis of language, but he regards their account of why language is metaphorical as mistaken. He cites Max Müller's description of how the Latin *spiritus* originally meant "blowing, or wind"; then was applied to breath as the physical sign of the principle of life and movement in man and animals; and then became metaphorical as it was applied to the soul, the spiritual principle of a human being. Barfield says Müller is looking at the matter backward, projecting "impossibly modern and abstract concepts . . . [on] the mind of primitive man" (74). What really happened, according to

Barfield, was that primitive man had a single term that meant "blowing," "life," and "soul" simultaneously. There was no separation between literal and metaphorical senses of words (75). It is only in relatively modern times that human beings have developed the ability to create abstractions and therefore split apart the complex cluster of meaning. We have some "unsplit" words even today. Barfield's example is *stomach:* when we say, "I have no *stomach* for such cruelty," we are not using a mere metaphor for a psychological, nonmaterial condition; we are referring to the mental and physical conditions simultaneously or, more accurately, to a single condition that cannot be classified as exclusively one or the other (80n.).

Barfield denies the validity of the Ogden-Richards dictum that clear thinking depends on the accurate use of nonmetaphorical, referential language—that is, language that refers to objects, preferably things that modify the sensory receptors. People who hold this belief, Barfield says, do not realize that scientific terms are just as figurative in origin as any other words. He adds, "Those who profess to eschew figurative expressions are really confining themselves to one very old kind of figure" (134). He cites several etymologies to prove that there is no such thing as perfectly literal language, because all the thousands of abstract terms and nuances of meaning were originally references either to objects or to human or animal activity. He calls such terms "fossilized metaphor," observing that "an apparently objective scientific term like *elasticity*, . . . and the 'metaphysical' *abstract* . . . are both traceable to verbs meaning 'draw' or 'drag'" (64).

Barfield also denies the validity of separating scientific language from poetic language and ascribing truth only to the former: "The fashionable distinction between Poetry and Science as modes of experience [is] essentially parochial" (138). The revolutionary changes in scientific thought are shifts in consciousness—poetic, metaphorical insights—that apply new concepts to the phenomena of the physical world. Bacon's insight in applying the term "mechanical" to natural principles, Newton's shift of the term "gravity" away from the simple meaning of "weight," Kepler's application of "focus" (etymologically, "hearth") to geometry—all these are examples of "the poetic diction of science" (137–38). These scientists increased the store of human knowledge by giving us new metaphors. The much-touted scientific method, says Barfield, is not a way of knowing, but rather a way of testing what has been discovered by insight into metaphorical language (139).[11]

The unity of metaphor and concept, of language and experience, of poetry and science is possible, Barfield says, because language is related to nature. Language is metaphorical and mythical because it reflects the true character of the universe. He refers to Emerson's view that such relationships as dark-evil, winter-old age, and breath-spirit are "constant, and pervade nature" (92). Barfield's view leads to the recognition of what we now call Jungian archetypes, although he did not know Jung's work at the time.[12]

The force of Barfield's view of metaphor, archetype, and myth may be seen by comparing several famous epigrams. First, Max Müller's "Mythology is a disease of language" implies that man's (deluded) belief in divinities is caused by the inevitable distortions in knowledge derived from language. Barfield contradicts Müller, stating that mythological words such as *panic, hero, fortune,* and *fury* are derived from primitive man's insights into the original, unified meanings given by nature (89). Ogden and Richards's position is in agreement with Müller's: the mythological words represent a distortion in knowledge derived from a mistaken belief that language has independent power and reality, a distortion that gives rise to empty metaphysical terminology. Their epigram is, "Metaphysics is a hybrid of science and poetry," which, like all hybrids, "is sterile" (*Meaning* 82n). It is a foreshadowing of A. J. Ayer's emendation of Müller: "Metaphysics is a disease of language." In contrast, Barfield, whose theory of language and metaphor asserts the validity of both language and myth, says, "Mythology is the ghost of concrete meaning" (*Poetic Diction* 92).[13]

The extent to which Lewis adopted Barfield's position is best seen in his essay "Bluspels and Flalansferes,"[14] composed after *The Pilgrim's Regress* and first published in *Rehabilitations* in 1939 and later reprinted in *Selected Literary Essays*. In it he concludes, with Barfield, that the original metaphors are indeed archetypes—that the universe is indeed organized according to "a kind of psycho-physical parallelism" without which "all our thinking is nonsensical" (265). He refuses assent to Barfield's assertion that one cannot refer to *physical* objects, or rather one's percepts of them, without using metaphor. But he does conclude that the person who speaks about anything other than a physical object has no choice but to speak metaphorically. Any time we think of causes, relations, or mental states, we inevitably use metaphor. At best we have a choice of metaphors, or the possibility of rapidly shifting from one to another (262–63). Although modern psychologists claim to give us an unmetaphorical account of the soul, their technical terms such as "complexes, repressions, censors, en-grams and the like" are metaphorical in origin, so that they are speaking of "*tyings-up, shovings-back, Roman magistrates,* and *scratchings*" (261).[15] The tough-minded, anti-mystical, "literal" philosophers (like Ogden and Richards) use more meaningless verbiage than Plato, one of "the great creators of metaphor," or the writers of religious literature such as Bunyan and Dante (264, 265).

Lewis also opposes Barfield's formulation by denying that poetry, the exercise of the imagination, leads to knowledge. Imagination, he says, is the organ of *meaning,* not truth. Before a statement can be judged as true or false, it must have meaning. Imagination provides the meaning, but reason must determine whether the statement is true or false. He does not, in this relatively brief essay, define what he means by "reason"; however, Adey concludes from "Bluspels and Flalansferes" that Lewis finally did accept Barfield's belief about imagination (82). Perhaps the distinction between meaning and truth is primarily a way to separate himself from Barfield's anthroposophy. It is certain that he makes use of the "psycho-physical parallelism" of the archetypal metaphor and adds to our verbal repertoire in Barfieldian ways in *The Pilgrim's Regress.*

Two Kinds of Metaphor in *The Pilgrim's Regress*

C. S. Lewis's first attempt to defend Christianity as he understood it was *The Pilgrim's Regress.* In it he responds to the philosophic and literary developments of the period between the wars, showing that the intellec-tuals' reasons for rejecting traditional literature and Christianity were based on illusion. The pilgrimage that the hero undertakes is philosophical as well as literary, a quest for what we may know as well as what we may enjoy. Manlove's remark, "Of course the book is about language in a sense . . . " (23), suggests that the novel is related to the postwar struggle over the nature of language. Lewis's choice of Bunyan's *Pilgrim's Progress* as a starting point is also significant for a postwar work, for, as Fussell points out, the Great War had frequently been described with Bunyan's imagery (137–39). Furthermore, when Lewis wrote *The Pilgrim's Regress* in 1932, he was beginning his academic masterpiece, *The Allegory of Love* (1936), in which he says, "We cannot speak, perhaps we can hardly think, of an 'inner conflict' without a metaphor; and every metaphor is an allegory in little" (60). It is not surprising, then, that *The Pilgrim's Regress,* which describes the inner conflict leading to his conversion, develops the chief metaphors that Lewis used for the rest of his life.

The complexity of the inner conflict requires two kinds of metaphor, which Barfield helps us understand. In *Poetic Diction* he distinguishes between the unitive metaphor, "*given,* as it were, by Nature," and the analytic metaphor, in which an individual "register[s] as *thought*" a perceived relationship (102–03). Although Barfield does not explicitly say so, the former are commonly called archetypes and the latter are what Ogden and Richards would call metaphors. The structure of *The Pilgrim's Regress* can be seen as an interplay between archetypal metaphors that are just "there" and individually created metaphors.

In *The Allegory of Love* Lewis discusses these two ways of using language, although the relationship to Barfield's formulation is not immediately apparent because of the difference in terminology. He describes the archetypal metaphor as part of human nature or perhaps thought itself:

> It is of the very nature of thought and language to represent what is immaterial in picturable terms. What is good or happy has always been high like the heavens and bright like the sun. Evil and misery were deep and dark from the first. Pain is black in Homer, and goodness is a middle point for Alfred no less than for Aristotle. (44)

He calls the use of such metaphors "sacramentalism or symbolism" and contrasts it with "allegory," the personification or reification of abstractions, which he describes as a process of invention (44–45). He adds, "Symbolism is a mode of thought, but allegory is a mode of expression" (48).

What Lewis calls allegory is not quite commensurate with the individual metaphor, but both are invented rather than given, created intellectually, and based on individual concepts rather than the collective unconscious. They are what Ogden and Richards would call metaphor, for instead of being part of the spiritual structure of the universe, which Ogden and Richards would regard as an untenable idea, individuals create them by abstracting common features from two unlike things. Metaphysical conceits, for example, are individual metaphors. They are often based on wordplay. For instance, the main character in *The Pilgrim's Regress* is called "John," another form of "Jack," Lewis's nickname. "John" is also a common word to designate an unspecified man, as in "John Doe." Allegorically, then, John is both C. S. Lewis and Everyman. When allegory uses individual metaphors, the reader's pleasure comes from identifying the referents, breaking the code, for they tend to have a one-to-one correspondence with the things they signify rather than a mythic, cognitively unknowable, polysemic significance.

In seeing how Lewis uses both types of metaphors it is helpful to use another metaphor: *The Pilgrim's Regress* is a building in which the structural elements—the foundation, the studs, the main bearing beam—are archetypal metaphors, while the individual rooms and details such as window facings are individual metaphors. The chief structural metaphor is John's journey, for the quest or journey has always been an archetypal metaphor of mental and spiritual development. John leaves his parents' home in Puritania, located at the foot of a mountain range in the East, to find an island which rises out of the sea in the West. The mountain range is an archetypal metaphor for divinity, because God has always lived in a high place. Furthermore, law comes to John's community from the mountains, just as Moses received the Ten Commandments on top of Mount Sinai. And the mountains are where people go when they die, just as people are said to go to be with God.

John hates and fears the Eastern Mountains; he turns his back on them to travel toward the Island, which he first glimpses through a window in a garden wall. According to his vision it is inhabited by creatures like Barfield's primitive Man—"wise like gods, unconscious of themselves like beasts" (*The Pilgrim's Regress* 24). The innocence of the Island is the opposite of the law-ridden, Puritanian habitation of the Landlord (God), and John desires to reach it with all his heart.

In order to attain the Island, John needs to stay on the road, the Middle Way running straight from East to West: he needs to walk in that goodness which is "a middle point for Alfred no less than for Aristotle" (*The Allegory of Love* 44). But John departs from the Middle Way. When he goes Northward, he experiences the abuse of intellectuality, of "objective" thought, which is archetypally cold. When he goes Southward, he experiences the abuse of subjectivity and the emotions, which are archetypally warm.

After John has been traveling for a while, he comes upon the Grand Canyon. It is an archetypal metaphor for Original Sin, the rift between man as he is now and man as an inhabitant of the Island—wise like a god and unselfconscious like a beast. John crosses the chasm with the aid of the Wise Old Woman, Mother Kirk. But when he has continued west as far as he can go, he learns that the Island is really just the other side of the Eastern Mountains, for John's world is round (and constructed with a fine medieval disregard for perspective). Thus the geography conveys complex spiritual and intellectual relationships, enacting Barfield's belief that metaphor reflects the true structure of the universe.

The discovery that the Island is really the Eastern Mountains is an especially suitable development of the basic metaphor. From a distance, a mountain seems to rise from the plain as an island rises from the water. But the biggest difference is that a mountain is part of a range, connected with others, as Christians are supposed to be, while an island is separate from others, like the egocentric dreams of youth. This relationship is suggested in the description of John's view of the Island in the company of others: "humility was mixed with their [the breezes'] wildness, and the sweetness came not with pride and with the lonely dreams of poets nor with the glamour of a secret, but with the homespun truth of folk-tales, and with the sadness of graves and freshness as of earth in the morning" (172). John finds that there is no approach to the Island, which is also the mountain on which the Landlord (God) lives—and which we now realize is Heaven—without crossing the brook back in the land of his childhood; he must retrace his steps along the Middle Way. This retracing is a major feature of the archetypal journey, as Tolkien recognized in the subtitle of *The Hobbit*, "There and Back Again."[16] John's archetypal journey homeward thus gives the book its title.

In addition to the interweaving of the archetypal metaphors of mountain range, Island, and there-and-back journey, Lewis introduces another mountain, or rather pseudo-mountain: the Spirit of the Age, a giant who in repose looks like a mountain and, as the Spirit of the Age, is a substitute for God, the real mountain. When John rejects the Eastern Mountains by denying the existence of the Landlord who dwells there, he inevitably falls under the power of the giant, the substitute mountain. Giants have traditionally stood for ignorance, pride, and rebellion against God in both Christian and Norse literature.[17] In this case Lewis has cleverly combined the archetypal metaphor of the giant with the individual metaphor of the giant's X-ray eyes, which suggests a preoccupation with one's own consciousness associated with the twentieth century.

The geographic metaphor lends itself to the efficient use of other archetypal metaphors, those of weather and the seasons. When John departs from the Middle Way into the intellectual sterility of North, the sky is gray but the rain clouds barren, for it never rains. When he travels southward, he finds warmth and sunshine. The seasons convey the same sorts of meanings. It is warm, spring or perhaps summer, when John first meets the brown girl; when he becomes disillusioned with her, it is fall; and when the vision of the Island disappears, it is winter. These archetypal metaphors provide a solid basis for the non-archetypal cities and homes that John visits.

The cities and homes and the incidents that occur in them are individual metaphors, the architectural details that adorn the basic structure of *The Pilgrim's Regress*. There are three major clusters of individual metaphors. They concern three aspects of twentieth-century thought: literature, philosophy, and religion. Each of these is involved, in its own way, with the twentieth-century effort to understand the nature and function of language. Lewis's approach is frequently satirical; in fact, he has such a fine eye for twentieth-century follies that *The Pilgrim's Regress*, rather than the Cambridge Inaugural Address, should have been entitled *"De Descriptione Temporum."*

The first literary movement that Lewis satirizes is the romantic/Victorian attempt to use aesthetic experience as a substitute for religion. The Halfways family is so called because John can get halfway to his Island with their art and the feeling it arouses. Old Mr. Halfways identifies himself as a romantic by quoting Keats: "What the imagination seizes as beauty must be truth."[18] His home is in the city of Thrill, and John experiences repeated thrills when Mr. Halfways sings. The name "Thrill" may be a sly reference to a quotation from Clive Bell's *Art* (1927), an assertion that works of art yield "a specific thrill" which is found only in art and which is unlike all other experiences.[19] Romantic literature validates John's desire for the Island as something real, but it also disappoints him. During Mr. Halfways's song he has a sentimentalized, self-serving experience of sexuality in the arms of Media Halfways, the daughter, but he gets only a momentary glimpse of his Island. Since romantic literature has failed him, John turns to Mr. Halfways's son, Gus, whose near-worship of his powerful car signifies a modern critic's near-religion of modern poetry. Wordplay carries the allegory: Lewis refers to the car as "the machine," which reminds us that Ogden and Richards call language an instrument and that Richards begins his *Principles of Literary Criticism* with the words, "A book is a machine to think with . . . " (1).

Imagery augments the verbal allegory: the city of Thrill with its "romantic" landscape—spires and turrets, ruined wall, and ivy; Mr. Halfways's churchlike home, with its vaulted roof and stained-glass windows; and the old man's priestly appearance, flowing robes and long beard. These details not only suggest the substitution of literature for religion, but also the neo-, or perhaps pseudo-, medievalism of the Pre-Raphaelites. The accouterments of Thrill contrast graphically with those of Eschropolis,[20] the modernist city to which John goes with Gus, just as the modernist poets aggressively revolted against romanticism. Eschropolis is the home of "the Clevers," the Bloomsbury intellectuals, and they meet in a trendy room that is "full of steel and glass and the walls nearly all window" (50).

While he is with the Clevers, John hears three styles of modern poetry. Again, the allegorical significance is verbal, communicated by labels: neo-Victorian by Victoriana,[21] the experimental reduction of word and sentence forms to grunting by Glugly, and the near-pornographic by Phally. All three styles are anti-romantic on the surface but derived from the same desire to wallow in sentiment, the same hunger for thrill as the bad nineteenth-century poetry. The poetic styles of Glugly and Phally can be seen as sly references to the language issue and its relation to I. A. Richards's literary criticism. In the first edition of *Principles of Literary Criticism* (1924), Richards defends Glugly-like poetry when he says that a poem can be almost devoid of sense and form and still be good (130). Phally probably represents D. H. Lawrence, whom Richards describes as having tried to "reconstruct in himself the mentality of a Bushman."[22] Richards later praised T. S. Eliot's "The Waste Land" for both Glugly-like and Phally-like qualities—the lack of logical and grammatical coherence and the "persistent concern with sex."[23]

But John is too naive to grasp the subtlety of the Clevers' literary productions. They chase him out of town shouting, "Puritanian! Bourgeois! Prurient!" (55), accusing him of their own obscenity. Thus Lewis shows that modern literature is unable to fulfill the desire for the transcendent represented by the Island.

Lewis's treatment of philosophy does not at first seem so involved with postwar language issues. The objects of satire include eighteenth- and nineteenth-century rationalism, hedonism, and subjective idealism as well as linguistic analysis. Again there are no archetypal metaphors; names provide a sufficient key to the allegory. Mr. Enlightenment's name, for example, identifies him with rationalism. He lives in the city of

Claptrap, the home of "our most influential publicists and scientific popularizers"—reminiscent not only of the runaway wartime press, but also of the Ogden and Richards observation about the dissemination of ignorance by the propagation of half-understood terminology and ideas. Mr. Enlightenment contributes to John's ignorance with his quick listing of "Christopher Columbus, Galileo, the earth is round, invention of printing, [and] gunpowder" as automatic proofs of the falsity of religion. He also demonstrates his half-understanding of the inductive method: "If you make the same guess often enough it ceases to be a guess and becomes a Scientific Fact" (37).

Mr. Enlightenment, like Ogden and Richards, shows an enlightened hostility toward religion, but Lewis makes him argue against it illogically. He says the Stewards (i.e., the clergy) are "simple old souls" who are gullible because they "have no knowledge of modern science." On the other hand, they have shrewdly invented the Landlord (God) to increase their own power (35). How they can be so stupid and so smart at the same time is unclear, but John is eager to be free of his guilt over not following the Landlord's rules and his fear of being punished in the Black Hole. Because Mr. Enlightenment's assertion that there is no Landlord and no Black Hole offers this freedom, John eagerly accepts his explanations.

Next comes the satire of Freudian psychology, which Lewis believes to be an outgrowth of Enlightenment philosophy applied to the study of man as an object. He expresses the relationship by making Sigismund (later called Sigmund) the son of Mr. Enlightenment. Like the behaviorism that was also increasingly accepted at the time, Freudianism militated against classical logic. If human beings are governed by subconscious motivations, then the old idea that someone might think through an issue logically and act on his conclusion is quite false.

As inheritors of the language cynicism following World War I, we take it for granted today that advertisers, politicians, and filmmakers appeal to us on a subliminal level and that most of our decisions—or if not ours, other people's decisions—are made out of subconscious motivations. Lewis, steeped in classical rhetoric and philosophy, was outraged by this denigration of logic in the name of "science." He ridicules it in an episode in which John becomes a prisoner of the Spirit of the Age. In this chapter, entitled "Poisoning the Wells" (after the logical fallacy in which one denies an assertion by attributing it to a noncredible source), Sigismund refutes both John's romanticism and the religion of Puritania (completely opposite attitudes) by attributing both to wish fulfillment, a noncredible source. When John tries to argue against Sigismund's fallacy, the jailer punishes him on the theory that his objection is mere wish fulfillment and therefore not worthy of an answer.

The jailer as the henchman of the Spirit of the Age also leads one of the prisoners, Master Parrot, in a mock catechism. As a catechumen in modernism, Master Parrot discounts antimodern arguments by attributing them to the arguer's self-serving, usually unconscious motivations—a version of the *ad hominem* fallacy which Wayne Booth calls "motivism" and which Lewis called "Bulverism" in later essays. The name "Master Parrot" may be a sidelong reference to Ogden and Richards's description of the intellectual disease of "psittacism" (216–17). Ogden and Richards attribute the parrot disease to traditionalists, but Lewis shows that modernists can have it as well.

In this episode we see the strength of allegory in enabling the author to present a complicated intellectual relationship compactly. By the father-son relationship of Mr. Enlightenment and Sigmund, Lewis shows that the study of the mind, which used to be a part of philosophy and governed by classical logic, has become the science of psychology, governed by empirical research. But the resulting objectivization of the mind is, in his view, inherently false. As Reason, his rescuer from the Spirit of the Age, tells John, "[The giant] showed you by a trick what our inwards *would* look like if they were visible. That is, he showed you something that is not, but something that would be if the world were made all other than it is. But in the real world our inwards are invisible" (70). In other words, to study empirically "a longing out of the dark part of a man's mind" one must give it an artificial self-consciousness, so that it seems monstrous; thus, the psychologist teaches us an unreasonable self-hatred. The seeming freedom of Enlightenment philosophy has led to a misapplication of the inductive method, and that has led to a greater bondage than that from which Enlightenment was supposed to deliver us.

In addition to the bondage of Freudian psychology, Enlightenment leads to the barrenness of linguistic analysis. Its goal, to purify philosophy of all misunderstanding and metaphysical excess, is embodied by the Three Pale Men. They are Manichaeans in their hatred of the body and bodily sustenance, in their pursuit of utter purity of thought. Their spare supper of bully beef and biscuit, perfect in form but not very nourishing, resembles

Barfield's characterization of linguistic analysis, which he considers another name for logical positivism. It is "an extensive gloss" on the principle that a perfectly logical language, one whose propositions really obeyed the laws of thought, could do so only by abolishing meaning completely.[24] I. A. Richards said something similar in *Principles of Literary Criticism*. He found fault with the "hard-headed positivist" because his insistence on "recognized facts" afforded him "insufficient material for the development of his attitudes"—that is, emotional experiences (*Principles* 282). In the headings of the second edition of *The Pilgrim's Regress* Lewis identifies the Three Pale Men as counter-romanticism, which perhaps narrows the meaning too much; however, linguistic analysis is counterromantic in that it prefers referential to emotive language and seeks to eliminate the "illusions" of Platonism.

Of the Three Pale Men, Mr. Angular purifies the Church of everything that one might discover through logic (since the Spirit of the Age believes that logic is tautologous and self-seeking); Mr. Neo-Classical purifies literature of the feeling that motivates one to read it in the first place; and Mr. Humanist purifies culture of everything that might make it fruitful. Patrick identifies Mr. Angular with T. S. Eliot, Mr. Neo-Classical with T. E. Hulme, and Mr. Humanist with Paul Elmer More, Irving Babbitt, and Norman Foerster.[25] These identifications are not particularly helpful, for Mr. Angular, taken simply as a High Church clergyman, runs away with the scene, and his significance as an Anglo-Catholic is self-evident. The others are characterized primarily by their genealogy, which is so complex and lengthy that it slows down the story—perhaps the only passage in which this aspect of the allegorical method is ineffective. Because of the ineffective technique here, it is necessary to describe their intellectual significance again in a lecture by History the Hermit. Finally, during John's Regress, we learn that all three are really one person: the Enemy's anorexic daughter Superbia, who polishes her bare rock in disgusting parody of Aphrodite before her mirror.

Two other philosophical characters, Mr. Wisdom and the Hermit, are presented less satirically, for they embody approaches to philosophy that really helped Lewis find his way to a satisfying Christian worldview. Mr. Wisdom speaks for philosophic idealism; unfortunately, however, the allegory is less effective because Mr. Wisdom's position is presented as lecture rather than narrative action. He says that man has three sources of information: the Roads, the Rules, and John's vision of the Island. The

Roads stand for the way the mind works, the way the pilgrim must travel over the land. The Rules stand for the moral imperative; they too are the way the mind works and are similar to the card John was given as a child. The vision of the Island is man's longing for the transcendent, which Mr. Wisdom says is "real" but unattainable, because the individual is both "the Imaginer [and] one of his imaginations" (134).

But John finds that Mr. Wisdom's *evangelium eternum,* the "perennial philosophy," is not really tenable. In the one satirical passage of this episode he learns that Mr. Wisdom's children do not live on the food served at his table, but they survive by getting nourishment from other sources—communism, Judaism, theosophy, romanticism, even drugs and the occult—after which they, perhaps feebly imitating Milton's devils (2:528–32), turn to nonphilosophical amusements such as "serious leapfrog." Thus, Mr. Wisdom validates John's questions but has no real answers for him.

History the Hermit adds to the information provided by Mr. Wisdom about the Rules: they came by revelation to the Shepherd People, the Jews. He also explains the vision of the Island: it is one of many pictures—imaginative longings—sent to non-Jews as messages from the Landlord. Three of the pictures are the mythological gods of the ancients, the courtly love cult of the medievals, and the love of Nature of the romantics. This passage is too lecture-ridden to be really effective, but Lewis skillfully uses the contrast between Rules and Pictures to express a complex theory of history compactly. In contrast, History's description of the Three Pale Men by literalizing three old proverbs is overly mannered: "One time they had a notion to eat better bread than is made of wheat. Another time their very nurses took up a strange ritual of always emptying the baby out along with the bath. Then once the Enemy sent a fox without a tail among them . . . [and in imitation] they . . . cut off their noses" (149–50). The restatement of the proverbs is simply not clever enough to be effective.

Lewis's sharpest satire of philosophy is directed against the modern version of hedonism professed by Mr. Sensible. It turns into a satire of the secular, superficial life of the British upper class, for only the wealthy can afford to hold this philosophy. Mr. Sensible is a man of independent means—that is, he lives on the labor of others. It is easy for him to practice moderation of the passions, since he has no real troubles to tempt him toward immoderate passions; but we notice that he does not moderate his anger and cruelty toward his servant Drudge. And because he is very lazy, his supposed moderation is nothing more than a lack of commitment, his supposed tolerance nothing more than fuzzy-mindedness. After dinner he makes a little speech in Latin thanking the Landlord, simply because religion is one more element in the good life. But his class, his economic prosperity, his way of life are in their autumn, as the light snowfall attests. His obedient servant Drudge, like the British lower classes, decides to leave in favor of Marxism, and Mr. Sensible is outraged but helpless. When John returns in the Regress section of the book, he finds that Mr. Sensible just isn't there; he was a nonentity all the time, and all his catchwords were borrowed from others.

In satirizing religion Lewis deals with the three types of Anglican churchmanship: the Anglo-Catholic, the evangelical, and the broad. Lewis portrays Mr. Broad as the kind of clergyman who could be the vicar of the church Mr. Sensible attends sporadically. He represents the religious side of Mr. Sensible's philosophy; he, too, devotes himself to living well and to appreciating the beauty of nature. He speaks to John encouragingly, but refuses to be confined to any doctrinal statement. The satire is clever, but seems anticlimactic after the fuller portrayal of Mr. Sensible.

The most effective portrayal is that of the evangelical clergyman, the Steward of John's childhood. Like many evangelical ministers, he uses the role of the good fellow interested in fishing tackle and bicycles to make friends with John, but then adopts an unnatural manner when he talks about the Landlord. His official message sounds like the preaching of simplistic evangelists: that God is very good, but very touchy, and is eager to punish people for breaking the rules. But the rules are self-contradictory— like a naive, literalist reading of the Bible—and the Steward's official moralism forces one into hypocrisy: "Better tell a lie, old chap, better tell a lie. Easiest for all concerned" (22).

If the portrayal seems severe, that of Mr. Neo-Angular, the Pale Man who represents the Anglo-Catholic stance, is no kinder. His name, Neo-Angular, simultaneously suggests the "Anglo" of "Anglo-Catholic" and his sharp-edged, "angular" personality. His snotty insistence that John must talk to Mother Kirk only "through a qualified Steward" satirizes the Anglo-Catholic concern with proper authority and valid apostolic succession. His pronouncement that John's motive for wanting to cross the canyon is unimportant satirizes the Anglo-Catholic emphasis on the objective validity of a sacrament, in contrast to the evangelical emphasis on the subjective experience of faith. And his advice that John should not talk to Reason, but simply learn the dogmas of the Church, is a weak Anglo-Catholic copy of the kind of anti-intellectual dogmatism that was common in Roman Catholicism before Vatican II.

Thus, Mr. Angular's futility, the Low Church Steward's hypocrisy, and Mr. Broad's lack of commitment all add up to a mordant criticism of religion. It would seem that Lewis agreed thoroughly with Ogden and Richards in their denunciation of the religious use of language to enslave people's minds. But his criticism of the Christianity that he himself believed simply demonstrates his honest confrontation of modern issues and attests to the power of the metaphors he used in *The Pilgrim's Regress.*

Like the places, the persons in the story are of two kinds: archetypal figures and humor characters. Reason, for example, is the archetypal figure of the warlike virgin, an Athena-like person with Athena-like character-istics: she is "a woman in the flower of her age: . . . a Titaness, a sun-bright virgin clad in complete steel, with a sword naked in her hand" (63–64). Just as deduction cannot produce new knowledge, Reason, or rational analysis, is virgin and has no children. As she tells John, "I can tell you only what *you* know. I can bring things out of the dark part of your mind into the light part of it" (67). She is toughminded, advising John not to draw a conclusion without evidence, even though he might die for lack of an answer. And, like Athena, she is powerful; she breaks her own chains, confounds and slays the Spirit of the Age, and rescues John. But she does not care about his feelings, and when he finds it tiring to keep up with her, she does not offer to adjust her speed to his.

The archetypal figures are not uniformly successful as characters. Mother Kirk is the Wise Old Woman, but she is not as fully realized as Reason. As we expect from her archetype, she is said to be crazy, or second-sighted, or a witch, but nothing in her manner or conversation bears out these reports. She wears a "country cloak," but she does not use it as Reason uses her steel mail. She tells Vertue and John the story of the Fall of Man and calls it an old wives' tale, but it lacks the stark narration and terror of a real old wives' tale. Her statement that she is the Landlord's daughter-in-law is doctrinally correct in that the Church is the Bride of Christ, but emotionally it is incompatible with her advanced age. Christ is still thirty-three, young and vigorous, and it is hard to feel that an old woman is a proper bride for him. Her name is also somewhat unfortunate. "Mother" is a common title of respect for an old woman in some speech communities, and "Kirk" ought to suggest a Scottish, and therefore a country, perhaps Protestant, church; but when they are combined it is easy to conclude that Mother Kirk symbolizes Roman Catholicism rather than "Mere Christianity."

The archetypal figures tend to be characterized by their appearance and action, while the humor characters are characterized by their repetition of catchphrases. Vertue, Mr. Sensible, and Drudge are humor characters. Vertue's catchphrases are "Keep to the road," a reference to the Middle Way, and "The great thing is to do one's thirty miles a day," a metaphor for self-determination and persistence. The limits of right behavior are expressed at the end, however, when he drops his catchphrases to say, "I am cured of playing the Stoic, and I confess that I go down in fear and sadness" (196). Mr. Sensible, with his misapplied Latin and Greek quotations, exemplifies a classical education in superficiality, while Drudge, with his "Coming, sir!" displays a necessary servility.

Mr. Wisdom and History should be archetypal Wise Old Men, but they are described and developed even less than Mother Kirk, so that they become merely voices for the author. The characterization of the angel who accompanies John and Vertue on the trip back to the Eastern Mountains is also weak. He could have been majestic and otherworldly, or lowly and humorous, but he falls between the two stools. His remark that the Landlord is not decent, and "that is why so few of your national jokes have any point in my country," is only mildly humorous, and his tribute to the Virgin Mary falls short of majesty: "Be sure that the whole of this land, with all its warmth and wetness and fecundity with all the dark and the heavy and the multitudinous for which you are too dainty, spoke through her lips when she said that He had regarded the lowliness of His handmaiden" (184). Mostly, the angel just lectures, sounding like Lewis.

Another weakness is confusion of form. Until Vertue and John reach the House of Wisdom, the story is a journey after the manner of Bunyan's *Pilgrim's Progress*. When they resume their journey, it has become a *prosimetrum* after the manner of Boethius's *Consolation of Philosophy*.[26] In Boethius, the verses heighten, summarize, or broaden the application of the dialogue between Lady Philosophy and Boethius. They are an integral part of the argument. In *The Pilgrim's Regress* the verses are more pleasing in themselves than contributory to the argument. Various characters—the Hermit, John, Vertue, the guardian angel, Superbia, the dragon—speak the verses, and the fact that such different characters have such similar poetic styles detracts from the small illusion of reality that even an allegory should display,

In addition to the ineffective wavering between the genres of journey story and *prosimetrum,* Lewis also confuses levels of allegory in one important passage, apparently because he has not quite made up his mind on the nature of myth. During the underground journey, the voice of God commenting on the validity of myth causes us to lose—or perhaps to realize that we never grasped—the allegorical significance of John's underground journey:

> "Child, if you will, it *is* mythology. It is but truth, not fact: an image, not the very real. But then it is My mythology. The words of Wisdom are also myth and metaphor: but since they do not know themselves for what they are, in them the hidden myth is master, where it should be servant: and it is but of man's inventing. But this is My inventing, this is the veil under which I have chosen to appear even from the first until now." (171)

The passage expresses two major concepts: the theological point that the visible universe reveals an image of God and the philosophical one on the nature of language, of Master's metaphors and Pupil's metaphors, that Lewis was to make in "Bluspels and Flalansferes." But it does not quite fit into the story. What does "mythology, not fact" mean for John, the hero of the story? On the literal level of the story, is he not traveling underground? On that level, was Wisdom correct when he said the Island was by definition a place one could never reach? And in what sense can *words* "know themselves for what they are"? These questions distract the reader when he should be participating imaginatively in the journey.

But the most important weakness, perhaps, is Lewis's apparent refusal to face the woundedness of society between the wars. When the Clevers attribute their "savage disillusionment" to the War, John hard-heartedly replies, "That war was years ago. It was your fathers who were in it ... " (54). But Lewis is writing in 1932, only fourteen years after World War I. Some of the people he was satirizing as the Clevers were veterans. His personal reactions to the war appear mixed. When Lewis and Barfield call their philosophical argument "the Great War," the name commonly applied to World War I, the humor may include an element of denial of woundedness. Certainly there is some denial in *Surprised by Joy* when Lewis says, "It

[World War I] is too cut off from the rest of my experience and often seems to have happened to someone else" (196). On the other hand, in writing to a former student before the outbreak of World War II he says frankly, "My memories of the last war haunted my dreams for years" (*Letters* 166).

This denial of the ravages of war leads to a greater one—an artistically debilitating denial of the need to engage with the modern world in the last book of *The Pilgrim's Regress*. As John begins the return journey to the Landlord's mountain, he finds that the modern world he experienced on the way out has simply ceased to exist. Its disappearance may be defended as an effective allegorical representation of what Lewis's between-the-wars contemporaries say about their own situation: that they lived in a world empty of hope. T. S. Eliot said it in "The Wasteland" (1922) and "The Hollow Men" (1925). Jung, writing in 1933, notes, "About a third of my cases are suffering from no clinically definable neurosis, but from the senselessness and emptiness of their lives. It seems to me that this can well be described as the general neurosis of our time" (qtd. in Leech 105). Defensible as it is, however, this complete disappearance of the modern world unavoidably implies that the language of religion Lewis has adopted is so incommensurate with the language of modernism that no communication, and therefore no conversion, is possible. Lewis holds out no hope that the Landlord will send some other picture to those who do not see the Island.

But for all its insufficiencies, the book is worth reading. The description of Puritania in Book One recaptures the childhood experiences of many people: wearing uncomfortable clothes to church, puzzling over the rules, and recognizing the grownups' ambivalence toward belief in the face of death. The characterizations of Reason, Mr. Enlightenment, Mr. Sensible, and Mr. Angular are superb.

It is most worth reading, however, for the images and metaphors that Lewis would repeat and develop in his subsequent fiction. The geographic layout of *The Pilgrim's Regress* is reworked to make Narnia, with Aslan's Mountain in the East, the giants and witches in the North, and the temptation of religious syncretism (Tashlan) coming from the South. The Wood between the Worlds is implied in the "place very ancient, folded many miles deep in the silence of forests" of *The Pilgrim's Regress* (171). The Island of Desire reappears as Meldilorn in *Out of the Silent Planet* and, multiplied, as the floating islands of *Perelandra*, for Malacandra is northern, Perelandra southern. The Island also appears as the garden of the Hesperides in *The Magician's Nephew* (Noel 7), and the underground journey reappears in *Perelandra* and *The Silver Chair*. Although Lewis later became a better writer and used these images and metaphors more skillfully, we see their inherent power in *The Pilgrim's Regress*.

In the subsequent books we also see Lewis dealing with the problems of literary genre, language control, culture, and religion in the context of modern cynicism toward language. It is under these rubrics that we go on to examine the rest of the major fiction.

· 2 ·

THE CONTEXT

OF LITERARY CRITICISM & GENRE

ONE MANIFESTATION of the disillusionment with language following World War I was the gap between the literary high culture and popular literature. Paul Fussell's study, *The Great War and Modern Memory*, shows that an "astonishing number" of the troops took literature seriously and saw their experience in literary terms (esp. 135–39). C. S. Lewis was a fledgling scholar at Oxford rather than an ordinary soldier, but his reading of George Eliot, Balzac, Boswell, and Milton while in France (*Greeves* 204) did not set him apart from the others.

But after the war it was different. The young men who read literary classics and wrote poetry in the trenches had been killed by the thousands, and those who survived often seemed to be afflicted with an intellectual malaise. In his preface to *Late Lyrics and Earlier*, Thomas Hardy writes:

> Whether owing to the barbarizing of taste in the younger minds by the dark madness of the late war, the unabashed cultivation of selfishness in all classes, the plethoric growth of knowledge with the stunting of wisdom, a degrading thirst after outrageous stimulation (to quote Wordsworth), or from any other cause, we seem threatened with a new Dark Age. (qtd. in Evans 6–7)

Hardy's phrase, "the plethoric growth of knowledge with the stunting of wisdom" recalls Ogden and Richards's point that "the twentieth century suffers more grievously than any previous age from . . . verbal superstitions" because "journalists and men of letters" now have more vocabulary but are unable or unwilling to use it properly (29).

Richards discusses the gap between the high and low culture in his *Principles of Literary Criticism,* and in 1960, Q. D. Leavis, wife of F. R. Leavis, set out to document it by surveying the holdings and checkout records of lending libraries. She found a growing dichotomy between "good books" and "best-sellers." She summarizes her findings as follows: in 1760, anyone who could read would be equally likely to read any novel. In 1860, the lowbrows read Dickens, Reade, and Wilkie Collins while the educated folk read George Eliot and Trollope, but the two kinds of readers still shared a world. In 1960, she concludes, "the general public . . . has now not even a glimpse of the living interests of modern literature . . . and . . . the critical minority . . . is isolated, disowned by the general public and threatened with extinction" (34–35).

C. S. Lewis's awareness of the problem is shown in his essay "High and Low Brows," first published in 1939.[1] He responded to the dichotomy in two ways: first, he wrote books (the Ransom trilogy) that could appeal to the readers of "best-sellers" with fast-paced adventure and to the readers of "good books" with style, classical background, and moral seriousness; second, he wrote literary criticism asking intellectuals to take a second look at what is called "genre" fiction—westerns, detective and action-adventure stories, historical and gothic romances, fantasy and science fiction.

Lewis's activity is highlighted by contrasting it with that of Dorothy L. Sayers, author of the Lord Peter Wimsey detective stories. In *Unnatural Death* (1927), Sayers makes her aristocratic sleuth comment, "It isn't really difficult to write books. Especially if you either write a rotten story in good English or a good story in rotten English, which is as far as most people seem to get nowadays" (32). Lord Peter's opinion, of course, is not necessarily that of his creator, but it does provide an additional witness to the cultural gap. The kind of story that might seem "rotten" to the general public would include mainstream novels such as James Joyce's *Ulysses* (1922), Aldous Huxley's *Crome Yellow* (1921), and Virginia Woolf's *Mrs. Dalloway* (1925)—books that abandon the canonical form and story lines of the nineteenth-century novel in order to experiment with new artistic techniques. Sayers was deeply conscious that her novels were "best-sellers" rather than "good books" (although she prided herself on using good English). She said she wrote them because she needed the money and turned to religious plays and essays as soon as she could. Critic B. Ifor Evans criticized her decision as an intellectual betrayal: "Some writers of erudition and genuine imaginative quality, such as Miss Dorothy Sayers, ... brought to an idle and meretricious form all the talents that might have been used in a healthier period for great creative writing" (14).

Instead of deprecating his writing of genre fiction as Sayers did, Lewis developed a whole critical viewpoint defending the reading of genre fiction. His essay "High and Low Brows" is a preliminary sketch of the completed literary theory expressed in *An Experiment in Criticism,* published only two years before his death. "High and Low Brows" supplies anecdotes validating Q. D. Leavis's distinction between good books and best-sellers, defines several genres that include both "serious" and "trivial" literature, and finally demands that popular books be judged by the same standards as the books of the high culture: "A man ought not to be ashamed of reading a good book because it is simple and popular, and he ought not to condone the faults of a bad book because it is simple and popular" (*Selected Literary Essays* 278).

Furthermore, Lewis casts doubt on the critical abilities of the proponents of "serious" literature, suggesting that future literati may regard Buchan and Wodehouse rather than Eliot and Auden as the primary artists of the early twentieth century (273). He reminds his readers that only in "quite modern times" has the reading of imaginative literature in the native language become an academic discipline; while approving the existence of English departments and examinations, he predicts that it will produce "the growth of a new race of readers and critics" who will know literature only as "an accomplishment rather than a delight" (276–77). Knowing that Lewis was a highly educated intellectual, we may find it hard to believe that he often preferred popular books to "serious" literature, but the plain prose of his critical essays can not be ignored; indeed, he expressed himself even more bluntly in private, writing to a former student, "the great *serious irreligious* art . . . is all balderdash" (*Letters* 182). He was in conflict with the literati of the high culture, which also entailed conflict with the literary theory arising out of *The Meaning of Meaning* and linguistic philosophy in general.

According to Tolkien, he and Lewis began to write fiction because nobody else was producing the sort of thing they wanted to read (Carpenter 65–66)—presumably the good story in good English. They decided that Lewis was to write about the far away and Tolkien about the long ago (Carpenter 66). Lewis also admitted that he wanted to present an alternative to science as the hope of mankind. He wrote to Sister Penelope,

C.S.M.V., in 1939, "What set me about writing [*Out of the Silent Planet*] was the discovery that a pupil of mine took all that dream of interplanetary colonization quite seriously, and the realization . . . that a 'scientific' hope of defeating death is a real rival to Christianity" (*Letters* 167).

In fulfilling their own desires, Tolkien and Lewis contributed mightily to the establishment of science fiction and fantasy. The "amazing story" is now recognized as a genre usable by serious artists, a genre that Anthony Burgess, Doris Lessing, and Margaret Atwood have found adequate for such works as *A Clockwork Orange, Briefing for a Descent into Hell,* and *The Handmaid's Tale.* In the preface to *Shikasta* Lessing remarks, "The old 'realistic' novel is being changed . . . because of influences from . . . space fiction. . . . [It] makes up the most original branch of literature now, . . . [and] literary academics and pundits are much to blame for patronising or ignoring it" (ix–x). Her comment vindicates Lewis's sense of what is worthwhile. In 1953, he wrote concerning Arthur C. Clarke's *Childhood's End,* "It is a strange comment on our age that such a book lies hid in a hideous paperbacked edition, wholly unnoticed by the *cognoscenti,* while any 'realistic' drivel about some neurotic in a London flat . . . may get seriously recieved [sic] . . . as if it really mattered."[2] It seems that B. Ifor Evans spoke too hastily when, in 1948, he accused Sayers and other "writers of erudition and genuine imaginative quality" of using "an idle and meretricious form."[3]

Again, and for the same reasons, the key figure to compare with Lewis is I. A. Richards, whom Lewis himself called "a critic whose works are almost the necessary starting-point for all future literary theory" (*Selected Literary Essays* 278n). Richards's *Principles of Literary Criticism* (1924), *Practical Criticism* (1929), and *Science and Poetry* (1935) supplied a defense of the subjects and techniques of modern mainstream authors built on the empirically oriented low view of language which he and Ogden set forth in *The Meaning of Meaning.* Lewis dealt with modern literary criticism and defended his high view of language in *Rehabilitations and Other Essays* (1939)[4] and *A Preface to "Paradise Lost"* (1942). *An Experiment in Criticism* (1961) is both his best answer to Richards's between-the-wars theorizing and a defense of the "idle and meretricious" science fiction he had published in 1938, 1943, and 1945.[5]

In *Principles of Literary Criticism* Richards is concerned with establishing literature as a thing of value without recourse to the ultimate, "metaphysical" realities asserted by Platonic philosophy and traditional Christianity.

To do so he must deny the existence of mind in any transcendental sense, describing it as just the activity of the nervous system. Furthermore, he denies the existence of mental faculties such as will, emotion, and cognition. To speak of the mind as *having* such faculties is mere reification—that is, the fallacy of treating something as a thing simply because one can express it as a noun. He maintains that mental abilities do not exist; instead, there is simply the activity of the nervous system. As proof, Richards refers somewhat vaguely to "the advance in neurology brought about by the War" (82–83).

Having replaced the mind with activity of the nervous system, he describes the nervous system as constantly responding to stimuli and directing behavior toward the fulfillment of needs (86–87). When the nervous system achieves an equilibrium, so that "certain positive and negative tendencies have instinctively attained their aim," one experiences pleasure (96). Art is valuable because it organizes experiences and thereby leads to the achievement of this equilibrium. Thus Richards accounts for artistic pleasure without postulating entities such as the mind, faculties of the mind, or the soul (105). Furthermore, he is able to assert that literature and the other arts are valuable (because they contribute to mental health through the achievement of equilibrium) without assenting to traditional ethical or religious values.

Richards creates a metaphor, most clearly stated in *Science and Poetry* (1935), to explain the value of art. He visualizes the human being as an arrangement of needles responding to magnets. The needles are our interests, and the magnets are stimuli coming from the environment. These stimuli upset the balance of the needles. Literature is sometimes one of the magnets that upsets the equilibrium, sometimes the force that restores it; but most often it is both (20–24). Literature also provides records of other people's experiences in the mental and emotional task of adjusting "attitudes" (40), a word Richards defines in *Principles of Literary Criticism* as "imaginal and incipient action" (112). (Apparently he uses "attitudes" in this way to avoid speaking of the mind, mental faculties, or the soul.)

Richards believes that literature and the other arts can and should take the place of religion in the modern world. Prescientific people were religious because they saw the natural universe as being controlled by spirits and powers. This view suited man's emotional makeup: "it gave life a shape, a sharpness, and a coherence that no other means could so easily secure" (*Science and Poetry* 53–55). Today nature is no longer alive with powers and spirits; mathematics and the sciences give us a better understanding of how things work, but they deny us emotional satisfaction and moral guidance (55–57). They cannot fulfill the basic need for a god, nor can they provide the adjustment of attitudes (55), which is just as valuable as ever, but "more difficult to maintain, because we still hunger after a basis in belief" (72). According to Richards, literature and the other arts fill the gap by providing substitutes for belief. Literature, for example, adjusts attitudes by providing sensory stimuli (imagery, rhythm, narrative) and "pseudo-statements," assertions which sound like the verifiable statements of scientific fact but are not factual and do not conflict with factual statements. When applied to a pseudo-statement, the word "true" simply means that it "suits and serves some attitude or links together attitudes which on other grounds are desirable" (64).

Richards states repeatedly that the purpose of all the arts is to furnish the community with value. He calls the arts "our storehouse of recorded values" (*Principles* 32) and claims that they provide data for "deciding what experiences are more valuable than others" (33). The slogan "art for art's sake" is erroneous; a critic cannot really avoid questions of value, and the attempt to do so merely passes the buck to the clergy or the government (34–35). He substitutes the term "value" for "beauty," which he regards as simply a report of one's own feelings in emotive rather than referential language. He exhorts us not to call a picture beautiful, but to say instead that "it causes an experience in us which is valuable in certain ways" (20). Sometimes the artist seems to ignore morality, but that is simply because the common formulations of what is moral are too narrow or crude to be applied to the work (62).

Certainly Richards's theories harmonize well with the mainstream novels that were being produced at the time. Michael Bell, in the introduction to *The Context of English Literature: 1900–1930*, lists four characteristics of modernism, all of which are related to Richards's aesthetic. First, modern literature depicts characters whose personal identity is questionable. Joyce's Bloom does not have the same kind of objective existence that George Eliot's Dorothea does. Eliot's Dorothea experiences the world and her individual self as existing in a kind of symbiotic relation; Joyce's Bloom reacts to random events (6–8). Here Joyce's literary technique seems to illustrate Richards's theoretical point that there is no mind, but only the activity of the nervous system. Second, modern literature focuses consciously on the nature of time. Like the montage in film or the multiple perspectives of cubism, the apparent passage of time in *Ulysses* traces an abstract pattern of timelessness (12–14). And third, in this timelessness random events are juxtaposed to create the novelistic equivalent of the collage and the found poem. These artistic techniques fit with Richards's needle metaphor. According to Bell, they are also responses to Marx, Lyell, and Darwin, whose teachings seemed to "swamp the individual fate into vastly collective processes" and deny the existence of free will (16, 17).

Finally, modern literature uses myth to add depth to the mental processes of the characters' response to a random, timeless world. Modern writers are interested in myth, Bell notes, because of its ambivalent truth value: "more than a story yet less than a proposition" (17)—in short, a myth is a pseudo-statement, in Richards's terminology. Joyce went back to Homer, creating an ironic juxtaposition of heroic Greece and unheroic Dublin, giving, as Richards says, "a shape, a sharpness, and a coherence" (*Science and Poetry* 53) to Bloom's life. Fiction having these characteristics, however, was appreciated only by a minority of readers; for the majority, such novels fell into Lord Peter Wimsey's category of "rotten stories in good English."

Richards was concerned about this deficiency in popular culture, which he explains in terms of adjustment of attitudes. The bad literature and art found in advertisements and movies are bad because they promulgate "immature and actually inapplicable attitudes to most things" (*Principles* 202–03). Continued exposure to these faulty productions, according to Richards, blurs and confuses the reader's responses so that he loses the potential for appreciating higher things (204). The proliferation of trashy, dishonest works for the consumption of the masses is especially a problem of the twentieth century. In earlier times it was possible to write multi-leveled works that could adjust the attitudes of both the common man and the sophisticate. But by the early twentieth century all the best themes that could be multileveled in treatment have been used up (213, 214). Whether Richards's cause-effect reasoning was correct or not, the Q. D. Leavis study showed that the decline of literary taste—or, more precisely, the gap between the high culture and the low—has occurred.

Lewis's *An Experiment in Criticism*, although not published until Richards's system had pretty much captured the field, suggests both a response to Richards's basic theory and a remedy for the cultural gap between good and bad literature.[6] The title suggests a connection with

Practical Criticism, in which Richards demonstrated that most people misread poetry through artistically irrelevant, conventional moral judgments and through preconceived notions about what the text should say. The title also indicates that Lewis will base his argument on the observable behavior of readers, just as Richards did in *Practical Criticism.* But instead of judging *readers* as highbrows or lowbrows on the basis of the books they read, he proposes to judge *books* by the kinds of readings people give them.

Having no need to deny the existence of the mind or its traditional faculties, Lewis does not begin, as Richards does, with a psychology of perception and behavior. Instead, he begins directly by classifying readers into three types: the literary few, the unliterary, and the semi-literary; then he describes each in terms of why, how, and what they read.

The why of the unliterary is that they read for ego gratification or simply to pass the time. Their how is to concentrate on the story line and pay little attention to style, and therefore they prefer a swift-moving narrative—a good story in rotten English. The why of the literary few is that they read for pleasure; their how, attentively, receptively, and passionately. And as for the what, they read what they like, regardless of whether it is in fashion. Lewis himself, one of the literary few, read the classics of Greek, Latin, and English literature, but he also read the adventure fiction sometimes referred to as "boys' books" or, even more bluntly, "trash." *An Experiment in Criticism* is his *apologia pro lectione sua* as well as his contribution to literary theory.

Lewis believes that the third type of reader, the semi-literary, can easily be led astray by people like Richards, people Lewis calls "the Vigilant school of critics."[7] The semi-literary read, not for ego gratification or intense pleasure, but because they have some capacity to appreciate literature. This capacity, however, is corrupted by Richards's belief—one that goes back to Arnold—that literature is valuable as a substitute religion. Without mentioning Richards by name, Lewis says that the person who goes to literature to have his attitudes adjusted is not seeking literature but mental health. Paradoxically, the person who takes literature so seriously is not a serious reader, just as a man who plays soccer for his health is not a real player (*Experiment* 11). Richards's doctrine that "the correct reading of good poetry has a veritable therapeutic value" has corrupted the why as well as the how of the semi-literary. It has produced a generation of "conscientious and submissive young people" who apply to literature the puritanical attitudes that their ancestors applied to religion (10). In Lewis's opinion, to use literature as a substitute for religion—to *use* it for anything—is to kill it.[8] Far from seeking the adjustment of our attitudes, we must begin by emptying ourselves of "pre-conceptions, interests, and associations" (18) so that we can surrender to the work.

In corrupting the why and the how, "the Vigilant school of critics" also narrows the field of what the semi-literary may read. Their substitution of the nervous system for the mind leaves no possibility for a specifically aesthetic mental faculty. If there is no aesthetic faculty, then there is no specifically *literary* good; thus the Vigilant critics are likely to disparage literature with spiritual values different from their own, as Richards disparages William Butler Yeats and Dante (*Principles* 197n, 222). This confusion of literary appreciation with morality also motivates Richards to state that people with "bad taste and crude responses" have "a root evil from which other defects follow" (*Principles* 62). Lewis disagrees, observing mildly that the literary few "include no small percentage of the ignorant, the caddish, the stunted, the warped, and the truculent" (*Experiment* 5–6). The Vigilant critics are so concerned with the bad effects of trashy literature that they rush to expose vulgarity, superficiality, and false sentiment. Their example has a bad effect on readers, according to Lewis, who believes that one must delay criticism, surrender oneself to the book, and risk being taken in by false and trashy work in order to appreciate literature truly. He sees the fear of being "taken in" as a particularly modern weakness,[9] reminding us that "we can find a book bad only by reading it as if it might, after all, be very good" (*Experiment* 116).

The Vigilant school narrows the field for the semi-literary by overvaluing realism of presentation and denying whole "escapist" genres like fantasy and science fiction. Having written stories which could be called escapist, Lewis shows that this blanket condemnation is incorrect, calling it the result of a taste "temporarily atrophied" by fashion (*Experiment* 70–71). He maintains that all reading, even of history or science, is an escape from "immediate, concrete actuality" (68); even the gritty realism of much modern fiction offers an escape from the reader's actual distresses. Furthermore, fiction with an unrealistic, marvelous surface is not more likely to give readers a false picture of life than is realistic fiction. He says, "Children are not deceived by fairy-tales; they are often and gravely deceived by school-stories. Adults are not deceived by science-fiction; they can be deceived by stories in the women's magazines" (67–68). Finally, the characterization of unrealistic, marvelous stories as "*childish* or *infan-tile*" (71) is simply wrong-headed, for the taste for the marvelous is not less valuable because it appears in childhood, and "to have lost the taste for marvels and adventures is no more a matter for congratulation than losing our teeth, our hair, our palate, and finally, our hopes" (72).

Lewis's defense of the nonrealistic leads to a discussion of myth, a kind of story that forms connections between unliterary, literary, and semi-literary readers. He maintains that the appreciation of myth is extraliterary rather than nonliterary. A myth is "a particular kind of story which has a value in itself—a value independent of its embodiment in any literary work" (41). Indeed, a book that seems sentimental and trashy to one person may convey a myth to another (48). Lewis mentions five modern examples of what he means by mythic: Stevenson's *Dr. Jekyll and Mr. Hyde,* Wells's *The Door in the Wall,* Kafka's *The Castle,*[10] the conception of Gormenghast in Peake's *Titus Groan,* and the Ents and Lothlorien in Tolkien's *Lord of the Rings* (42–43). All of these are more closely related to science fiction and fantasy than to the realistic novel.

Although Lewis does not specifically make the point, his argument leads to the conclusion that science fiction and fantasy may be capable of healing the gap between the Few and the Many. In *Principles of Literary Criticism* Richards mentions *Macbeth* as a work that can be enjoyed by both the sophisticated and the ignorant because it is multileveled. He speculates that drama declined in the seventeenth century because all the best themes that could be multileveled in treatment had been used up (213, 214). Analogously, one might argue that the nineteenth-century real-istic novel with its triple preoccupations of money, marriage, and manners could no longer satisfy twentieth-century readers, perhaps because all the typical novel plots that could be appreciated by both the Few and the Many were used up. If so, perhaps what Lewis sometimes calls mythopoeic fiction—science fiction and fantasy[11]—offers the best source of multi-leveled stories that are capable of appealing to the general public and the critical minority alike. The mythic elements that Joyce uses ironically in *Ulysses* can appear in a more accessible form in science fiction.[12]

Each of Lewis's three science fiction novels represents a different effort to explore the limits of the genre. In his essay "On Science Fiction," first given as a talk to the Cambridge University English Club in 1955, ten years after the publication of the third novel, he presents science fiction as one species of "fantastic or mythopoeic literature in general," because it deals with "the impossible—or things so immensely improbable that they have, imaginatively, the same status as the impossible" (*On Stories* 64). Lewis is very sensitive to the inherent imaginative qualities of different literary materials. In the essay "On Stories," for example, he discusses "the enormous difference" between the claustrophobic danger of the heroes in *King Solomon's Mines* and Bedford's danger of being left alone on the surface of the Moon to experience "'the infinite and final Night of space'" (*On Stories* 9). Although both the fairy tale and science fiction are mythopoeic, the latter's focus on space travel and some reasonably plausible "pseudo-scientific apparatus" (63, 64) makes it a different imaginative experience.

The two major subcategories of the genre are hard and soft science fiction, the hard stemming from Jules Verne and the soft from H. G. Wells. Hard science fiction is relatively more concerned with bringing the space travel and the pseudo-scientific apparatus in line with what is known to be possible—or at least not known to be impossible—at the time of writing. Lewis calls it "the fiction of Engineers" and says that he is "too uneducated scientifically" and too "out of sympathy with the projects" they describe to have any interest in it (58, 59). Soft science fiction is less concerned with technical accuracy and more human-centered. One subtype is the imaginary voyage.[13] It differs from hard science fiction's voyage in that it concentrates on the human mind as it experiences the new environment rather than the technical possibility of such travel. Wells's *The First Men in the Moon* is of this type, and Lewis's *Out of the Silent Planet* is a development of, and variation on, Wells's creation.

Another subtype is what Lewis calls "the Eschatological." Stapledon's *Last and First Men* and Wells's *The Time Machine* are examples (61). Lewis's *Perelandra* is eschatological in its attention to the nature and destiny of man, but a great deal of its interest is the experience of being on a strange planet. Lewis very much appreciated the pure fantasy set in a completely improbable world. He admired David Lindsay's *A Voyage to Arcturus* as an example of this type, saying, "it is [the] wonder, or beauty, or suggestiveness [of such worlds] that matters" (*On Stories* 64). *Perelandra* thus combines the eschatological and the improbable-world fantasies, although Lewis does more than Lindsay to make his planet seem probable.

A third subtype is the extrapolation of some ominous or ridiculous tendency in present-day society, such as the threat of overpopulation or the mind-numbing dominance of the media. It contains one or more inventions. Huxley's *Brave New World* is such an extrapolation, with the "Malthusian belt" and the "feelies." Extrapolation differs from hard science fiction in that there is little or no attention to how the apparatus works, and in that it is usually satirical. *That Hideous Strength* may be seen as an extrapolation from modern society's tendency to dehumanize people, destroy the environment, and exercise control over public opinion through the media. It certainly possesses the satirical focus of this subgenre,[14] and the Pragmatometer foreshadows present-day computer networks. It is similar in theme to Orwell's *Nineteen Eighty-Four,* its near contemporary, which is an extrapolation based on the intrusiveness of twentieth-century media.

Lewis says that what he seeks in science fiction and fantasy is a new "quality" or "flavour," an expansion of consciousness through "sensations we never had before" (*On Stories* 66). Each book of the Ransom trilogy provides such sensations, and, furthermore, each one of them contributes in some way to the twentieth-century preoccupation with the nature of language. *Out of the Silent Planet* half-casually introduces the language issue with Ransom, the hero, as a philologist; *Perelandra* explores the relationship between language and consciousness in a primitive woman. And *That Hideous Strength,* like *Nineteen Eighty-Four,* deals with language as a tool of social control. Of course, all three have concerns other than language: human-race chauvinism, alternatives to industrial man, the spiritual—as opposed to the empirically verifiable—pattern of the universe. All three are at cross-purposes with Bell's four characteristics of the modernist novel, for they depict heroes rather than questionable personal identities, insist on the importance of time and the nonrandomness of events, and use myth as something important in itself rather than as a resonating counterpoint of modern life. In creating the Ransom trilogy Lewis contributed substantially to the development of the "scientific romance" into a serious, philosophical mode of fiction which, being multileveled, can appeal to common readers as well as literati.

The remainder of this chapter is devoted to *Out of the Silent Planet* and *Perelandra,* with special attention to how Lewis developed Wells's basic concepts. Because it presents problems other than the development of the science fiction genre, *That Hideous Strength* will be treated in a chapter of its own.

Out of the Silent Planet

In showing that *Out of the Silent Planet* represents a significant contribution to the development of the science fiction genre, the first step is to observe how Lewis augmented Wells's *First Men in the Moon*,[15] changing the mere adventure story into one with a serious moral point. Since moral discussion in the early twentieth century so often led to questions of literary theory and the nature of language, the second step is to note the passages in which Lewis implicitly criticizes the views of I. A. Richards. Finally, the fundamental objection that *Out of the Silent Planet* does not belong to the science fiction genre at all because it is too scientifically inaccurate will be considered, although this objection is less often raised today as the gap between science fiction and mainstream fiction narrows.[16]

It has long been recognized that *Out of the Silent Planet* is closely related to *First Men in the Moon*.[17] In Wells's 1901 novel, Bedford, a hard-up young journalist and entrepreneur, meets Cavor, an absentminded scientist who has invented an antigravity material. Cavor builds a spherical container in which they can live and devises a method of controlling the antigravity effect by something like window shades. He wants to travel to the Moon, and Bedford goes along because he believes there is money in it. They experience the loneliness and personal detachment of being in space; they hear the pings of meteorites on the outside of their ship.

Upon landing, they find that the Moon has a cycle of vegetation based on the lunar day (fourteen of our days). Since the surface cannot support life continuously, the Selenites live *in* the Moon.[18] Captured by the Selenites, the travelers are overcome by fear and kill some of them in an effort to escape. Bedford gets back to the sphere and manages to return to Earth, taking some of the gold that abounds on the Moon. Left behind, Cavor learns a little of the Selenite language, builds a radio transmitter, and broadcasts descriptions of the culture. He reports that the Selenites are like ants with bodies specialized to perform just one task in their complex industrial society. Then he is taken before the planetary ruler, where he imprudently expatiates on the human talent for violence and war. The Grand Lunar prudently has him put to death. After Bedford returns to Earth, a boy meddles with the spaceship and causes it to fly off the Earth, so that no second journey is possible.

The parallels between *Out of the Silent Planet* and *First Men in the Moon* show how much Lewis appreciated the space travel premises established by Wells. Lewis uses the same characters: Dick Devine is Lewis's entrepreneur, Weston his scientist. He uses a similar spaceship, a sphere moved by natural forces and using shutters. He describes the experience of being in space, especially the sound of meteors pinging against the ship. Lewis's Malacandrians, like Wells's Selenites, live *in* their planet, for the surface cannot support life. Like the Selenites, the Malacandrians have body shapes specialized to perform different functions in the society. In Lewis's story as in Wells's, the turning point is the killing of an indigenous creature. In both stories there is an audience with the planetary ruler—the Grand Lunar of the Moon, the Oyarsa of Malacandra—who hears the case and passes judgment. Wells's Grand Lunar condemns Cavor to death; Lewis's Oyarsa lets the space travelers live but alters the spaceship so that it will disintegrate after it returns to Earth, thus preventing any new space voyages.

In a sense, *Out of the Silent Planet* is a sequel to *First Men in the Moon* because it recounts the space travelers' *second* trip to the planet. In another sense, it is an entirely different sort of journey because the entrepreneur and the scientist take along another traveler, Ransom the philologist. His presence overturns and replaces the thematic emphasis of *First Men in the Moon*. Ransom's vocation is the key to the deeper moral seriousness of *Out of the Silent Planet* and to its handling of twentieth-century language issues.

To elucidate this point, it is helpful to consider the difference between philology and the science of linguistics which developed out of philology in the early twentieth century, especially in the 1930s. The research procedures of Bloomfield and other linguists, usually applied to unwritten tribal languages, were modeled on behaviorist psychology; consequently the linguists emphasized objectivity and at first refused to deal with meaning at all. The discipline of philology, on the other hand, has been largely focused on the study of old documents—establishing the provenience of manuscripts, tracing the relationships between multiple copies of a document, and resolving disputed readings. Since there are no living speakers, philologists cannot proceed by observing speakers' behavior; they must work more subjectively, seeking to understand the language of the document from within, combining sympathetic identification with the manuscript and rigorous editorial procedures. Also, since the philologist works primarily with the classical languages—Greek, Latin, and Hebrew—that have been the carriers of Western culture, in Lewis's time they were deeply concerned with the relationship of language to culture. It is no accident that Jacob Grimm the philologist collected folklore or that Tolkien the philologist created cultures to go with his dialects of Elvish. As Barfield, also a philologist, has said, "If there was a language, there must have been a people who spoke it, and attention was soon focused on the character, civilization and whereabouts [of these people]" (*English Words* 10).

The introduction of Ransom, a character whose professional interest is in classical learning and nonempirical methodology, is the lever by which Lewis overturns common modernist views of the universe. He was writing to refute people like J. B. S. Haldane and Olaf Stapledon, in addition to Ogden and Richards and Wells, who simply assumed that scientific knowledge frees us from delusion and narrow-mindedness, brings uncounted material benefits, and makes traditional ideas of God and the soul unnecessary. Haldane says as much in *Daedalus: or, Science and the Future* (1923): "We must learn not to take traditional morals too seriously. And it is just because even the least dogmatic of religions tends to associate itself with some kind of unalterable moral tradition, that there can be no truce between science and religion" (90).

Lewis reverses this modernist creed by portraying Ransom the philologist as one who can understand and adjust to the real nature of the universe, precisely because he has absorbed the moral tradition from old documents, while Weston, the scientist, is deluded, narrow-minded, rigid, and illogical. Left alone in a completely strange environment, Ransom becomes a hnakra-punt, a respected member of the Hrossian community. Weston, arrogantly attempting to patronize the Malacandrians as savages, becomes a figure of fun. Lewis is not saying that philologists are more ethical than other people; in fact, he complains that because of "chronological snobbery" many scholars are remarkably unaffected by the ethical content of the documents they study. But the values are there; it is possible to embrace them, and Ransom does.

In the process of questioning the modernist creed, at every point Lewis adds philosophic depth to his reworking of Wells's story. Even such a small detail as the way the point-of-view character (Bedford in *First Men in the Moon*, Ransom in *Out of the Silent Planet*) happens to go on the voyage is philosophically significant. Bedford came to Lympne in Kent to escape his creditors and to recoup his losses by writing a play. He got acquainted with Cavor because the absentminded scientist disturbed him by walking outside his cottage and making a buzzing noise. In contrast, Ransom makes contact with Devine and Weston as a result of his commitment to the traditional virtues of temperance, justice, prudence, and courage taught in old books. Temperate and self-controlled, he "might have," but did not, pronounce "a malediction on the inhospitable little hotel which . . . had refused him a bed" (7). After avoiding the malediction, he meets Harry's mother and promises to call at the Rise to see what has become of the retarded young man, prudently reflecting that he is likely to find hospitality there. But the Rise proves so uninviting that he is tempted to pass by, and if he had nobody would have been the wiser; only justice compels him to carry out his promise to the old woman, and courage enables him to throw his pack over the hedge. Wells's Bedford comments on the way he met Cavor with a certain ersatz solemnity, "So utterly at variance is Destiny with all the little plans of men" (391); the effect is superficial because Wells never shows that destiny is operative. Lewis's book is not superficial at this point because Ransom's moral character, not someone's accidental mannerism, leads to his destiny.

Lewis magnifies the opposition between traditional values and the motivations of Devine and Weston by darkening their characters, by making them despicable where Bedford and Cavor are simply funny. Bedford is merely a journalist hoping to make a buck. He bilks his creditors and keeps his mouth shut about the death of the boy who meddles with the spaceship; but he is self-centered rather than malicious. Devine is also mercenary and dishonorable; but he actively hates common morality, instead of just ignoring it as Bedford does. Devine has cultivated cynicism so long that his life is twisted into a perpetual sneer. His flippant remarks about the far-flung line, the Dear Old Place, and the noble savage recall Screwtape's remark that "the habit of Flippancy builds up . . . the finest armor-plating against the Enemy [God] that I know" (*The Screwtape Letters* 52).

In like manner, Cavor is merely a stereotypical absentminded scientist. Where Weston is egotistical, Cavor is modest. As Bedford reports in astonishment, "when he [Cavor] said it was 'the most important' research the world had ever seen he simply meant it squared up so many theories, settled so much that was in doubt" (*First Men* 400). Weston's advanced knowledge only serves to make him overbearing toward other people. He describes Ransom's specialty as "unscientific foolery" (13), considers everyone except "the four or five real physicists now living" (25) as his intellectual inferiors, and scorns the Malacandrians. Cavor, in contrast, is generally humble, has a puppylike desire to make friends with the Selenites, and plans to communicate with them by means of geometric designs (*First Men* 448). Weston is ruthless in his willingness to sacrifice first Harry and then Ransom to the supposed Malacandrian deity. Cavor is somewhat ruthless, saying, "There must be risks! . . . In experimental work there always are!" (406). But compared with Weston, his near-stripping of the atmosphere from the Earth is the result of a charming absentmindedness.

Lewis further magnifies the opposition between Ransom and his captors by giving the good characteristics of Bedford and Cavor to Ransom. Although Bedford is essentially a very superficial young man, as he travels in the spaceship he experiences his own insignificance in the universe and gains some detachment; in *Out of the Silent Planet* it is Ransom rather than Bedford's counterpart Dick Devine who gains detachment. Cavor's good characteristic is his thirst for knowledge; in *Out of the Silent Planet* it is Ransom rather than Weston who possesses "the love of knowledge [which] is a kind of madness" (55). Devine and Weston cold-bloodedly plan to sacrifice Ransom to the sorns; Bedford and Cavor would be incapable of premeditated murder, although Bedford does kill some Selenites out of fear. Furthermore, Bedford and Cavor in their treatment of each other show no trace of the magnanimity that Ransom first displays when he freely volunteers to be cook/housemaid on the outbound journey.[19] Thus Lewis systematically darkens the characters he received from Wells's story.

It might be argued that in making Ransom so unmistakably good and his captors so evil Lewis has eliminated moral complexity from his story. On the contrary, Cavor and Bedford are a mixture of good and evil not because their characterization is complex but, rather, because Wells is downplaying or ignoring the moral implications of his adventure story. When Cavor believes that his workers were killed in the cavorite accident, he remarks that their lives are "not much good" (404). In the character of Weston, Lewis shows that this single-minded search for knowledge can lead to outright criminality, and he raises the emotional ante by making the issue the deliberate sacrifice of people we know—Harry or Ransom—rather than the destruction of property or anonymous people's lives. Weston's willingness to sacrifice Ransom is brutally expressed: "Still, he's only an individual, and probably a quite useless one" (19).

Lewis's description of the human experience of space is also more philosophically serious than that of Wells. On the outbound voyage Wells's Bedford begins to perceive monetary transactions as trivial. Concerning "those companies we were going to run" he says, "I don't see 'em here" (416). On the way home, alone, he experiences profound detachment, seeing the sphere as a "little speck of matter in infinite space" and himself as an ass, "the son of many generations of asses." Finally he comes to feel that he is "something quite outside not only the world, but all worlds, and out of space and time, and that this poor Bedford was just a peephole through which I looked at life" (488–89).

Ransom experiences a similar detachment, but for different reasons. On the outward journey he is delighted by the possibility of moving from endless day to endless night simply by going to a different part of the spaceship. He perceives that space is filled with radiance and beauty and decides that "[o]lder thinkers had been wiser when they named it simply the heavens" (32). In effect, Lewis takes Haldane's observation, "The universe is not only queerer than we suppose, but queerer than we can suppose" and amends it to "The universe is not only more beautiful than we suppose, but more beautiful than we can suppose." On the way home Ransom has learned from Oyarsa that space is full of the angelic eldila and that the suns and planets which interrupt space are less vital than the dance of the heavenly beings which they interrupt. He finds that "he and all his race showed small and ephemeral against a background of such immeasurable fullness" (147). The old concept of "the heavens" with the neo-Platonic doctrine of plenitude is more accurate than the modern one of "outer space." Although Lewis may not have succeeded in convincing the modern reader of the literal existence of the eldila, the concept of a full universe inhabited by a diversity of intelligent lifeforms has become almost a truism in contemporary science fiction. In developing and expanding upon the experience in space of Wells's Bedford, Lewis asserts the meaningfulness of the universe.

Where Wells's work contains a vivid touch of something more than scientific romance, Lewis builds on it. For example, in Bedford and Cavor's first hours on the Moon they watch the lunar sunrise, see the seeds begin to sprout, and experience the force with which living beings seek to live. It is well done. Years before time-lapse photography, Wells imagines that the growth of the plants would look like the creeping of mercury in a thermometer, a remarkably accurate description that mediates to the reader the wonder of life. Lewis adds to his description of the strangeness of vegetable life on a different world a reference to the way human consciousness works. He uses Barfield's assertion that "the most elementary distinctions of form and colour are only apprehended by us with the help of the concepts which we have come to unite with the pure sense-datum" (*Poetic Diction* 57). Ransom looks at the landscape of Malacandra and sees only "colours that refused to form themselves into things" because "you cannot see things till you know roughly what they are" (42). This detail, like so many of the others, adds philosophic depth to the space adventure.

Lewis's most important expansion and development of Wells's original idea comes in the description of the aliens' social organization. *First Men in the Moon* portrays an industrialized society in which the citizens are inevitably destined to carry out a certain function in society and shaped for it by an "elaborate discipline of training and education and surgery." One who is being trained as a mathematician, for example, loses "the faculty of laughter, save for the sudden discovery of some paradox" (512). Since sexual activity is of limited value to the society, most of the Selenites are neuter, and the mothers who procreate the young are incapable of nurturing them (516). The Selenites live only to work, and when their services are not needed they are put to sleep by drugs (515). Lewis's Malacandrians, like the Selenites, are specialized according to their function in the social system; however, their bodies are shaped by natural growth, not cruel and invasive biological engineering. All of them reproduce sexually, although the pfifltriggi are most interested in sex and the seroni least. The description of the Malacandrian ways of life shows that Lewis regards pleasure as an intrinsic element in the pattern of the universe. The primary function of all three species is to enjoy themselves; their economic contribution to society is definitely secondary. The hrossa are devoted to making poetry and the sport of hnakra-hunting, and on the side they fish and grow vegetables; the seroni delight in scholarship—scientific theory, history, and philosophy—but they also work as herdsmen; the pfifltriggi are primarily artists and jewelry makers, although they also do some building and manufacture some needed objects (like the oxygen mask that Augray the sorn gives to Ransom). The Malacandrians have chosen (or perhaps Oyarsa has chosen for them) to accept a lower standard of living in exchange for freedom and leisure.

This arrangement reflects a deep conviction of Lewis's that biologists and social scientists err in attributing too much to the economic or materialistic motive, even in the animal world.[20] As he remarks in a letter to Barfield,

> Talking of beasts and birds, have you ever noticed this contrast: that when you read a scientific account of any animal's life you get an impression of laborious, incessant, almost rational economic activity (as if all animals were Germans), but when you study any animal you know, what at once strikes you is their cheerful fatuity, the pointlessness of nearly all they do. Say what you like, Barfield, the world is sillier and better fun than they make out . . . (*Letters* 217)

Thus, Lewis would argue that his imaginary Malacandrians with their playfulness are closer to commonsense observations about our own world than Wells's intense, narrow-minded Selenites.

Another instance of Lewis's deepening of the moral implications of the adventure involves Ransom's observations of Malacandrian population control. In *First Men in the Moon* Cavor does not find out exactly how the Selenites control their population, although the implication is that the planners simply would not allow unneeded workers to be produced. At any rate, the Grand Lunar is shocked by Cavor's suggestion that human wars are useful in reducing the surplus population. In contrast, Ransom learns that the Malacandrians voluntarily limit their numbers. Once a couple produces progeny, the partners abstain from sex (as Malthus advised), content to remember their mating and to gain wisdom from it.

Although Lewis's separation of good from bad is simple, his description of the social system is more artistically complex than that of Wells. The descriptions Cavor transmits to Earth are simple, transparent, accurate. What you see is what you get. Ransom's observations are constantly being corrected. His mindset as a philologist saves him from the grosser errors of Weston; nevertheless, he tries to understand the planet in terms of earthly, materialistic standards and repeatedly learns that he is wrong. For example, he first decides that the hrossa's remarks about the seroni who live above them are references to their mythology. Because of their primitive living arrangements, "he took it for granted they were on a low cultural level" (64). Later, when he learns that the seroni are the intelligentsia, the scientists, he assumes that they must "[use] their scientific resources for the exploitation of their uncivilized neighbours" (70), as the white men on Earth have done.

Wells's criticism of imperialism is confined to Bedford's remark that the moon plants are an excellent food, second only to the Irish potato, his plan to "annex this moon" and thus assume "the White Man's Burden," and his drunken desire to prove "that the arrival of Columbus was, after all, beneficial to America" (441). Lewis not only ridicules Weston's imperialism in his interview with the Oyarsa, but he also shows Ransom's imperial pride being humbled. First Ransom considers whether it is his duty to instruct his primitive hosts in the true religion and is greatly surprised when he finds himself "being treated as if *he* were the savage and being given a first sketch of civilized religion" (68). Next he finds that the hrossa are far above human beings in ethical behavior. They share food with other Malacandrians, are naturally chaste, and meet death without fear. Ransom begins to realize that technological advancement and ethical advancement do not necessarily coincide, as Wells with his love of science and technology often implies. Ransom's education[21] along this line continues when he goes among the seroni and finds that technological advancement is not necessary for intellectual achievement either. Although the seroni live very simply, in caves, they are scientifically sophisticated and express surprise at Ransom's ignorance. Finally, at Meldilorn, he learns that the Malacandrian civilization is so old that it predates the existence of life on Earth and realizes that man's assumption of superiority is simply naive.

Thus within the framework of the given Wellsian narrative Lewis communicates his philosophical disagreement with social Darwinism, with the modern social scientist's common assumption that economics is destiny, with the modern pride in technology. This depiction of the moral dimensions of scientific advancement is one of the tasks that science fiction, among all forms of literature, is uniquely qualified to accomplish, and Lewis's work helped to push the genre in that direction.[22]

In addition to the more serious moral dimension, Lewis also implicitly criticizes Richards's ideas; however, such questions about the nature of language and literary theory are not as important in *Out of the Silent Planet* as they become in *That Hideous Strength*. First, Ransom's education in beauty refutes the idea that there is no such thing as an aesthetic faculty in man and therefore no such thing as beauty aside from one's own experiences. In outer space Ransom finds beauty that is "out there" whether any human being sees it or not, and he is able to recognize it by giving up his previous belief that space is cold and dead. Later on he perceives that the Malacandrians are beautiful when he learns to look at them properly.

At first Ransom went back and forth between two views of the hrossa: on the one hand, they were "abominable—a man seven feet high, with a snaky body, covered, face and all, with thick black animal hair, and whiskered like a cat"; on the other hand, "an animal with everything an animal ought to have—glossy coat, liquid eye, sweet breath and whitest teeth—and added to all these, as though Paradise had never been lost and earliest dreams were true, the charm of speech and reason" (58). The context of the story makes it clear that the second point of view is truer than the first, for the same thing happens more quickly in his contact with the sorns. Taking shelter in Augray's cave on his way to Meldilorn, Ransom finds that the sorn is "less terrifying than he had expected" and "more grotesque than horrible" (92). Later on he sees three of the creatures in motion, coming "swiftly down like full-rigged ships before a fair wind," and "the grace of their movement" moves him to see them as "'Titans' or 'Angels'" rather than monsters. He calls his previous attitude toward them "not so much cowardly as vulgar," adding, "So might Parmenides or Confucius look to the eyes of a Cockney schoolboy!" (101). It is clear that he has now learned how to look at them in the right way. He never quite warms up to the "insect-like or reptilian" pfifltriggi (who come nearest to fulfilling the science fiction convention of the Bug-Eyed Monster), but he does appreciate their quality. In fact, the one he meets reminds him of "a little old taxidermist whom [he] knew in London" (113). In *Perelandra* Ransom completes this reeducation, learning that his abhorrence of an enormous insect is not consonant with the true nature of the universe but is due to demonic influence on his mind. Richards exhorts us to say that something that would in ordinary language be called beautiful "causes an experience . . . which is valuable in certain ways" (*Principles* 20). Lewis makes it quite clear that the perception of beauty depends on one's willingness to take in the universe as it really is. In these two earlier novels we see an implicit affirmation of objective standards of beauty; Lewis later makes the affirmation explicit in *The Abolition of Man* and *That Hideous Strength*.

In addition to insisting that the universe is objectively beautiful, Lewis implicitly criticizes Richards's literary theory in the description of the hrossa's artistic activity. It consisted of "a kind of poetry and music which was practised almost every evening by a team or troupe or four *hrossa*" (66). Lewis does not make it clear whether the performances were improvisations on familiar themes, like the folk tales and ballads that philologists collected in the nineteenth century, or whether they were quite original. They apparently were not repetitions of traditional compositions, like the Homeric bards' performances of the *Iliad* and *Odyssey,* for Hyoi tells Ransom that poetry cannot be repeated: "For the most splendid line becomes fully splendid only by means of all the lines after it; if you went back to it you would find it less splendid than you thought. You would kill it" (73). Later on the sorns tell Ransom, "The hrossa . . . say that the writing of books destroys poetry" (101). These passages obliquely comment on the New Critics' close analysis of poetry, with the implication that the attempt to objectify literary responses—to treat them as objects of scrutiny— falsifies the experience.

In context Hyoi is comparing the desire to go back and hear the poem again with the desire—in his view false and perverted—to repeat the pleasure of mating, or of eating and sleeping after bodily needs have been satisfied. Hyoi explains that one remembers pleasures, but the memory is the fulfillment of the original experience, not a repetition of it. The memory is not an objective examination of what happened, but a meditation on it, modified by the experiences one has had in the interval. On first reading, the Malacandrian belief that one cannot go back, either in life or in literature, seems like mere local color—something to make Martian culture strangely different from the terrestrial. But the idea occurs again in *Perelandra,* where Ransom is restrained from repeating a gustatory pleasure, and even in *The Voyage of the Dawn Treader,* where Lucy is unable to turn back the page and reread the story in the book of magic. When one attempts to repeat a pleasure, it becomes something else; in *The Pilgrim's Regress* John's desire to hear Mr. Halfways sing the same song over turns desire for beauty into lust for Media Halfways. It is perhaps not overreading to see in this detail Lewis's continued distaste for modernist literary structures with their abstract patterns of timelessness and collages of random events. For Lewis, Story—a succession of events in time—was important, not just as a source of pleasure but also as an emblem of the universe's essential nature. On another level, the passage is an expression of Lewis's dislike of the social sciences and their attempt to objectify human actions, since the test of objectified, scientific methodology is that the results shall be repeatable. (In *Practical Criticism*, for example, Richards tries to make the results of literary criticism more repeatable.)

Finally, the interview between Oyarsa and the men from Earth contains a veiled commentary on Richards's view of language. Readers easily recognize that Weston's grand generalities become ridiculous when they are translated into the simple words and sentences permitted by Ransom's limited knowledge of the Malacandrian language. Like the description of the steamship in Pidgin English which Barfield quotes in *Poetic Diction*, Ransom's rendering of Weston's speech results in a heightened consciousness of what he is really saying. But the joke becomes more pointed with the realization that Weston makes the false rhetorical moves attributed to traditional metaphysicians in *The Meaning of Meaning*.

Ogden and Richards condemned metaphysicians for using words that have no referent, for using statements that seem to make sense simply because the sentence is grammatical. Such statements often include reification and personification—treating abstractions as though they were concrete things and people. Weston is guilty of reification when he says, "I bear on my shoulders the destiny of the human race," when destiny is not an object that can be carried. He is guilty of personification when he says, "Life is greater than any system of morality; her claims are absolute" (135, 136). Lewis agreed with Ogden and Richards that these rhetorical moves are fallacious. There is no such thing as Life, but only living creatures, so that Weston's "Life is greater than any system of morality" becomes "He says that living creatures are stronger than the question whether an act is bent or good," followed by an alternate translation and finally Ransom's apologetic "I cannot say what he says, Oyarsa, in your language" (136). Weston adds personification to his fallacy of reification, calling life "She," and Ransom is forced to say meekly, "I'm sorry, but I've forgotten who She is," evoking Weston's irascible "Life, of course" (136). Ransom's ineffectual translation simply demonstrates that Weston intends to serve the cause of life by killing as many living creatures as possible.

The passage also suggests that the Malacandrian (or Old Solar, as it is later called) language is True Speech, the language that reflects the nature of the universe,[23] similar to the concrete but metaphorical speech Barfield attributes to prelogical man in *Poetic Diction*. Above all, Lewis's description of the extraterrestrial language reflects the Platonic theory of correspondence between words and forms that Ogden and Richards denigrate as "language superstition" and the source of "bogus entities." Since the Malacandrian language corresponds to the way things really are, Weston's nonsense is partially untranslatable.

Furthermore, the language philosophers account as meaningless any assertion that cannot be put in operational terms. Weston's assertion that his motive is "a man's loyalty to humanity" is meaningless, because his project of preserving humanity by sending human beings throughout the universe cannot be operationally described. Since he admits that the physical being of man would have to be changed, and since the ability to think and reason is not distinctive to man, there would be no way to determine that his project had actually preserved humanity. If the term "humanity" has nothing to do with an individual person's mind and body, then it is empty verbiage of the kind that Ogden and Richards deplore. Likewise, his concluding rhetorical flourish, "What lies in the future, beyond our present ken, passes imagination to conceive: it is enough for me that there is a Beyond"[24] sounds like the bravery of modern man in a world where belief in God is no longer possible. But according to language philosophy, the word "Beyond" is just as much without referent as the word "God."[25]

Weston is, in fact, a prime example of the fallacy of assuming that a scientist who is expert in his own field is also knowledgeable in other fields; he may know how to build and operate a spaceship, but he does not understand the rules of logic or "the meaning of meaning." When Weston is talking about his own subject, he is incisive—"If it makes you happy to repeat words that don't mean anything—which is, in fact, what unscientific people want when they ask for an explanation . . ." (25–26)—but having scorned the study of "unscientific foolery" (13) like philology and philosophy, he is unaware that the words he uses to express his purpose are as empty as the unscientific description of a scientific phenomenon.

Since the argument is being made that Lewis developed and deepened the science fiction genre, it is necessary to deal with a major obstacle to classifying *Out of the Silent Planet* as belonging to that genre—its scientific inaccuracies. Lewis admittedly made some ludicrous errors. For example, he apparently was unaware of the difference between weight and mass, so he depicts his space travelers compensating for weightlessness by wearing metal belts with huge weights on them. He also assumes that once the spaceship gets out of the gravitational field of Earth, "down" will be felt as the direction toward the center of the ship; in fact, the spaceship could not carry enough mass to give a human being a sense of gravitation. And he says the sun side of the ship is bathed with golden light, even though he knew the radiation of the sun could not be perceived as golden without something to refract it (see *The Discarded Image* 111).

Moreover, like the spherical world in *The Pilgrim's Regress,* the spaceship is badly out of perspective. In England, Ransom first sees it as "a huge round shape that rose black against the stars, which he took for the dome of a small observatory" (11–12). A sphere forty or fifty feet in diameter would fit this description. Inside the sphere is another sphere, a storage area. In space, the surface of the inner sphere becomes the floor of the rooms. If the walls of the rooms were about ten feet high, then the diameter of the inner sphere would be twenty or thirty feet. The ceiling of each room would indeed be, and appear to be, about twice the area of the floor. But adjoining rooms would not appear to be lying on their sides, as Lewis describes, because the eye level of a man would be at least five feet off the floor and the smallness of Ransom's room would interrupt the view.[26] One would have to be a mouse to experience the optical sensations Lewis describes.

The description of daily life aboard the ship is even more unrealistic. By comparison, Wells's provisions for traveling in space at first seem quite carefully considered. Bedford lists "compressed foods, concentrated essences, steel cylinders containing reserve oxygen, an arrangement for removing carbonic acid and waste from the air and restoring oxygen by means of sodium peroxide, water condensers, and so forth" (410). Lewis never mentions the need for oxygen or air purification, and his space travelers seem to live fairly well on canned food. Many unanswered questions arise: since Ransom is the cook, what kind of heating equipment does he use? What refrigeration? When he "washed up the remains of their evening meal," where did the water come from? When he dried his hands "on the roller-towel behind the galley door," what was done with the towel when it became dirty? What laundry facilities did the spaceship have? But Wells's seeming practicality is illusory; he is as remiss as Lewis in providing laundry and toilet facilities, and his failure to strap down the travelers and their impedimenta is a gaffe as serious as the ones Lewis makes.

In fact, both authors are more interested in a good story than in mechanical accuracy. Lewis describes life in space as a spiritual and emotional experience rather than a physical and mechanical one; and even

Wells moves quickly to the emotional significance of these provisions and arrangements: "I remember what a little heap they made in the corner, tins and rolls and boxes—convincingly matter-of-fact" (410).

In the Golden Age of science fiction, the 1940s and 1950s, Lewis's errors were, paradoxically, more intrusive than they are today. Now that we know what astounding technology is needed to support human life in space, now that we have seen men swimming through their space vehicles and have eaten the freeze-dried foods developed for use in space, Lewis's spaceship seems no more blameworthy than Dante's putting Mount Purgatory where Australia ought to be, or, more recently, Robert A. Heinlein's equipping his characters with slide rules rather than pocket calculators.[27] Technological development has become so rapid that distinctions between plausible and implausible gadgets have virtually disappeared. And as the science fiction and fantasy genres become more and more respectable, the "smug hostility" of the fans toward the literary critics who are "ignorant of the genre" (Conquest 43) subsides. By concentrating on the philosophical and ethical questions raised by space travel, Lewis contributed to this result.

Even so, Lewis's arrangements are no more preposterous than those of many other science fiction writers of his time. In numerous stories it is assumed that getting away from the Earth's gravitational field would bring into being the spaceship's own up/down orientation. Numerous other writers also fail to remember the difference between mass and weight. If we compare him with Heinlein, whose training in engineering and ballistics ensures correctness in matters of gravitation and velocity, we find that the master of hard science fiction, like Lewis, ignores scientific theories when it suits his purpose. For example, in *Time for the Stars* one identical twin, traveling on a starship at just under the speed of light, experiences the contraction of time and remains young while his brother ages normally on earth. In *Starman Jones*, on the other hand, the starship repeatedly attains such speeds without any apparent effect on Ellie's age relative to her "dirtside" boyfriend, Putzie.

It seems reasonable to conclude that Lewis's mistakes are not sufficient grounds for saying that *Out of the Silent Planet* is not science fiction. What we demand of science fiction is that the author portray extraordinary states of consciousness and non-ordinary social systems resulting from strange environments. The description of Ransom's stages of coping with the new environment of the spaceship is very well done. When he first regains consciousness after having been drugged and knocked out, he sees stars "pulsing with brightness as with some unbearable pain or pleasure" (21). His senses contradict each other, for the walls look slanted but feel perpendicular to the touch.[28] He exerts his muscles, and his body responds unexpectedly. He wonders momentarily if he is dead, and "his nerves [resist] a bottomless dismay" (24).

Lewis's description of the spaceship, out of perspective as it is, also contributes to the spiritual and emotional purposes of science fiction. He shows us that it is "a little world made cunningly"—like the Earth, where we live on the surface of one sphere within the larger sphere of the atmosphere. His description creates a momentary, wondering realization that the Earth itself is a kind of spaceship, a reaction that real-life astronauts experienced in the 1960s.

In the description of Malacandrian society Lewis shows how strange it would be to live without the competition and jealousy we take for granted. But we are less aware of the didactic thrust of the description because he focuses on another strangeness, that of a sophisticated society not based on literacy. This is another example of Wells's influence, for the Selenites have official rememberers rather than books. Oyarsa and the sorns function as rememberers to some extent, but the two cases are not otherwise parallel. For Wells, the existence of rememberers is one more instance of industrial specialization; for Lewis, the lack of books is the occasion for a subtle comment on the nature of literature and literary criticism.

The usual source of plausibility in science fiction is the inclusion of information about a single branch of science. For example, Heinlein's *Beyond This Horizon* contains a great deal about genetics and the relation of genetics to personality, but nothing about his usual favorite, ballistics. Lewis's major source of plausibility in *Out of the Silent Planet* is philology—an organized body of knowledge, if not an empirical science. Because Lewis knows a great deal about philology and has studied old texts such as Bernardus Silvestris's *Cosmographia,* he is familiar with a cosmology that turns early-twentieth-century astronomy inside out. His story is based on the speculation "What if the astrological myths of the ancients were essentially true?" In space Ransom feels extraordinarily well and attributes it to heavenly influences, so he finds it "night by night more difficult to disbelieve in old astrology" (31). On Malacandra, he learns of the existence of the eldila, who seem similar to the Silvans, Pans, and Nereids described by classical poets. Much later, at Meldilorn, Ransom finds that the old astrology was correct in assigning to each planet a heavenly being to control its orbit and to rule it. He finds that the personalities traditionally attributed to Mars, Venus, and Mercury are not simple inventions of terrestrial poets but are traditions of the solar system. This discovery is validated back on Earth when the fictional Lewis writes to Ransom about the word "Oyarses" in the *Cosmographia*.[29] The fact that Ransom found a version of this word being used on Malacandra witnesses to the truth of his experiences there.

Philology also adds to plausibility in the account of the first meeting with Hyoi, when Ransom systematically begins to break words into their roots. He learns that *Malacandra* is *mala-* plus *-handra* and that *handramit* is *handra-* plus *-mit*. Any student of language would proceed in exactly the same way. Some critics have objected that it is extremely unlikely that an extraterrestrial language would be so Earthlike and so easy to learn.[30] However, most linguists today believe that certain basic aspects of structure, such as the existence of morphemes (roots and other elements of words) and ways of combining them, are simply essential to the whole concept of language. Thus, the language of Tweel in Weinbaum's "A Martian Odyssey," which has no fixed referents, is not credible.[31] Other critics object that Ransom would not have been able to recognize so quickly that Hyoi's noises were language. However, Samarin's research on glossolalia (speaking in tongues) showed that both linguistically trained and untrained people were able to recognize that the glossolalia was not ordinary human language.[32] Therefore the first contact between Ransom and Hyoi is linguistically plausible.

For most readers, the important feature of science fiction is the sense of wonder it evokes. The smallest bone of plausibility is sufficient to quiet the yelping of critical disbelief. Lewis, like other good science fiction writers, supplies both the wonder and the plausibility. Of course, like other science fiction writers, he minimizes technical difficulties in order to keep the story moving. For example, he solves the problem of the spaceship's means of propulsion with Weston's ungracious and thoroughly characteristic refusal to explain: "If it makes you happy to repeat words that don't mean anything . . ." (25). He minimizes the question of whether Ransom could have instantly recognized Hyoi's speech as language (after all, Samarin's research had not been done at that time) by shifting the reader's attention away from the recognition and focusing on Ransom's state of mind. Instead of saying, "This seems incredible, but Ransom recognized the noises as speech," he says, "If you are not yourself a philologist, I am afraid you must take on trust the prodigious emotional consequences of this realization on Ransom's mind" (55). Then he covers himself further by having Ransom complain, in the postscript, about "the ruthless way in which you [Lewis] have cut down all the philological part" (155).

Despite its lack of empirical science, *Out of the Silent Planet* has the tone of science fiction. It uses conventional science fiction techniques of making plausible but spurious connections with reality. Ransom's knowledge of ancient documents and his procedures in learning the language contribute a great deal to the air of plausibility, especially for readers who have studied an Indo-European language other than English. If the novel had not promoted religious values, which are automatically assumed to be nonscientific, the question of its place in the science fiction category might never have been raised.

Perelandra

An excursus into the eschatological subgenre of science fiction, *Perelandra* builds on Wells's *The Time Machine.*[33] As he did in his first novel, Lewis starts with Wells's premises and builds on them to produce a more philosophical and artistically serious work of fiction. Lewis follows his model much less closely than he did in *Out of the Silent Planet,* but he does use Wells's narrative structure and plot outline. Furthermore, the theme of *The Time Machine* is the destiny of man as brought about by natural processes, especially those of evolution. *Perelandra* also deals with evolution, accepting the scientific theory of how it happened but denying the moral and philosophic implications that are popularly thought to follow from it. Lewis continues in *Perelandra* his refutation of the language philosophers, but this element is not as important as it is in *Out of the Silent Planet.* Language itself remains important, however, because in this book Lewis develops the method of characterizing his heroine through her language that he uses so masterfully in *Till We Have Faces.*

The first clue to the relationship between *Perelandra* and *The Time Machine* is the similarity in narrative structure. In both, the center of the story is a flashback. Wells's Time Traveler has a good friend who listens to him explain his theories and discuss his projected journey. The friend returns to the house a week later when the Time Traveler appears, suffering from a lame foot and bringing a flower from his travels. They share a meal and then the Traveler recounts his adventures. In *Perelandra* the good friend is the fictive Lewis. Ransom explains the background and the linguistic situation to Lewis and discusses his projected journey. More than a year later, Lewis returns to the house accompanied by a physician. Ransom emerges from his space capsule suffering from a wounded heel and bringing flowers from Perelandra. After a meal, he tells his story.

Ransom's story is also quite similar to that of the Time Traveler. Like the Time Traveler, he arrives at a place with a mild climate in the midst of precipitation—hail for the Time Traveler, warm rain for Ransom. Both find people who live on fruit and apparently have no goals beyond leisure and play—the Eloi for the Time Traveler, Tinidril for Ransom. The Time Traveler's friendship with Weena, whom he loves in his own way and tries to protect, is analogous to Ransom's friendship with Tinidril and his efforts to protect her from the Un-man. Both travelers are forced to fight underground, the Time Traveler with the Morlocks and Ransom with the Un-man, and both recoil from the unpleasant touch of the enemy. Both receive a vision of the final destiny of man. The Time Traveler takes his machine to the end of time and finds that man has been replaced by a few clawed creatures on a planet whose sun is about to go out. Ransom hears a kind of oratorio about the Great Dance, and "what had begun as speech was turned into sight" (218). Finally, both the Time Traveler and Ransom are forced to leave the locale and return to our world and time. The Time Traveler attempts a second trip and disappears permanently, his friend surmising that he journeyed into the past, "among the blood-drinking, hairy savages of the Age of Unpolished Stone, into the abysses of the Cretaceous Sea." The trip to Perelandra is Ransom's second trip. Although it is not a trip into the past, he finds naked, primitive people in a situation resembling Earth's past.

Like *The Time Machine*, *Perelandra* is an eschatological novel because it deals with the nature and final destiny of man. Wells introduces this dimension of his story by having the Time Traveler face a colossal statue of the Sphinx, the being who posed the riddle of man to Oedipus. He then answers the question by having the Time Traveler continue his journey all the way to the time when man no longer exists. As a thoroughly modern person, Wells thought of man's destiny in evolutionary terms, and the way to discuss it was to follow man into the future. An 1895 reviewer of *The Time Machine* astutely observed that time is "the most important of the conditions of organic evolution" (Hutton 34). As a twentieth-century man, Lewis cannot ignore evolution and the nature of time; but as a Christian, he thinks the key to the nature and destiny of man is to be found in the past, in original sin. Whereas the Time Traveler goes to the future, Ransom—in effect—goes to the past.

It is not at first evident that *Perelandra* fulfills the functions of a story of time travel. The conclusion of *Out of the Silent Planet,* "If there is to be any more space-traveling, it will have to be time-traveling as well," suggests that Lewis is thinking of Wells's book as the basis of his proposed sequel, and many critics see the Dark Tower fragment as a fulfillment of this virtual promise.[34] The contextual meaning of the sentence, however, is merely that as a philologist Ransom intends to search for additional information about the solar system in old books, since the reference to "Oyarses" in Bernardus Silvestris has illuminated his experience on Mars. Even if Lewis did begin the Dark Tower fragment to fulfill the promise, it seems plausible that he would have abandoned it as the better story of *Perelandra* occurred to him.

Lewis could have sent his hero backward in time to our own Garden of Eden; instead, Ransom goes to Venus, where the history of mankind is just beginning. Venus is a newer world than Earth because Lewis is following (as science fiction novels conventionally did in the 1930s and 1940s) the Laplace hypothesis that the planets were formed when a vast cloud of gas and dust began to contract and spin, throwing off blobs of matter that became planets. If this had happened, the outer planets, being thrown off first, would be older and the inner ones younger. Ransom's space travel is thus a kind of time travel because it takes him to a world similar to our own at an earlier stage of planetary development. In accordance with his interest in theology and especially in Milton's *Paradise Lost,* Lewis places Ransom's arrival time after the creation of humanity but before any temptation and Fall.[35]

Since *Perelandra* is structurally similar to *The Time Machine,* and since it is thematically similar in that both deal with the ultimate destiny of humankind, a structural analysis of *The Time Machine* should illuminate Lewis's novel to some degree. John Huntington's analysis divides *The Time Machine* into three major parts based on the Time Traveler's three hypotheses about the future. Each one focuses on a single aspect of evolutionary theory. There is a kind of dialectic as the Time Traveler formulates each hypothesis and then finds that he must modify it (41ff). In *Perelandra,* Ransom experiences three encounters with the Green Lady that are analogous to the three evolutionary hypotheses, and in each case his interaction with her shows how the kind of universe previously described in *Out of the Silent Planet* opposes the commonly held implications of evolutionary theory.

The Time Traveler's first hypothesis is that the Eloi are feeble and childlike because at some time in their past, human life had become so secure that strength and intelligence were no longer needed, thus circumventing the evolutionary mechanism of survival of the fittest.[36] Analogously, Ransom's first conversation with Tinidril addresses the concept of survival of the fittest. She shows Ransom that the Malacandrians are not inferior, or unfit, because they are a dying race, for "they are their own part of history and not another" (*Perelandra* 63). Thus, she refutes the conclusion popularly drawn from evolution that whatever is newer is better, that change is always progress. Tinidril sees a difference between substantive change and the randomness of mere passage of time: "Among times there is a time that turns a corner and everything this side of it is new," but the old is not "rubbish to be swept away" (62, 63).

Ransom's second conversation with Tinidril is analogous to the Time Traveler's second evolutionary hypothesis, one concerning man as a social being. In Victorian times, the evolutionary mechanism of survival of the fittest was used to explain class distinctions. Thus the Time Traveler's second hypothesis is that nineteenth-century class distinctions have resulted in two races, with the Eloi having developed from the aristocrats and the Morlocks from the working class. Ransom's second conversation with Tinidril also deals with class distinctions. The Lady finds out that she is of higher rank than Ransom, since she is the mother of her world while he is merely one of the children in his world. She begins to treat him with "deliberate courtesy, even . . . ceremony" (67). At the end of the conversation she dismisses Ransom (he had ended the first one) and the account concludes, "The *audience* was at an end" (71; emphasis added).

This second scene also presents Lewis's belief in hierarchy, mentioned only in passing in *Out of the Silent Planet* (102). Although Lewis admitted that democracy is the best form of government for flawed and fallen man, he believed, with Milton, that hierarchical authority is the natural state of unfallen man, because authority comes from God. This scene shows Tinidril, in the absence of other humans to rule, exercising her skills of queenship over the animals for their benefit, "mak[ing] them older every day" (65). Just as she rules the beasts, Maleldil rules her; thus it is in this conversation that she becomes aware of her obedience to God: "I thought that I was carried in the will of Him I love, but now I see that I walk with it" (69).

This conversation on hierarchy and class distinction must, however, be placed in the whole context of the book. Lewis does not, like Samuel Wilberforce, an early Christian spokesman against evolution, believe that man's superiority is based on having been created as a separate species. Later in the book, when Ransom is riding on the fish, he speculates that "the King and Queen of Perelandra . . . might on the physical side have a marine ancestry" (102). Neither does man's domination over animals, or some men's social superiority to others, justify cruelty. Lewis shows Tinidril, the unfallen woman, treating the animals almost like human beings.[37] The cruel, senseless torture of flying frogs and the killing of birds to make a useless feather cloak for Tinidril are the works of the Un-man, not actions justified by human superiority.

The Time Traveler's third hypothesis, according to Huntington, is that the Eloi are cattle for the Morlocks. But this third section of *The Time Machine* is more involved with the issue of man's relationship to scientific knowledge, especially the use of technology to control the environment. As the Time Traveler goes exploring, he uses matches to keep the Morlocks at bay and to create a small circle of security for himself. That matches symbolized science and technology for Wells is shown in this quotation from "The Rediscovery of the Unique":

> Science is a match that man has just got alight. . . . It is a curious sensation, now that the preliminary splutter is over and the flame burns up clear, to see his hands lit and just a glimpse of himself and the patch he stands on visible, and around him, . . . darkness still.[38]

The matches, which symbolize technology, are for the Time Traveler like the Fixed Land is for Tinidril: both represent security and control.[39] In Ransom's third encounter with her, she proposes to go to the Fixed Land because she knows that the height of the mountain will give her a better view of the sea. Technology augments the natural powers of man, and the high mountain will augment her search for Tor.[40] Later on, during the temptations, the Un-man argues that living on the Fixed Land would have prevented her from being "suddenly separated" from her husband (104). He also points out that if she lived on the Fixed Land she could keep things, such as the feather robe he made for her or the hand mirror.

He urges her to "become mistress of your own days" and not live "from day to day, like the beasts" (138).

The excursion that Ransom and Tinidril make to the Fixed Land segues into the temptation segment, so that Lewis seems to be saying that human beings cannot be both innocent and technologically sophisticated. Furthermore, during the temptations the Un-man argues that technology came about because of the Fall, and Ransom does not contradict him. But what Lewis is really saying is that technology is subordinate to moral choice. At the end of the book, dwelling on the Fixed Land is no longer forbidden, and Tor the King announces plans to build a great meetinghouse there. He also plans to take such complete control over the environment that "[w]hen the time is ripe for it . . . we will tear the sky curtain and Deep Heaven shall become familiar to the eyes of our sons" (211). Thus Lewis answers Haldane's fear that a worldwide religious revival might strangle research before human beings learned to control their own evolution (see Hillegas, *Nightmare* 141).

The King's confidence contrasts with the insecurity of the Time Traveler. Although, as Huntington points out, the matches create some safety for him, they often let him down. The forest fire he starts with matches nearly destroys him as well as his enemies, and his campfire goes out while he is asleep. When he is trying to fight off the Morlocks long enough to activate the Time Machine, the safety matches from the museum fail him because they can be struck only on their own box (Huntington 48–50). But because King Tor is unfallen, his science and technology will not fail him.

At the time that Lewis was creating his Venusian Eden, he was working on the university lectures that later became *A Preface to "Paradise Lost"* (Green and Hooper 166–68). He adopted several features from Milton's expansion of the biblical story, features so well known that most people do not realize they are in Milton but not Genesis. The most important is the concept that the divine prohibition was purposely attached to a morally indifferent action—eating a fruit in *Paradise Lost* and sleeping on the Fixed Land in *Perelandra*—so that the issue might be one of pure obedience. Another Miltonian concept is that Eve was not really tempted by the serpent, but rather Satan in the serpent's body. Similarly, it was not Weston who tempted Tinidril, but a demon inhabiting his body. Milton also shows that Eve's imagination was corrupted before she actually willed to disobey God, for Satan crouched beside her as she slept and influenced her dreams, just as the Un-man corrupts Tinidril's imagination by telling her tragic stories. Finally, Lewis adopts Milton's idea that the temptation occurred while Adam and Eve were separated. However, Milton's Eve insisted on working apart from Adam, showing that her fall was already beginning, while Tor and Tinidril's separation is due to a storm at sea, something completely out of their control.

These resemblances to Milton—and to the Eden story in general—have seemed so all-encompassing that critics have not looked for another source. The Miltonic source is undeniable, but as the previous analysis has shown, the narrative frame, sequence of adventures, and evolutionary theme come from *The Time Machine* rather than the story of the Fall. Lewis also adopts a number of small details from *The Time Machine,* though he changes their significance. For example, both the Time Traveler and Ransom wanted a bath and a meal as soon as they returned, but for the Time Traveler it is an evening meal and for Ransom it is breakfast. This small detail harmonizes with the differences between the two experiences: the Time Traveler saw the nightfall of human existence; Ransom saw the morning. It expresses Lewis's belief in eternity, that the end of time is the occasion of a new beginning. Ransom says to King Tor, "[W]hat you call the beginning we are accustomed to call the Last Things," and Tor replies, "I see no more than beginnings in the history of the Low Worlds [the inhabited planets]. And in yours a failure to begin. You talk of evenings before the day has dawned" (212, 213). Thus Lewis expresses in an apparently random detail his Christian hope.

Other changes in small details express his confidence that humanity is at home in the universe. For example, the Time Traveler rides in a machine that he built himself, and he is constantly nauseated by a falling sensation. Ransom rides in a celestial coffin without fear of death and experiences the falling sensation only as his container approaches the planet. Similarly, the Eloi pelted the Time Traveler with flowers out of simple-minded playfulness; Tor and Tinidril purposefully covered Ransom with flowers to protect him on his homeward journey. At the end of the Time Traveler's journey, the Traveler is "dusty and dirty" with a "ghastly pale" face and an expression "haggard and drawn, as by intense suffering" (*The Time Machine* 10–11). Ransom, on the other hand, is "glowing with health and rounded with muscle and seemingly ten years younger" (*Perelandra* 30). Both men have lived on fruit during their time away, but the Time Traveler reacts by craving meat, while Ransom reacts by refusing it. It is evident that Ransom was more at home in Perelandra than the Time Traveler is in the future, just as he was more at home in Malacandra than were Devine and Weston.

Thus Lewis went beyond his source by adding moral seriousness, reversing popular views on the meaning of evolution, and telling a story in which human beings win over the discouraging, depressing philosophy of the Un-man.[41] His eschatology asserts a wonderful beginning at the end of time. But he accomplishes more: he creates an imaginary planet with lyrical appeal and artistically pleasing self-consistency, and he subtly portrays the education of Tinidril by using linguistically accurate observations about language. In "On Science Fiction" Lewis expressed a fondness for the pure fantasy set in a completely improbable world, like Lindsay's *A Voyage to Arcturus.* Because of the lack of a dominating mechanical gadget, *Perelandra* seems less scientific in tone than *The Time Machine* or even *Out of the Silent Planet;* nevertheless, it is not completely improbable because the planet is created by combining common speculations about the actual physical state of Venus with Neoplatonic and astrological lore. For example, in Lewis's time it was known that the surface of the planet is hidden under a thick cloud cover, called the albedo, which accounts for its extraordinary brightness as seen from Earth. Lewis apparently realized that as the Sun shone through the albedo, the surface of the planet would be bathed in golden light, an effect something like that of Yale's Beineke Library: there are no windows, but the Sun shining through thin marble provides golden interior light. Once Ransom has fallen through Venus's cloud cover, he sees that "the prevailing colour . . . was golden or coppery" (34). Thus Lewis combines the scientific fact of the albedo with the astrological tradition associating gold and copper with Venus.

Astronomers in Lewis's time speculated that Venus might be largely water.[42] Again, Lewis connects this quasi-scientific fact with the mythological Venus, who was born from the sea and who was depicted in medieval-renaissance art and literature as floating in the sea. For example, in "The Knight's Tale" Chaucer describes how

> The statue of Venus, glorious for to se,
> Was naked, fletynge [floating] in the large see,
> And fro the navele doun al covered was
> With wawes grene, and brighte as any glas. (1:1955–58)

We are not surprised to find that the waves of Perelandra, though golden on top, are green on their slopes.

The combination of the cloud cover with the sea is connected with another bit of medieval-renaissance iconology, the conventional portrayal of Venus as a woman looking in a mirror:

> [Ransom] saw the golden roof of that world quivering with a rapid variation of paler lights as a ceiling quivers at the reflected sunlight from the bath-water when you step into your bath on a summer morning. He guessed that this was the reflection of the waves wherein he swam. . . . The queen of those seas views herself continually in a celestial mirror. (35)

Thus Lewis connects the scientific behavior of light with the mythological behavior of Venus. Another seemingly offhand remark, "The sky was pure, flat gold like the background of a medieval picture," sets the stage for Ransom's meeting with Tinidril, who combines the characteristics of the goddess of love and the Virgin Mary.

The islands of vegetation that float in the Perelandrian seas are just barely plausible in a scientific sense, but the traditional association of the goddess Venus with softness and comfort makes it easier to accept "land" that is resilient and mattresslike. Lewis also uses the tradition that Venus is the goddess of pleasure in his description of Ransom's first day on the planet. His first drink of water is "a quite astonishing pleasure" (35). He is swept up and down, from crest to hollow, in the pleasantly lukewarm waves, at a speed no earthbound theme park could attempt. He is able to climb onto a floating island just before his strength is exhausted, and the "thrill of true fear" (39) intensifies his pleasure. Learning to walk on the island is fun, falling sends him into a "fit of the giggles" (40), and he finds "an exuberance or prodigality of sweetness about the mere act of living" (37). Breathing is not just a physical necessity, but spiritual, "a kind of ritual" (41), suggesting that spirituality is pleasurable.

On the planet of pleasure even negative experiences are pleasurable in their intensity and fullness. The sunset, the time when, as Dante observes, the seafarer longs for the dear friends he has left behind (*Purgatorio* 8:1–3), brings to Ransom the thought that perhaps he is the only person on the planet, "and the terror added, as it were, a razor-edge to all that profusion of pleasure" (43). In Wells's book, the Time Traveler first hypothesizes that mankind has eliminated the unpleasantness of normal existence and thereby doomed itself, on the assumption that only the struggle for survival can keep the race from degenerating.[43] Lewis substitutes pleasure, with the spiritual overtones it has for him, for the survival of the fittest and shows that some discomfort is not incompatible with pleasure.

But being a modern man, Ransom has to be taught how to have pleasure. His journey to Malacandra began the education which continues more intensely on Perelandra, the world of the goddess of pleasure. One thing he learned on Malacandra was that the hrossa did not repeat sexual experiences, or even poems. Similarly, on Perelandra Ransom learns not to repeat the pleasure of drinking from the gourd-fruit and not to look for the especially tasty redhearts among the breadlike berries. He learns to exercise the virtue of temperance out of respect for the pleasure rather than as the result of a puritanical ban.

Ransom's education in pleasure is preliminary to a major segment of the book, his three conversations with Tinidril. In *Out of the Silent Planet*, we are reminded that Ransom is learning the language by the insertion of non-English words in most sentences and by his use of simplified sentence structures. In *Perelandra* the language is the same as Malacandrian, which he has now learned to call Old Solar. Since he is already fluent in it, his conversations with Tinidril are reported in straight English. Nevertheless, the conversations are strange, unearthly. In *Out of the Silent Planet* the strangeness came from the inhuman body shape of the hross and the extraterrestrial language. In *Perelandra* the strangeness comes from the realization that Tinidril, even though human in shape and speaking the same language, is separated from Ransom by her race, her whole emotional makeup, her sense of humor, her lack of background in social living. Her peal of laughter at the first sight of him is followed by a calm and unearthly stillness that "might be idiocy . . . [or] immortality" or some completely alien mode of consciousness (56).

Nightfall prevents their further communication, but the next morning Ransom sees her again. Lewis suggests the numinous quality of her presence and her unfallen state by describing her in terms reminiscent of Dante's encounter with Matilda at the entrance to Eden (*Purgatorio* Canto 28). Just as Dante saw Matilda on the other side of a brook, Ransom sees Tinidril on an adjacent island, "as if on the other side of a brook." Matilda was singing and plaiting flowers; so is Tinidril. Matilda's head was bowed in modesty, but then she looked straight at Dante. Tinidril walks with bowed head, but when Ransom calls her, she looks him "full in the face" (59).

As he and Tinidril begin to converse, Ransom begins to realize that the Lady is so strange because she is unfallen. Lewis's portrayal of the situation derives much from Barfield's theory of metaphor, which holds that primitive man used language in spiritual and physical senses simultaneously. In expressing her thoughts, Tinidril uses her physical experiences—gathering fruit, eating, swimming, playing with the animals—spiritually. Ransom's first efforts to communicate with her fail because he tries to move outside her experience. For example, he asks if he may come over to her island. Having no concept of individual possession, she responds, "Which do you call my island?" Weston/Un-man is also unable to converse with her at first, even though he is now fluent in Old Solar. Like Ransom, he must learn to speak of physical activities with spiritual significances.

One of the difficulties in communication is caused by Tinidril's ignorance of what is today called pragmatics—the rules of carrying on conversation. For example, when Ransom joins the conversation between Tinidril and the Un-man, she fails to greet him because she had never participated in a conversation of more than two speakers, "[a]nd throughout the rest of their talk, her ignorance of the technique of general conversation gave a curious and disquieting quality to the whole scene" (113). She doesn't understand the need to return the conversational ball even when one has nothing new to contribute, and so observes with a child's directness, "You had nothing to say about it and yet made the nothing up into words" (75). Lewis uses Tinidril's lack of communication skills to express her naivete and to show the unearthly strangeness of the situation. Thus, his sensitivity to language contributes to the verisimilitude of the work.

Because she is in unity with her world and Maleldil, the Lady has no need for the hints and indirections common to all human speech. Human children learn these conversational rules gradually, and her lack of them makes her seem young indeed as she inquires, "If that is what they mean, why do they not say it?" (75). But innocent as she is, Tinidril is not stupid. Her growth in language is both the reflection of her growth in knowledge and, in accordance with Barfield's treatment of language as a source of knowledge, the means of her increasing sophistication. The care with which Lewis depicts this growth repays detailed analysis.

In order to be tempted like Eve, Tinidril must acquire several concepts. First, she must understand the concept of time, for it is necessary to the Christian doctrine of choice with which Lewis is concerned. *The Time Machine,* because it presents changes in mankind as occurring through a natural response to evolutionary forces, handles time like frames on a film, which might as well run backward as forward (Ramsaye 196–97). Second, she must understand the concept of choice itself. In the second conversation with Ransom she asks, "But how can one wish any of those waves not to reach us which Maleldil is rolling towards us?" (68). As she grows in self-consciousness, she comes to see that she could have a desire that was different from Maleldil's. Finally, she must become conscious of the operation of cause and effect in order to understand the importance of her choice. Until her obedience to Maleldil is based on these three concepts, it cannot be fully informed and mature.

Lewis traces the education of Tinidril by showing how she actively builds concepts by making one metaphor the foundation for another. Just as Barfield describes it in *Poetic Diction,* she uses her innate poetic ability to perceive comparisons and thus gain knowledge. Her mind is not a tabula rasa on which engrams are scratched, but an agent of significance. Her understanding of time, for example, comes from describing it metaphorically in terms of the waves: "This looking backward and forward along the line and seeing how a day has one appearance as it comes to you, and another when you are in it, and a third when it has gone past. Like the waves" (60). Since "waves do not always come at equal distances," she does not expect to be able to divide time into equal segments and thus is able to tell Ransom that the importance of a time derives from events and not physical measurement. She sees that the measurement of time is of a piece with an empirical approach to her own experience— "stepping out of life into the Alongside and looking at oneself living as if one were not alive"—and doubts whether it is wise (60). She begins to relate time to choice when she understands that "times do not go backward" and that "among times there is a time that turns a corner" (62).

The second conversation deals more fully with the concept of choice. Tinidril takes the first step in understanding choice when she accepts the idea of measuring time: "the first picture does stay in the mind quite a long time—many beats of the heart . . ." (69).[44] Again she builds on the metaphor of the waves, realizing that she does not simply accept the shape of the waves coming toward her as the floating islands do, but rather plunges into events like a swimmer. The second step is to relate choice to cause and effect. She has experienced the possibility of eating one fruit rather than another and uses it to understand her choice to fully accept the "wave" of meeting Ransom when she expected to meet her husband: "Oh, that is how I came to understand the whole thing. You and the King differ more than two fruits" (69). In the first conversation Ransom had introduced in passing the concept of cause and effect when he said, "Do different trees bring forth like fruit?" (61). His teaching of the concept in terms of fruit prepares the way for the Un-man, who defines "Bad" for her by fruit, describing Ransom as "One who rejects the fruit he is given for the sake of the fruit he expected or the fruit he found last time" (114). More complex concepts are attached to the metaphor as she calls a remark of the Un-man's "a tree without fruit" (105), meaning the manipulation of words without referents, and later rejects self-centeredness by saying, "A fruit does not eat itself, and a man cannot be together with himself" (137).

The discussion of choice in terms of trees and fruits is artistically satisfying as an expression of the pervasive influence of Genesis and Milton in the story. But portraying Tinidril's mental growth is so central to the novel that it is described in several other ways as well. She speaks of growing older, of feeling her consciousness expand like the branching out of a tree, of realizing that she is to Maleldil as the beasts are to her. She describes her previous unawareness as sleep (68) and says that the Un-man's words are "like a bubble breaking on the tree" (114), an experience that was for Ransom like "the verse in Pope, 'die of a rose in aromatic pain'" (47). As the temptation sequence proceeds, her metaphor clusters gain complexity in accordance with her increased knowledge.

Although Lewis's affirmation of Barfield is more important to the total effect of this book than his rejection of Richards, there is some attention to the issues raised in *The Meaning of Meaning* and a subtle denial of the connection between morality and poetry that Richards set forth in *Principles of Literary Criticism*. The dialogue between Weston and Ransom on the Fixed Land connects *Perelandra* to *Out of the Silent Planet* by showing that Weston's megalomania has opened him to demonic possession. Again, in contradiction to the language philosophers' accusation that Platonic and Christian metaphysics comes from empty language, it happens that Weston's scientific viewpoint results in generalities, as it did in the audience with the Oyarsa of Malacandra. Again, it is Ransom who insists on pinning the generalities to referential terms. When Weston says, "Greatness always transcends mere moralism," Ransom asks, "Would you still obey the Life-Force if you found it prompting you to murder me?" (95).

The conversation between Weston and Ransom on the Fixed Land, preceding the temptation of the Lady, is balanced by another exchange after the temptation as they ride their fishes in the trackless ocean. Weston lectures again, but his grandiose manner is gone. He has given up "trying to believe that anything you can do will make the universe bearable." Instead of using generalities like "spirituality," "emergent evolution," and "Life-Force," he uses concrete images like the dead grandmother, Africans in masks, and "dirty priests in back streets in Dublin" (167). His despairing but honest agnosticism here suggests that his previous pride of science on Malacandra and of Bergsonian evolution[45] on the Fixed Land of Perelandra was nothing more than a terrified avoidance of the Christian God.

Far from assenting without ambiguity or reservation to Richards's belief that beauty "causes an experience in us which is valuable in certain ways" (*Principles* 20), Lewis shows the Un-man using Story—poetry and history—to break down Tinidril's resistance to temptation. The stories do not engage her mind's active ability to make metaphor; they simply suggest images to her. The Un-man uses Story to lure her into the "Alongside" more frequently and for a longer time. He builds up her image of herself as a noble queen of tragedy, creating a "picture of the tall, slender form, unbowed though the world's weight rested upon its shoulders," an image complemented by an image of the "pitifully childish and complacently arrogant" male (126). Ransom worries that "if her will was uncorrupted, half her imagination was already filled with bright, poisonous shapes" (134).

Whether by her own active understanding of metaphors or her passive acceptance of the Un-man's images, the prolonged conversations cause Tinidril to "grow older." As she does so, the cluster of meanings around the phrase becomes more complex. To be capable of growing older is to be a creature, not God. Thus she calls herself Maleldil's beast (76) and says concerning the animals, "We make them older every day. Is not that what it means to be a beast?" (65). To grow older is to become somewhat independent of Maleldil, "to learn things not straight from Him but by your own meetings with other people and your own questions and thoughts" (105). To grow older is to have power as well as knowledge, for the Lady says, "The King is always older than I, and about all things" (105).

But, as Barfield points out in *Poetic Diction*, language, being grounded in metaphor, can never be unambiguous, and ambiguity of the word "older" causes Ransom to lose to the Un-man. Approving of one of Ransom's explanations, the Lady asks, "Piebald, if you are so young, as this other says, how do you know these things?" Ransom asserts that he is not so young. Then the Un-man says, "I am older than he, and he dare not deny it . . . . And in the order of creation I am greater than he" (118–19). The fact that "old" means having a great number of years as well as wisdom leads to Ransom's defeat and the damaging admission that Adam's fall brought about the glorious incarnation of Christ. Having lost the battle of wits, Ransom must turn to physical combat.

The scene in which he accepts this necessity hinges on the Barfieldian assertion that language reflects the nature of the universe. It is not, strictly speaking, the philosophical concept of the "psycho-physical parallelism" Lewis discussed in "Bluspels and Flalansferes" but is simply a realization that the same God who wills all other events also wills language events. Ransom hears the voice of Maleldil say, "It is not for nothing that you are named Ransom" and "My name is also Ransom" (147, 148). Ransom knows that his name is derived from "Ranolf's son" and has no etymological connection with "ransom," which came into English in about the thirteenth century from French and ultimately from Latin. He reflects that we human beings call certain things accidental simply through lack of knowledge. His family name is one that can be punned upon because he has been chosen as the ransom of Perelandra; in an ultimate sense, there are no accidents.

The same thing is true of evolution. The random variations are not really random. Ransom's experiences with the geography and inhabitants of Perelandra other than the Lady are all designed to make this point. When he is riding on the fish in pursuit of the Un-man, he has a momentary loss of faith in the importance of his task, feeling that Venus must not have been created for its human inhabitants, since most of it is trackless ocean haunted by "the wholly inscrutable to which man and his life remained eternally irrelevant" (164). He struggles to deny "The Empirical Bogey . . . in which everything that can possibly hold significance for the mind becomes the mere by-product of essential disorder" (164). Then he reminds himself that the material universe seems awesome to human beings because they make it majestic by the "comparing and mythopoeic power" (164–65) inherent in human nature.

Lewis's eschatology is expressed in the concluding segment of the book, a ceremonial investiture of the King and Queen with a new kind of dominion over their world. The ceremony takes place in a mountain valley shaped like a cup, red with delicate flowers, a valley in which Tinidril and her husband glow like emeralds with a light as great as a terrestrial dawn. Like so many details in *Perelandra*, the significance of the colors reverses that of Wells's picture of the end of time. There the red is the harsh red of the dying sun, the green is slime, and instead of dawn there is a decline into black night, silence, and bitter cold. Instead of the degeneration of mankind into Eloi and Morlocks, and finally into the last clawed creatures, *Perelandra* shows the exaltation of Tor and Tinidril into their true place— between the angels who keep the planets in orbit and "the warm multitude of the brutes" in the Great Chain of Being.

Although Lewis accepts the mechanism of evolution, he denies the despair and hopelessness arising from the popular interpretation of it. The prose poem that concludes the book celebrates "the Great Dance." It makes again the points that emerge from both *Out of the Silent Planet* and *Perelandra*: the universe is stranger and more beautiful than we suppose, beyond our understanding; time is swallowed up in eternity; and there is no disorder, no randomness, because everything that exists is, by the grace of God, the center of the universe. Lewis shows the three human beings transcending time and material existence as they join the angelic intelligences in hymning the Author of these things, and thus he answers, for himself and his fellow religionists, the questions posed by Wells's *The Time Machine.*

The prose poem is not entirely successful. Lewis's point, that nothing is random, everything is center, is more glorious than Wells's picture of the inevitable destruction of man and man's determination "to live as though it were not so" (66). But because making Lewis's point requires multiple examples, the passage seems wordy and magisterial in tone. It is less vivid than the two withered flowers that sum up *The Time Machine,* the witnesses "that even when mind and strength had gone, gratitude and a mutual tenderness still lived on in the heart of man" (66). Lewis's answer to "the Empirical Bogey" is more complex than Wells's pessimism, more difficult to express, and he does not quite bring it off. But it is a *stunning* failure, and the book as a whole is a success, as science fiction and as a good story in good English.

· 3 ·

THE CONTEXT

OF LANGUAGE CONTROL

B Y 1943, the date of the preface to *That Hideous Strength,* the low evaluation of language set forth in *The Meaning of Meaning* (1923) had become a landmark on the intellectual scene. Ogden and Richards's warning that people were vulnerable to behavioral control through language had become a widely held concern. One of the first presentations of the role of language in social engineering was Aldous Huxley's *Brave New World* (1932). A satire of mass man controlled by the media, it showed how the constant repetition of socially approved slogans molded opinions and behaviors. Only the Savage, with his grounding in the traditional language of Shakespeare and the Bible, could think as an individual. A different contribution to the question of whether mankind was to control or be controlled by language was *Science and Sanity* (1933), in which Alfred Korzybski provided mental exercises for escaping from the misconceptions of traditional thinking.

It was only a matter of time until university graduates trained in the new language philosophy as well as Richards's New Criticism would be teaching a simplified version of the concepts in secondary schools. In 1939, two Australian schoolmasters, Alec King and Martin Ketley, published a textbook for secondary English classes.[1] It was entitled, significantly enough, *The Control of Language,* and in the preface they acknowledged Ogden and Richards as their masters (xviii). A review copy was sent to C. S. Lewis; his annotations of it express his adverse reaction. For him, the success of the low view of language on the university level was bad enough; its introduction into secondary schools, with the inevitable over-simplifications and the greater defenselessness of the younger students, would lead to the loss of humane discourse. If carried to its logical conclusion, it would lead to the destruction of everything that makes human beings truly human. Thus, when Lewis prepared the Riddell Memorial Lectures (delivered in February 1943 and published as *The Abolition of Man*), he did not attack the low view of language as presented by his academic peers, but rather as it was manifested in *The Control of Language.*

These two books provide the relevant context for *That Hideous Strength.* Indeed, Lewis says in his preface to the novel that it is "a 'tall story' about devilry [with] a serious 'point' which I have tried to make in my *Abolition of Man*" (7). In the novel, Lewis's two main characters, Mark and Jane Studdock, are people whose thought patterns have been disordered by modern assumptions about language, assumptions like those underlying *The Control of Language.* In describing their struggles and interactions with others, Lewis provides a diagnosis of modern society and suggests a remedy for its ills. The action moves among three settings—Bracton College, Belbury, and St. Anne's. These are described with details that make them symbolic of the high and low views of language. Lewis's *Abolition of Man* draws much from Barfield's *Poetic Diction,* and when the story is seen in this perspective it becomes evident that Merlin rather than Ransom is the paradigmatic character, the one who shows both the proper use of language and the proper attitude toward scientific knowledge. The novel is in some sense a contribution to the science fiction genre, although it defeats the expectations of the genre in many respects.

The Control of Language and *The Abolition of Man*

The Control of Language, better known to readers of Lewis as "The Green Book," the name he gave it in *The Abolition of Man,* is a modest textbook consisting of 273 pages of text plus a preface. Lewis's copy of it, with his annotations in margins and on the flyleaf, is available in the Wade Collection at Wheaton College. Lewis may not have read all of it, since his last annotation refers to page 142 and his last underlining is on page 147. The first six chapters present Ogden and Richards's language philosophy, appropriately simplified for secondary students; the last part of the book, which applies the language philosophy to specific reading and writing tasks, is more traditional, less indebted to Ogden and Richards, and therefore less opposed to Lewis's own point of view.

Although the authors no doubt hoped to give their subject a fresh new approach, the overall thrust of the book is within the mainstream of English composition instruction. In the hands of the ordinary teacher of secondary English, it might be nothing more than another text to help students read more attentively and write more specifically. Its primary enemy seems to be adolescent generalizations and hot air. In fact, the book is much less radical than Lewis's attack on it implies. It would not deserve the attention Lewis gives it except for his conviction that its principles lead to the corruption of feeling and the eventual dehumanization of humanity. Even so, Lewis himself says that King and Ketley are "better than their principles" (*Abolition* 33).

Lewis does not discuss King and Ketley's principles and refute them on a coldly logical basis. Indeed, he ignores several of their confusions and self-contradictions, such as the fact that they apparently do not know what they believe about metaphor. Is it a decorative veneer or part of the very essence of language? On the one hand they describe good writing as "an author's thoughts as they are born—naked, out of the mind, not disguised and dressed up stylishly" (208), but in another passage they imply that style and content are sometimes inseparable, saying that figurative language is used because it expresses things that cannot be expressed directly (226). They explain that scientists do not use metaphors because they write about material things rather than feelings, but then they cite "'worm' drive" and "'tread' of a tyre" as examples of the use of metaphor in technology (229). They advise the student to avoid metaphors "when you are writing straight-forwardly," but they also note that dead metaphors are inevitable (240–41). At this point Lewis might have appropriately rephrased Barfield's lines in *Poetic Diction:* "The authors have written a short and not very clever book about meaning without managing to grasp its essential feature—the relation to metaphor" (cf. 134).

Similarly, Lewis might have castigated King and Ketley for their uncritical adoption of Richards's views on the use and value of literature. They present its use as therapy rather than pleasure and praise poetry as "a very good training in the understanding of how to live, how to be a human being and not just a bundle of appetites and fears" (272).[2] As for the value of literature, King and Ketley's pedagogy is designed to make status seekers and literary puritans of their students, a pedagogy Lewis deplored in "High and Low Brows." Their chapter on how to write "scientific" criticism (their term for New Criticism) encourages the pupil to detach "general standards of value from the welter of . . . feelings and prejudices" (130). However, the authors also say that general standards of value are gradually acquired "from your own experience, with the help of the experience of others" (140), and that scientific criticism "is of the utmost importance . . . if you believe in a democratic society" (141). In other words, the hapless students are to approach literature with objectivity while remaining aware of the opinions of others. Whether the "others" are their classmates or their grade-giving instructors is not made clear; but if the latter, it is difficult to see how "scientific" criticism could promote democracy.

Instead of responding to these absurdities, Lewis comments on just three faults of the textbook: the authors teach the distinction between referential and emotive language as a way of leading students to scorn words expressing value judgments; they encourage students to treat emotions cynically and even suppress their own emotions; and they substitute ephemeral values for traditional ones.

Lewis's first attack on King and Ketley, for their handling of Ogden and Richards's distinction between referential and emotive language, is not as telling as it might have been. The authors say that "sublime" and "pretty" are emotive, statements about one's own feelings, while "brown" and "green" are referential (17–18). This leads to the story of Coleridge at the waterfall in which Coleridge said it was right to call the waterfall "sublime" but not "pretty" (see *Abolition* 14). In their effort to simplify the concept for secondary pupils King and Ketley say "That is sublime" means "I have sublime feelings." Lewis comments in the margin, "confusion worse confounded" (19), and in *The Abolition of Man* he makes so much fun of it that he skips over King and Ketley's more important self-contradiction. They say that "beautiful," applied to a horse, can be both referential and emotive. It is an expression of feeling, of pleasure, and therefore emotive, but it is referential if the hearer knows the standard of beauty for horses (20–21). Thus they are unaware that they have opened up the possibility that "sublime" might be referential if one knew the standard of sublimity for waterfalls. Like their source, *The Meaning of Meaning*, King and Ketley's language philosophy lacks criteria for classifying some adjectives as referential and others as emotive, and Lewis fails to call attention to the lack.

He does, however, deal effectively with the authors' implied scorn of value judgments in the sentence, "We appear to be saying something very important about something: and actually we are only saying something about our own feelings" (*Control* 20). Lewis expatiates on the significance of the word "only" and comments, "The very power of [King and Ketley] depends on the fact that they are dealing with a boy: a boy who thinks he is 'doing' his 'English prep' and has no notion that ethics, theology, and politics are all at stake" (16). Lewis's objection is not that schoolmasters are exercising such power—after all, the classical definition of the orator as "a good man speaking well" implies that rhetoric has moral implications— but that the authors' moral and philosophical basis of teaching is fundamentally wrong. In following Ogden and Richards, they think that words without physical referents name "bogus entities."

By teaching the students to be cynical about value words, King and Ketley also encourage them to devalue and suppress emotions. For example, when they assign a personal essay, they trivialize students' creativity by touting the assignment as a break from the modern world. They also declare that "pure narrative, written in scientific prose, is the backbone of all kinds of narrative" (179) and that an inherently interesting fact does not need the hype of emotional language. Lewis's marginal comment is, "The fact might include an emotional value" (35). In their fear of language as a tool for control they are unable to describe the correct role of emotion in human life. They say, "There are many occasions . . . when it is right for us to rouse feeling," but it should not be done when the topic has already aroused "deep feelings and emotional prejudices" in the audience. The student is advised to avoid communicating his own such feelings and to write so as to promote calm, rational thought (84). In other words, the authors encourage the student to suppress his sincere excitement and write on a more superficial, cowardly level. Lewis's marginal notes point out that "Plato, St. Paul, Hooker, Sidney, Pascal, Browne, and Burke" as well as politicians and advertisers have attempted to arouse people's emotions.

By teaching the young people to regard all impassioned appeals to "feelings that are regarded as useful or valuable" (56), as sentimentality and poor writing, King and Ketley subtly substitute values of their own for traditional values. Their hostility to these values is expressed in a passage, which Lewis marked, describing the prose of "uninteresting persons" as "weak love of the past for what it was not" (111). On the flyleaf Lewis lists the authors' implied values. He notes that they call the words "gentleman" (63) and "coward" (64) vague, but say that the word "wise" when applied to peaceful men is not vague (65). They praise "democratic community life" (67) and a "community of reasonable adults" (71), but state that "feeling for England is a feeling for nothing in particular" (77). Like Ogden and Richards, they refer to the "lying propaganda" used during "the Great War" (61–62) and imply that it is undemocratic for a writer "to try to persuade us . . . [to do or feel] what we cannot clearly understand" (67). On the other hand, they say that propaganda is necessary for children, since they cannot choose rationally what is best for them, and blameworthy "only when too much of it is given" (62). ("Too much," needless to say, is never quantified more precisely.)

Lewis's attack on *The Control of Language* may be seen as a way to focus and dramatize the points of his lectures rather than a direct engagement with the ideas that King and Ketley had derived from *The Meaning of Meaning*. Instead of arguing dispassionately against the low view of language, Lewis appeals to the emotions, stirring up pity for the schoolboys who are to be turned into soulless automatons and divorced from the heritage of human literary experience. At times, however, he does swipe at his academic peers. In long footnotes to *The Abolition of Man* he argues with Richards's definition of value (in *Principles of Literary Criticism*) as the satisfaction of impulses (46–47n) and with C. H. Waddington's attempt to base value on fact in *Science and Ethics* (49–50n). He also charges that Richards has failed "to explain why a bad treatment of some basic human emotion is bad literature" except by attacking the emotion itself (23).

The three chapters of *The Abolition of Man* all deal with the relationship between language, facts, and values in some respect. The first chapter argues that aesthetic value is not merely subjective, but a reflection of the way the universe really is, so that dismissing value words as merely subjective is false. The second chapter shows that ethical value is neither subjective nor based on mere survival, but an essential part of human nature, just as language is. Finally, the third chapter considers how aesthetic and ethical human nature is related to the external nature studied by science and includes a philological discussion of the word "nature." In other words, the three chapters deal with the Beautiful, the Good, and the True, employing a version of Platonism reminiscent of Barfield's *Poetic Diction*.

In chapter 1, entitled "Men Without Chests," the central issue is King and Ketley's separation of language uses into referential and emotive and the effect of that separation on the development of the students. Since

King and Ketley's discussion of these language uses is self-contradictory, Lewis could have said (and did occasionally say in other contexts)[3] something similar to Barfield's statement in the 1952 preface to *Poetic Diction:* "It is a failing common to a good many contemporary metaphysical theories that they can be applied to all things except themselves but that, when so applied, they extinguish themselves" (16). Instead of discussing this philosophic weakness, however, Lewis merely asserts that value judgments do have a verifiable existence—that "the universe [is] such that certain emotional reactions on our part [can] be either congruous or incongruous to it" (*Abolition* 25). His support is not philosophical argument, but authority: "Platonic, Aristotelian, Stoic, Christian, and Oriental" traditions, the latter referred to "for brevity simply as 'the *Tao*'" (28–29).

Lewis's use of the term "Tao" has nothing to do with Taoism and is therefore somewhat misleading, especially to present-day readers, who are likely to have some previous knowledge of Taoism. For Lewis, Tao designates the natural law, the ethical principles agreed upon by all civilizations in all times. In an appendix to *The Abolition of Man* he gives some examples of these principles: respect for human life; fulfillment of obligations to family; the practice of justice, mercy, and truthfulness; and the preference of death to dishonor. Apparently Lewis uses the term to get away from the associations the term "natural law" has with Christian ethics, for he is attempting to write nontheistically rather than from a Christian viewpoint. To this end he lists examples of these universal principles from Egyptian, Babylonian, Hindu, and Native American sources (from general reference works, not his own scholarship) as well as Judeo-Christian, Graeco-Roman, and Teutonic ones.

Lewis's decision to confront a secondary school textbook rather than original works of the language philosophers shows that he regards the issue not as an abstract, academic discussion of philosophy but as a debate on educational policy. Lewis's main point is that the principles taught by King and Ketley stunt the emotional growth in young people and thereby stunt aesthetic appreciation and, ultimately, the ability to reason.[4] This relationship is partly suggested by Barfield, who in *Poetic Diction* associated the acquisition of knowledge with the pleasure of the felt change of consciousness. Lewis cites Plato's *Republic* concerning the need to nurture young people by beauty before the age of reason so that they may recognize the affinity between reason and beauty, and delight in reason as they have delighted in beauty. He says that King and Ketley's biggest error is their assumption that modern young people need to be taught to avoid being swayed by emotion and pleasure lest they be swayed by propaganda. On the contrary, says Lewis, "by starving the sensibility of our pupils we only make them easier prey to the propagandist when he comes" (24). He paraphrases a passage from *The Republic:*

> We were told it all long ago by Plato. As the king governs by his executive, so Reason in man must rule the mere appetites by means of the "spirited element." The head rules the belly through the chest—the seat, as Alanus tells us, of Magnanimity, of emotions organized by trained habit into stable sentiments. (34)

If it is the trained emotions that make people human, then an education that stunts and perverts the emotions produces "Men Without Chests," humanoid animals rather than human beings. Such "education" is merely conditioning, and the conditioners themselves are not truly human. Thus, in his own way Lewis arrives at the main point of Huxley's *Brave New World.*

His strong conviction about the connection between emotion, aesthetic response, and rationality is dramatized in *That Hideous Strength* by the characterization of Mark. As a person who has learned to hold back his emotions, Mark is unable to detect the falsity of Belbury and becomes a propagandist, a newspaper writer of the sort castigated by King and Ketley (56) and earlier by Ogden and Richards (29). Later on, when Frost is attempting to secure Mark's complete commitment to "objectivity" (crime), he is placed in an ugly room that starves his aesthetic responses. When, after his escape, he is able to respond with honest pleasure to a boys' adventure story, it indicates that his dishonesty and irrationality have been cured.

In chapter 2, entitled "The Way," Lewis, having previously established the objective validity of the Beautiful, goes on to defend the objective existence of the Good, of ethical behavior. First he states that King and Ketley do not believe that their own values are merely subjective; if they did, they would not have bothered to write a book upholding them. With an uncharacteristic dip into both chronological and class snobbery, he characterizes their unstated values as those "which happened to be in vogue among moderately educated young men of the professional classes during the period between the two wars" (40–41). In a long footnote he reproduces his list of their values from the flyleaf of his copy of *The Control of Language:* peacefulness, democracy, tolerance, cleanliness. He concludes, "Comfort and security, as known to a suburban street in peace-time, are the ultimate values; those things which can alone produce or spiritualize comfort and security are mocked" (41n).

After showing that King and Ketley apply the subjectivity of value statements to everyone's values but their own, Lewis focuses on the *dulce et decorum* tradition of "death for a good cause" as "the *experimentum crucis* which shows different systems of thought in the clearest light" (42). (It is also, of course, the crux that other early-twentieth-century authors had used in debunking traditional attitudes toward language.) He asserts that all these systems are actually derived from the Tao, for it is the source of proper feelings and objective value, the basis of all ethics, otherwise known as "Natural Law or Traditional Morality or the First Principles of Practical Reason" (56).

His discussion is shaped by a submerged comparison of natural law to language.[5] Like language, natural law is in some sense a given in the human mind, although it must be learned. Like language, it differs in detail in various cultures and is subject to a certain amount of change. And like language, it is recognized by the "native speaker"—or, as Lewis puts it, "the well-nurtured man, the *cuor gentil*" (61). In some sense it serves man the way instinct serves other animals (90).

The submerged comparison applies to reason as well as morality. Just as the low view of language derives meaning from associations based on sense impressions, so also people like King and Ketley[6] believe that reason is nothing more than "the connecting by inference of propositions, ul-timately derived from sense data, with further propositions." Although Lewis does not make the point completely clear, we may infer that what he means by reason is the combination of logic and natural law symbolized by the warlike virgin in *The Pilgrim's Regress.* And just as Barfield in *Poetic Diction* argued that percepts alone cannot lead to meaning, so Lewis argues that inferences based on sensory information alone cannot lead to the ethical decision to sacrifice oneself, to accept *dulce et decorum* as a principle of behavior. *Ought* can never be derived from *is.*[7]

The givenness of the Tao, like Barfield's psycho-physical parallelism of metaphor and the universe, is shown by the fact that human beings cannot really step outside it. Like language, Lewis's Tao is the human mind's basis of operation. Lewis says, "The human mind has no more power of inventing a new [ethical] value than of imagining a new primary colour" (56–57); thus modern thinkers who believe that they are introducing scientific, or more reasonable, systems are merely taking fragments of the Tao out of context and treating them as if they were the whole (56).

Nevertheless, like language, the Tao must be learned. In chapter 1, Lewis spoke of the Roman father who taught his son that it is *dulce et decorum* to die for his country, "communicating" his own emotion to his son (31). Here he cites Aristotle's dictum that "only those who have been well brought up can usefully study ethics" (59). Since the Tao is learned, it is, like language behavior, subject to change. Also, the perceptions of value that people obey in following the Tao will undergo some modification, analogous to the changes of language accomplished through the creative use of it by poets.

In an example reminiscent of Barfield, although not found in the first edition of *Poetic Diction*, Lewis compares the modern thinkers who wish to replace the Tao to the linguistic theorists who attack a language from the outside, "advocating wholesale alterations of its idiom and spelling in the interests of commercial convenience or scientific accuracy," while traditionalists who accept the Tao and work to develop it are like the great poet who "works from within" (57). It is the difference, says Lewis, between Shakespeare and Basic English (58). Barfield, we remember, explained the role of Shakespeare in the development of the language, while Ogden invented Basic English. Lewis's detail about spelling reform as an alteration of the language by people who do not love it appears, differently stated, in Barfield's preface to the second edition of *Poetic Diction* (1952): "[T]hose ... who are driven by an impulse to reduce the specifically human to a mechanical or animal regularity, will continue to be increasingly irritated by the nature of the mother tongue and make it their point of attack" (23).

In *That Hideous Strength*, Jane has been well nurtured in the sense that she has received training in proper sentiments—the Good—through her study of traditional literature. She has not learned to suppress her emotions to the extent that Mark has. Thus when she goes to St. Anne's she almost immediately fits into a society based on the Tao, the natural law. Just as the story of Mark illustrates the principles set forth in chapter 1 of *The Abolition of Man*, the story of Jane illustrates the description of the Tao in chapter 2.

Having dealt with feeling as the basis for moral actions and with the Tao as the source of human standards for such actions, Lewis turns in chapter 3 to a consideration of human nature and the extent to which it is part of Nature. If the absolute standards of the Tao are, as Lewis asserts, built into human nature, then any attempt to study or control human nature apart from these standards is dehumanizing. King and Ketley, in teaching young people to scoff, whether at the aesthetic response of awe in the presence of a waterfall or at the ethical response of willingness to die for the fatherland, are contributing toward the destruction of human nature.

But perhaps we do not need human nature in the traditional sense. Perhaps the rise of scientific knowledge and control over the environment has made it unnecessary. What of those who say, "Having mastered our environment, let us now master ourselves and choose our own destiny" (63)?

In chapter 3 of *The Abolition of Man*, Lewis considers this possibility. First he shows that man's mastery of the natural environment must be subject to natural law. The argumentative technique by which he reaches this conclusion is the same one that demolished Weston's speech before the Oyarsa in *Out of the Silent Planet*—translating the general nouns of high-flown discourse into more specific ones. The phrase "man's power over Nature," Lewis says, really means that some men exercise power over other men with Nature as the instrument. Anyone who exercises power over Nature outside the natural law (the Tao) is denying power to other persons and in effect dehumanizing them. Those who choose to rebel against tradition deny power to our predecessors, and those who take control of natural processes deny power to our successors.

Lewis gives three examples of control over natural processes—the airplane, the radio, and the contraceptive.[8] His choices seem quixotic now, but he was writing during World War II, when these technologies were obvious symbols of the power that Nazi Germany was exercising over Europe. At that time the airplane was not a quick, routine form of transportation, but the source of bombs; the radio was a symbol of propaganda through mass media, the way some human beings control the values of the society; and contraception was a symbol of the selective breeding advocated by the Nazis.[9] Lewis asserts that if the "some men" who exercise these powers over other men refuse to acknowledge and themselves be governed by the Tao, then their motivations will be determined by the natural processes of their heredity, their conditioning, the state of their digestion (or, in the case of King and Ketley, by the values "which happened to be in vogue" when they were being educated). If they are successful in establishing their control, they will put mankind into a closed circle.[10] Thus, the almost-trivial teaching of cynicism by King and Ketley is part of a movement to destroy humanity as we know it.

But is not objectivity, the denial of feelings, necessary to experimental science? To study a thing scientifically means to understand it analytically, to quantify it, to suspend value judgments about it, to ask "how" rather than "why." In a quick expedition into the history of science Lewis describes the painful repressions of feeling that the scientific method has brought: "We do not look at trees . . . as Dryads . . . while we cut them into beams: the first man who did so may have felt the price keenly. . . . The stars lost their divinity as astronomy developed, and the Dying God has no place in chemical agriculture" (82). Lewis states explicitly that he is not against science and technological development; nevertheless, he wants his audience to be aware that these things have their price. With more passion than consistency, he calls such development "the magician's bargain: give up our soul, get power in return" (83). Another quick raid into the history of science supports his point. Both magic and science as we know it were part of the sixteenth and seventeenth centuries' push to understand and control Nature. Both magic and science are *scientia,* or knowledge, in contrast with *sapientia,* or wisdom. *Scientia* asks "how to subdue reality to the wishes of men" and finds the answer in technology. *Sapientia* asks "how to conform the soul to reality" and finds the answer in "knowledge, self-discipline, and virtue" (88). Science is not evil, but the founders of science, such as Bacon and Paracelsus, had mixed motives, and "[i]ts triumphs may have been too rapid and purchased at too high a price" (89).

Thus, Lewis accepts the natural sciences. But he vehemently resists the social sciences' notion that human beings must be studied objectively. He warns that if Man treats himself "as a mere 'natural object' and his own judgements of value as raw material for scientific manipulation" (84), then Man will become no more than the determinism-bound slave of natural processes. To explain the values of the Tao as the end product of such processes is to undercut the very belief in the value of knowledge on which science is based.

In his conclusion, Lewis calls on modern scientists to do their work in the consciousness that the quantified abstractions they study are not the whole of reality, that the analysis of the object of study into parts limits understanding of the whole. The brevity of his argument does not allow him to expatiate on Barfield's insight that the objective scientific method is not a means of making discoveries, but a way of checking an insight already reached by a leap of metaphor (*Poetic Diction* 139). However, he does mention the noninvasive scientific techniques of Rudolf Steiner and the botanical discovery made by Goethe through metaphor.[11] He appeals to modern scientists for "reconsideration and something like repentance" (89), asking them to develop similar noninvasive means of study: "The regenerate science which I have in mind would not do even to minerals and vegetables what modern science threatens to do to man himself" (89–90).

Lewis's reading of *The Control of Language* was a call to battle for him. He was outraged at the way the "ghastly tissue of empty abstractions" (Barfield's phrase) set forth by Ogden and Richards in *The Meaning of Meaning* had infiltrated secondary education. In the ordinary schoolboy "'doing' his 'English prep'" from such a textbook, Lewis saw a threat to the traditional idea of literature that teaches through delight, to the natural law accepted by all cultures, and to the prescientific inhibition against sacrificing the wholeness of plants, beasts, and human beings to the attainment of knowledge. Lewis's angry reaction to this threat resulted in one of his finest demonstrations of rhetorical pyrotechnics, *The Abolition of Man,* and the convictions he expressed there are dramatized with great intensity in the last novel of the Ransom trilogy.

In the novel, just as regenerate aesthetics is modeled in the education of Mark and the restoration of ethics in Jane, so regenerate knowledge is modeled by Merlin. As Dimble says, he "represents what we've got to get back to in some different way" (286), and in this sense he symbolizes science. One of the reasons *That Hideous Strength* has been so frequently misunderstood is the failure to grasp the symbolic import of Merlin. But the book also presents many other difficulties and needs to be examined as a whole.

That Hideous Strength

That Hideous Strength is a complex, difficult, and somewhat unsatisfactory novel. Lewis himself was frustrated by it. He called it "bosh" and "rubbish" and wrote to E. R. Eddison that "the thought of trying to mend it, and of abandoning it, seem equally unbearable."[12] A number of readers are confused by the replacement of Ransom the space traveler by Ransom the hieratic Pendragon, bored by poorly integrated expository passages, disappointed by the *deus ex machina* resolution of the plot. According to critic W. W. Robson, the book is "unpleasant and unsatisfactory, a work containing things that an admiring and judicious reader would rather forget," but it is the favorite of the three interplanetary novels for many readers.[13] Longer by two pages than the first two novels put together, it is still written so tightly that the abridgement, *The Tortured Planet,* succeeds only in wrecking the style and obscuring the theme; it certainly cannot replace the original. The masterful account of the college meeting, the suspenseful narration and skillful interlace of plot lines, Wither's bureaucratic doubletalk, the characterizations—sometimes sharp and sometimes sympathetic, but always witty—are the excellences of a first-class novel, whether science fiction or mainstream.

One of the obstacles to a just appreciation of *That Hideous Strength* is trying to read it as the third book of an interplanetary trilogy. While the first two books are patterned according to the fiction of H. G. Wells and focus on the narrowness of his scientific viewpoints, *That Hideous Strength* is patterned on the fiction of Charles Williams and focuses on the corruption of language and the use of it to control and dehumanize people. Although *Perelandra* is a departure from the premise of *Out of the Silent Planet,* it does not depart from the first book as much as *That Hideous Strength* departs from the second.

Even when *That Hideous Strength* is read separately, however, it is possible to miss the importance of language as a central theme. The plot is structured around the contrast between happenings at Belbury, the home of the evil National Institute of Coordinated Experiments, and at St. Anne's-on-the-Hill, the home of the modern Pendragon and his small band of followers. The main characters are Mark and Jane Studdock, a young couple whose marriage is breaking up. Mark, a young Fellow of Bracton College, is lured to Belbury by the promise of money, power, and the chance to belong to an inner circle. Left alone by Mark, Jane joins the household of St. Anne's. The Pendragon and ruler of St. Anne's is our old friend Ransom, who is also called the Director and the Fisher-King. It is a mostly prescientific community where the major pursuits seem to be philology and truck gardening, but whose real purpose is to oppose Belbury. Apparently, no clearer example of Snow's two cultures could be found. St. Anne's is good, literally on the side of the angels (the planetary Oyéresu), and Belbury is bad, literally on the side of the devils (the Macrobes). Thus it is easy for someone like J. B. S. Haldane, who is already biased against Lewis's Christianity, to believe that Lewis equates good with pre-science, bad with science. He says, "Mr. Lewis's idea is clear enough. The application of science to human affairs can only lead to hell" ("Auld Hornie" 18).

But this is not what Lewis is saying. Although the lifestyle at St. Anne's is prescientific, the community includes—in addition to Dimble the literary scholar—a sociologist, a medical doctor, and MacPhee, who apparently is or was a scientist. And although Devine of Belbury talks about finding scientific solutions to human problems, the N.I.C.E.'s real purpose is to seize power. Mark thinks he has been asked to come to Belbury to do research in sociology, but he finds that his real job is the control of language—that is, to control the public by writing mendacious articles for high-grade periodicals and sensational trash for low-class rags. Thus, the source of power at Belbury is "the control of language," for Lewis's main point concerns the Ogden-Richards/King-Ketley view of language and how that view leads to the abolition of man. This is the "serious 'point'" of *The Abolition of Man* that Lewis mentions in the preface to *That Hideous Strength* (7). Opposition to modern science is part of the novel, but simply because the abuse of language through rejection of the Tao leads to the corruption of science.

Some critics have minimized the novel's opposition to science by asserting that Lewis is not against science but technology, or perhaps against "scientism."[14] Others have suggested that the evil of Belbury stems from the social sciences rather than the hard sciences. But a careful reading of *The Abolition of Man* shows that Lewis does oppose science as we know it. One of his important points is this: in a linguistic environment in which the language of observable fact is considered more important than the language of aesthetic and ethical values, scientific research becomes "tainted" and needs "reconsideration, and something like repentance" (89). Lewis contrasts existing modern science and its technology, which he calls a twin of Magic, with a possible science based on seeing into Nature, creating an I-Thou relationship with it, rather than dissecting it. He objects to technology because it ignores traditional values in order to "subdue reality to the wishes of men" (88) and to the social sciences because they apply to human nature the falsifying processes of analysis and objectivization: "It is in Man's power to treat himself as a mere 'natural object' and his own judgements of value as raw material for scientific manipulation" (84). These processes arise because science and its twin, magic, were "born in an unhealthy neighborhood and at an inauspicious hour" (89). Ogden and Richards's rubrics for controlling language, simplified by King and Ketley, exemplify the unhealthiness by turning language, like science, into a dead thing to be analyzed rather than a relationship, manifesting itself through metaphor, between the human mind and the universe.

The title itself—*That Hideous Strength*—points to language as the main issue. As the title page explains, the phrase is a quotation from a commentary on Genesis, describing the tower of Babel. The builders of Belbury, like the builders of Babel, rebel against God by seizing power; then they create confusion by using language to corrupt the press and render helpless the general public. God responded to the builders of Babel by confounding their speech, and the same thing happens to Belbury. Belbury is not destroyed because it is scientific, but because it is proud and cruel; St. Anne's mission is not primarily to model the opposite of scientism, but to locate and nurture Merlin, the instrument of God to destroy Belbury.

Although Merlin is endowed with the powers of five Oyéresu—Mercury, Venus, Mars, Jupiter, and Saturn—he uses only one, Mercurial power of language, against the enemy. He is admitted to Belbury as an expert on ancient languages—a small touch of irony, since he is so much more than an expert. Once inside, he tricks Frost and Wither by using the power of Mercury to make the tramp speak, so that they think the tramp is Merlin. He uses it again to turn Horace Jules's after-dinner speech into nonsense, recreating Babel and causing the dinner guests to destroy themselves in panic. He pronounces judgment upon the Belburians for their corruption of language, calling in Latin, "They that have despised the word of God, from them shall the word of man also be taken away" (351). The Mercurial power of language that he has used is the one closest to the Tao and the most basic to humane values, as Lewis made clear in *The Abolition of Man*. The only action against Belbury that is not derived from language is the release of the animals to turn against their captors; that action Merlin accomplishes through his personal affinity with Nature.

One obstacle to the perception of language as the theme is the novel's mixture of genres. Lewis was apparently experimenting with the technique of Charles Williams's "supernatural thriller," in which something wild and incalculable—the stone from Solomon's crown, the archetypal Tarot deck, the Holy Grail—breaks into ordinary life.[15] The premise of *That Hideous Strength* is that an ordinary English couple, Mark and Jane, become involved in a supernatural war between angels and devils. But Lewis is trying to fill an even wider canvas than Williams, and the result is a clash of artistic conventions. When Lewis describes the college meeting and the mental processes of Mark and Jane, it seems like a conventional real-istic novel, a comedy of manners, though written by a man who has strong views on modern *-tions*, especially educa*tion*, contracep*tion*, and antivivise*ction*. When the focus is on Merlin, the novel has some of the fascination of the time travel subgenre of science fiction, especially in Merlin's reactions to the twentieth century. When contrasting the ways of life at St. Anne's and at Belbury, it seems to belong to the utopia and anti-utopia subgenres of science fiction. The appearance of Merlin and the mythological beings, the Oyéresu and their earthly wraiths, which would be the center of a Williams novel about the ordinary person's astonished reaction to the supernatural, are very nearly crowded out of Lewis's picture.

Nevertheless, the concern with language in general and the abolition of humanity through the control of language in particular is the meat of this Mulligan's stew.[16] It is cooked with psychological realism in the parallel accounts of Mark and Jane's reeducation, archetypal symbolism and subtle allusion in the description of the novel's three settings, and a mixture of realism and symbolism in the contrast between Merlin and the modern scientists. A discussion of these three major ingredients will solve many, though not all, of the difficulties caused by the blend of genres and establish more fully the theme of the abuse of language.

Several critics have emphasized the carefully done contrasts between Belbury and St. Anne's.[17] But Lewis devotes a great deal of attention to a third setting, Bracton College and the wood attached to it. The third setting is necessary because Lewis is not presenting a simple good-evil contrast but, rather, offering an argument against the King/Ketley approach to language and the miseducation it produces. Bracton College is a part of the University of Edgestow, an institution where modern ideas (what Lewis calls *trahison des clercs*, and presumably including the low view of language) have led to the rejection of the Tao. As one speaker points out, all the cruel, inhuman practices of Belbury had been advocated by lecturers at Edgestow, although "they never thought any one would *act* on their theories" (371).

The initial description of the college seems to be mere local color, but it is actually a veiled comment on its moral bankruptcy. The authorial voice says, "It was founded in 1300 for the support of ten learned men whose duties were to pray for the soul of Henry de Bracton and to study the laws of England. The number of Fellows has gradually increased to forty, of whom only six (apart from the Bacon Professor) now study Law and of whom none, perhaps, prays for the soul of Bracton" (17). Bracton, who died in 1268, was the author of the legal treatise *De legibus et consuetudinibus Angliae* (On the Laws and Customs of England), described as the most "detailed and accurate [account] of native English law in the whole legal literature of the Middle Ages" (Sandquist 2:356–57). Lewis's choice of law as the raison d'être of Mark's college may have been influenced by Charles Williams, who quotes this flaming sentence from Bracton in *Many Dimensions:* "Therefore let the king attribute to the law that which the law attributes to him, namely, domination and power. For where the will rules and not the law is no king" (214).

But Lewis also was familiar with Bracton from his medieval studies. He cites the same sentence in a briefer and soberer form in *The Oxford History of English Literature in the Sixteenth Century* (48).[18] What he calls the Tao is sometimes identifiable with Bracton's *jus gentium,* the law used by all groups of people, and sometimes with Bracton's *jus naturale,* the Way Things Are (*De legibus* 2.26, 27). He may also have been influenced by Barfield, who was a lawyer as well as a philologist. Barfield's essay, "Poetic Diction and Legal Fiction"[19] states explicitly the relationship between language and law (Lewis's Tao) that is only implicit in *The Abolition of Man.* Barfield compares the creation of metaphor to the creation of legal fictions—for example, the one by which a company is deemed to be a person. Like metaphors, legal fictions expand human consciousness by increasing the applicability of the law. He sets up a formula: "metaphor [is to] language [is to] meaning [as] legal fiction [is to] law [is to] social life" (*Rediscovery* 58). In other words, metaphor expands language and contributes to the total body of meaning as legal fiction expands law and contributes to the totality of social life. He adds, "the *nature* of law, as law, is the same, whether it be moral, or logical, or municipal" (58, 64).

Thus, the failure to study law at Bracton College is not a minor detail but a key to the theme of the book. As Barfield explains, legal studies provide us with unique insight into the workings of the human mind. Such studies are even more important in the twentieth century than in previous times, when all the traditional ideas of human society are being questioned, and the former "respectful attitude to legal studies has long since been abandoned" (63). The way to achieve freedom is not to rebel against the law, but to expand it through metaphor. With language also, those like Ogden and Richards who try "to cut away and expose all metaphorical usage" do not "escape the curse of Babel" (*Rediscovery* 64). Seen in the context of Barfield's understanding of the law, the description of Bracton College, seemingly so offhand, alludes to a profound complex of ideas about the relationship between law and language, law and morality. Even the fussy academic parenthesis "apart from the Bacon Professor" (*Strength* 17) is significant, for Barfield also reminds us that Bacon, a lawyer as well as the founder of the scientific method, formulated the concept "laws of nature" by analogy with jurisprudence (*Rediscovery* 61–62).

The failure to study law is closely connected with the denial of validity to logical reasoning. Linguistic philosophers such as A. J. Ayer disparage logic as mere rearrangement of words and useless tautology. Barfield defends the usefulness of logic, quoting F. W. Maitland's description of law as "the point where life and logic meet" (*History* 48). He agrees with Ayer that logic is tautologous but asserts that it unfolds the meanings already "implicit in words," meanings that have been created by the poets. We do not use tautologies to convey information but to "[bring the] opponent to his senses. It is shock-treatment, designed to show him that ... he has, for the moment at least, abandoned his sovereign unity and ceased to function as a human being" (*Poetic Diction* 31–32). Therefore, in failing to study law the Fellows of Bracton College have abandoned their duty as intellectuals to provide a defense against the Controllers of the N.I.C.E.

Lewis dramatizes Barfield's discussions of law and logic, as well as his own discussion of the Tao, in the college meeting scene. He shows that the Fellows have replaced both law and logic with petty political maneuvering. Since they no longer study the law, they no longer debate logically. Pursuing power for its own sake, they violate the absolutes of the Tao; in their meeting, in Bracton's words, "will rules and not the law." The point is carried a little further at the dinner after the meeting. Curry says he would like to do research but is too busy with college politics. As Feverstone puts it, "In order to keep the place going as a learned society, all the best brains in it have to give up [research]" (36). Ironically, Curry's field is military history, and a Bractonian approach to it would be of vital significance to a civilization that had experienced two major wars in twenty-five years.

The Fellows of Bracton College have also forgotten the relationship between feeling and the law, set forth by Lewis in *The Abolition of Man*. The authorial voice hints at this in a philological comment about sounds: "Bracton" has voiceless stops, [k] and [t]; "Bragdon," the name of the wood containing Merlin's Well, is the same except that the stops [g] and [d] are voiced. The narrator says, "How Bragdon the wood was connected with Bracton the lawyer was a mystery, but I fancy myself that the Bracton family had availed themselves of an accidental similarity in the names" (*Strength* 21). But as Ransom found out on Perelandra, in Lewis's universe there are no accidents; the connection may be a "mystery," but it is not insignificant. Just as the remark about failing to study the law is disguised as mere description, so also this comment on an accidental phonetic similarity is a disguised reference to the relationship between feeling, "the ordinate condition of the affections" (*Abolition* 26), and the ability to live out the Tao in the search for knowledge.

According to Patterson, there is a symbolic opposition between Bracton College, which represents thinking, and Bragdon Wood, which represents feeling in the sense of moral judgment (5–6). Her careful tracings of the literary and historical allusions in the description of the College and the Wood support her Jungian interpretation of the novel; they are also relevant in understanding the novel as a warning against the abolition of man through the loss of a high view of language.

Bragdon Wood is, as Patterson points out, an enclosed garden and as such an ancient symbol of Paradise.[20] The only way to get into it is through the College quadrangles, "a series of widenings and narrowings" (Patterson 7). First comes the Newton quadrangle, "dry and gravelly" (*Strength* 20), named for Sir Isaac Newton (1642–1727). His discovery that the same law governs the fall of an apple and the swing of the planets in their courses was intensely exciting to eighteenth-century intellectuals. It suggested that the universe was truly a uni-verse, a rational whole that could be understood by human beings using their capacity to reason. Pope captured this excitement in his "Epitaph Intended for Sir Isaac Newton":

> Nature and Nature's Laws lay hid in night:
> God said, Let Newton be! and all was light.

Newton himself was a Christian as well as a scientist, valuing his work on theology and biblical chronology as much as his discoveries of gravity and the calculus. In naming the quadrangle for him, Lewis is alluding to a time when "the activities of the scientist were subject to moral and religious commandments."[21]

After the Newton quadrangle comes "a cool tunnel-like passage" (*Strength* 20) opening into Hall, a place for civilized dining and conversation, on the left, and the buttery, a service area for it, on the right. The passage leads to the cloister of the medieval quadrangle, where the grass is very green and the stone "soft and alive" in contrast to the dry and gravelly Newton quadrangle. The medieval quadrangle, named "Republic," is the original college, as the medieval synthesis of Platonism and Christianity was the basis of university education in England.[22] In *The Discarded Image,* published in 1962 but based on lectures given much earlier, Lewis says of the medieval synthesis, "Few constructions of the imagination seem to me to have combined splendour, sobriety, and coherence in the same degree" (216).

Onto this unity of thought and feeling, ethics and aesthetics, is attached Newton's science on the one side and seventeenth-century religion on the other side, symbolized by the Lady Alice Quadrangle, a "sweet, Protestant world" of "humble, almost domestic" buildings. The Lady Alice Quadrangle is reached by another narrow passage decorated with "slabs and urns and busts that commemorate dead Bractonians" (*Strength* 20). This seemingly random detail is a veiled reminder of an action mandated by the Tao, one of the seven corporal works of mercy, the burial and remembrance of the dead.

The quadrangle and the land adjoining it suggest the seventeenth-century Anglican balance between faith and rational inquiry. Between the Lady Alice Quadrangle and Bragdon Wood is the Fellows' bowling green, which suggests recreation and the balance of body and mind.[23] The green leads up to the gate in the wall; it is an Inigo Jones, suggesting serenity and balance in its classical purity. As the narrator enters Bragdon Wood, he pauses to describe the silence, his loneliness, the ancient mystery of Merlin's Well, "the heart of Bracton and Bragdon Wood ... on [which], I suspected, the very existence of the College had originally depended" (21). Again the narrator's antiquarian pedantry produces an anecdote hinting at the sanity, the balance of religion, science, and law that makes up the Bracton College tradition. During Queen Elizabeth's reign (that is, the time of the Elizabethan Compromise), the warden of Bracton College surrounded Merlin's Well, a numinous place, with a wall to prevent it from becoming the center of superstitious rituals. His action, preserving the relic but preventing its misuse, is typical of the Anglican *via media*. In contrast, Cromwell's men, in their religious zeal, attempted to destroy Merlin's Well and thus "purify" the place. Their action occasioned the gallant defense of the Well and the martyrdom of "the fabulously learned and saintly Richard Crowe" (*Strength* 22), an exemplar of noble adherence to the Tao who taunts the vandals with their low birth and rebellion against their lawful king. Crowe is a forerunner of the learned and aristocratic William Hingest, the twentieth-century Bractonian who is killed while trying to escape from Belbury.

As the narrator lies by Merlin's Well, he thinks of others who have lain there and who perhaps have followed the Tao in their times: Sir Kenelm Digby (1603–65), an amateur scientist, poet, and collector of manuscripts; William Collins (1721–59), a pre-romantic poet; George III (1738–1820), the mad king; and Nathaniel Fox, a fictional World War I poet.[24] Thus is summarized the tradition and quality of thought which the present Bractonians, especially the Progressive Element, reject—from the sacredness of Merlin's burial place to the ardent patriotism of the young poet who believed that it is *dulce et decorum* to die for England. This is the law that they do not study—not just the laws of England, but the Tao itself.

Bracton College is part of the University of Edgestow, the starting point for Jane and Mark, their home base. Its very name, "place of the edge," implies its position between Belbury and St. Anne's. Jane leaves Edgestow to arrive at St. Anne's-on-the-Hill, where the values represented by the stretch of land between Newton Quadrangle and Merlin's Well are preserved. Mark leaves Edgestow to arrive at Belbury, where the loss of values through rejection of the Tao culminates in dehumanization.

The contrast between Belbury and St. Anne's is obvious and has been explicated by many critics. It is less often noticed that Belbury also contrasts, almost point by point, with Bracton College. Bracton's architecture is Georgian, medieval, and seventeenth century; Belbury is "a florid Edwardian mansion . . . built for a millionaire who admired Versailles" and surrounded by concrete modern buildings (51). Instead of the dry gravelly surface of Newton Quadrangle, there are "winding paths covered so thickly with round white pebbles that you could hardly walk on them" (101). In Bragdon Wood, trees grow "just so wide apart that one saw uninterrupted foliage in the distance but the place where one stood seemed always to be a clearing; surrounded by a world of shadows, one walked in mild sunshine" (21). In the Ornamental Pleasure Grounds surrounding Belbury, the trees are "dotted about" meaninglessly among the winding paths and the flower beds in geometric shapes. The "slabs" of laurel look like the artificial foliage that Filostrato prefers; and instead of a high wall with an Inigo Jones gate, there is "a low brick wall surmounted by an iron railing" (101), the style that was the dubious glory of the Victorian and Edwardian ages of iron.

The animals of Bragdon Wood are mild, quiet sheep who perform a service by keeping the grass cropped; the animals of Belbury are imprisoned, awaiting vivisection, and they express their woe in "all manner of trumpetings, bayings, screams, laughter even, which shuddered and protested for a moment and then died away into mutterings and whines" (102). The grounds at Belbury are not really constructed for the refreshment and pleasure of human beings, and Mark seeks them only because he has been exiled from the deliberations of the "inner ring" inside the building.

The fact that the main building at Belbury is an imitation of Versailles with formal gardens is symbolic shorthand for a cluster of ideas. The name immediately reminds us of the absolutism of Louis XIV, which was outside the natural law as understood by Bracton; of the Treaty of Versailles, formulated with a remarkable ignorance of how "life and logic" meet in the Law; and of Cartesian dualism, the center of much modern thought as Platonism was the center of medieval thought. Lewis, of course, knew all about Versailles from his brother, Warren. Although W. H. Lewis's brilliant and charming book, *The Splendid Century: Life in the France of Louis XIV,* was not published until 1953, it was virtually finished in 1942, about the time C. S. Lewis was preparing the Riddell Memorial Lectures, later published as *The Abolition of Man.*[25]

The original garden of Versailles has been said to embody Cartesianism because it expressed "the 'natural' in terms of the universal laws of geometry."[26] The grounds at Belbury carry Cartesianism even further; in their anti-natural, aseptic resemblance to a municipal cemetery they suggest the mechanization and desacralization of Nature that Lewis discusses in *The Abolition of Man* and, later, in *The Discarded Image*. Cartesianism also promulgated the idea that animals are mere soulless automatons and that human bodies are also machines, but with an "incorporeal soul" in the pineal gland (Highwater 152–53). Highwater quotes a report from La Fontaine of how experimenters "systematically manipulated a living creature as if it were a senseless machine," beating dogs and nailing them down to boards to cut them open and study their inner mechanisms while they were still alive (149). Belbury's vivisection zoo carries out this attitude toward animals. Furthermore, Descartes' view of man as a machine with a soul is the first step toward the language philosophers' low view of language, treating it as a matter of mere word associations and paths in the brain (the engrams). Cartesian dualism is also the first step toward the N.I.C.E.'s goal of making Alcasan into a living but disembodied head. Because of the machinery necessary to keep the head alive, it is an automaton of sorts—a mind without a body. Frost, on the other hand, by endeavoring to destroy all feeling and motivation in himself, is trying to turn himself into a body without a mind.

Since the building of Versailles began in the seventeenth century, the architecture of Belbury is in a sense contemporary with that of Bracton's Newton and Lady Alice Quadrangles. Nevertheless, the parallels and contrasts between the two locations are seldom noticed by critics, perhaps because of the differences in narrative purpose and tone.

The description of Bracton College concentrates on the buildings and grounds, their beauty and history, as an ironic backdrop for the long account of the College meeting and the social gatherings before and after it. The description of Belbury concentrates almost completely on the inhabitants, with only a few side remarks about the buildings and grounds. Most of these observations are made by Mark as he struggles to keep afloat in the new social system. Since they are Mark's observations rather than the narrator's, they are without historical resonances, rooted firmly in the present. They are concerned with his physical comfort and whether he will be accepted into the N.I.C.E. He notices with approval the good fire in his bedroom and the private bathroom.[27] In the mirror on the wide staircase he sees his gaucherie; in Wither's office he responds to the blazing fire and the "warm and almost drugged atmosphere of vague, yet heavily important confidence" (54) by losing his ability to obtain a definite commitment from the Deputy Director; in the dining room he worries about finding a place to sit at the long table. All these details contribute to a general impression of a place which comforts the body while starving the spirit—a commune which is not a community. The contrast between Bracton College and Belbury emphasizes how much worse Belbury is. At the college, though the Fellows do not study law, Curry, the subwarden, is careful to orchestrate the debate so that they will vote correctly. They vote their self-interests, their emotions, and, in the case of old Jewel, their traditions. At Belbury, the lawlessness is so far advanced that Wither need not create even the pretense of debate. The inhabitants of Belbury are subject to none of the restraints that govern ordinary politicians who meet together to divide Gaul into three parts: no fear of retribution from the outside, no effective adverse publicity, no personal standards of right and wrong. The fear of Wither, or of any person perceived to be more powerful than themselves, is their only restraint. The abandonment of the Tao which has led to the corruption of scholarship by politics at Bracton College has resulted in the abandonment of all political behavior at Belbury.

The structure of Bracton College, contrasted with Belbury as seen by Mark, is repeated with variations in St. Anne's as seen by Jane. Just as Merlin's Well is a "holy of holies" to be approached by stages, so also St. Anne's, with the throne room of the Pendragon as its spiritual center, is approached gradually. There is a long description of the rustic train, its stops, and its passengers. St. Anne's is the end of the line, and even when Jane gets to the station, there is "still a climb to be done on foot" (51). Like Bragdon Wood, St. Anne's is enclosed by a wall. Instead of quadrangles, there are successive areas of the large garden. The first area has a brick path beside the wall with espaliered fruit trees, a "little lawn with a see-saw in the middle of it, and beyond that a greenhouse" (61). This area is analogous to the Newton Quadrangle of Bracton College. Espaliered fruit trees are characteristic of the gardens of the period, the see-saw represents balance, and the greenhouse also suggests the eighteenth-century idea of modifying, civilizing, and protecting Nature.

Then there is a rustic version of a quadrangle—Lewis calls it a "hamlet," consisting of "a barn and a stable on one side and, on the other, a second greenhouse, and a potting shed and a pigstye" (61). This area is analogous to the Republic Quadrangle in that it contains that summit of medieval thought, the Great Chain of Being. The greenhouse represents the vegetable soul of plants, the pigsty and the stable the animal creation, and the potting shed with its tools both inorganic being and the rational soul of man. This leaves the vegetable garden on the steep hillside with its narrow paths—at one point a path of single planks—to be the analogue of the strict Protestantism and Anglican balance of the Lady Alice Quadrangle.

While Mark sees Belbury through his desires for physical comfort and belonging, Jane sees St. Anne's through her literary training. As she walks along the various paths she thinks of literary gardens—*Peter Rabbit, The Romance of the Rose, Parzifal, Alice in Wonderland,* and "the garden on the top of some Mesopotamian ziggurat which had probably given rise to the whole legend of Paradise" (62). What all of these gardens have in common is the thrill of desire, of danger, of forbiddenness, of difficulty of attainment.[28] All the stories are about seekers, adventurers with passions far beyond Jane's modern lassitude and her thesis about Donne's "triumphant vindication of the body." The whole garden, together with its literary associations, illustrates Barfield's principle that we learn through pleasure and that poetry enables the recovery of unification through language. The garden produces physical nourishment, but the work of poets has enabled it to bring spiritual nourishment as well.

When Jane enters the Manor, she finds that St. Anne's is a place of logic and the Law, as Bracton College should be. On Jane's first visit to the Manor, Dr. Grace Ironwood uses the tautologies of logic to force her to see the significance of her visions. What Dr. Ironwood says to her may be paraphrased as the major premises in two hypothetical syllogisms: "If a condition is not a disease, then a doctor cannot cure it," and "If the content of a dream is consistent with information we already possess, then the dream is at least partly true." On the second visit, Dr. Ironwood introduces Jane to appropriate behavior in the presence of a lawful king, one who "attribute[s] to the law that which the law attributes to him." She is initially shocked and annoyed by Dr. Ironwood's curtsy to the Director, but then "her world was unmade" (142), and she "tasted the word *King* itself with all linked associations of battle, marriage, priesthood, mercy, and power" (143).

The Director's right to rule through heredity and the will of God rather than might or merit is emphasized more than once. For example, when MacPhee urges him to put the members of the organization to work or replace them, the Director replies, "Do you think I would claim the authority I do if the relation between us depended either on your choice or mine? . . . I have no authority to give any one of you permission to leave my household" (198). So complete is the hierarchy over which the Director rules by the grace of Maleldil that it comprises the whole terrestrial Chain of Being: the garden, with MacPhee as its steward; the mice, the pigs, and the pet bear; and all the members of the household.

Thus the highly concentrated and allusive descriptions of the three settings show that the primary contrast is not between Belbury and St. Anne's as representatives of science and humane letters, or of good knowledge and bad. Instead both of them are contrasted with Bracton College, whose buildings and grounds show what it ought to be—a place where education is rooted in the Tao. Likewise, the stories of the two major characters, Mark and Jane, are stories of reeducation in the relationship between language and mature humanity; both need it, even though Mark is a sociologist and Jane a literary scholar.

What happens to them in their reeducation is primarily a dramatization of the ideas Lewis defends in *The Abolition of Man*. In the first chapter, "Men Without Chests," Lewis asserts that people learn the Tao through learning to appreciate beauty; the attempt to corrupt Mark includes contact with ugliness in the Objective Room, and his reeducation is a process of becoming aware of his own likes and dislikes. In the second chapter, "The Way," Lewis discusses the absoluteness of the Good and the impossibility of substituting modernist ethics for tradition; Jane's reeducation occurs as she becomes aware that traditional standards of commitment and obedience meet her deepest needs. These two processes of reeducation in the novel also reflect the three stages of language in Barfield's *Poetic Diction,* and an awareness of his theory elucidates the changes in the two central characters. Barfield posits an initial unity in which the factual reference and the spiritual metaphor are indivisible; a second stage of non-poetic, abstract analysis; and a final restoration of unity through response to poetic language. *The Meaning of Meaning* and *The Control of Language* both present the second, analytical stage as the most real and important and reliable. They regard poetic diction as a potential trap, an occasion of falling into irrational conclusions and sentimentality. Being modern young people, both Mark and Jane have been trained to prefer the language of analysis. As a result, both have serious weaknesses of character that must be corrected.

The opening description of Jane's dissatisfaction with her lot shows that she is lacking in the "ordinate affections" described in *The Abolition of Man*. She is supposed to be writing a thesis in which she analyzes Donne's "triumphant vindication of the body" (14), but her experience of the body in the marriage bed completely separates the spiritual from the physical. Mark treats her almost like a Versailles-inspired automaton, a treatment that reminds her of Donne's definition of a woman as "Mummy possest" (*Strength* 16). Whenever he is home he is "always sleepy or intellectually preoccupied" (13); as Jane reflects bitterly, "only one thing ever seemed able to keep him awake after he had gone to bed, and even that did not keep him awake for long" (14). She thinks resentfully that the intellectual and spiritual companionship they had before marriage was only a ruse to bring her to physical surrender.

This marital disharmony is at least partly linguistic. As "sensible, modern people" Mark and Jane lack the mythic, metaphorical language they need to express their love. One might think that Jane's specialization in seventeenth-century literature would provide some clues, but she is unable to benefit from its wisdom. Her attitude toward scholarship resembles that of Damaris in Charles Williams's *The Place of the Lion*. Damaris is studying Platonism in medieval philosophy, but she is more interested in her own reputation than in Abelard and Bernard. She enjoys the game of creating abstract patterns of intellectual relationships without realizing that "intellect might make patterns, but itself it was a burning passion" (*Place* 168).

Jane is not as single-mindedly self-centered as Damaris, but she pursues her thesis as a way to "have her own work" apart from marriage rather than out of a burning passion for Donne. There is a sophisticated irony in her choice of Donne as a subject. Donne was a hot topic in the early 1940s, for his difficult, convoluted poetry made a good object for I. A. Richards's New Criticism. In addition, T. S. Eliot praised the seventeenth century as the last literary period before the modern separation of thought and feeling produced what he called "the dissociation of sensibility." But the seventeenth century has not helped Jane. No doubt she has developed some aesthetic appreciation in the process of earning her first degree, but she is trapped in the language of abstract analysis.

The first stage in her reeducation is her momentary experience of unified consciousness when she falls in love with Ransom. When she is taken to meet him, now enthroned as the Pendragon, successor to Arthur, in his throne room, she beholds the spiritual idea of kingship completely embodied in the individual person. She "tastes" kingship instead of just understanding it as an abstract concept, just as the word *pneuma* embodies both "spirit" and "breath." In "tasting," she "forgot who she was, and where" (143); she experienced something similar to ancient man's lack of self-consciousness, his participation in spirit and matter as a unity.[29]

This point about Jane's reeducation in language is obscured here by Lewis's use of the realistic mode of fiction when the fantastic mode is more suitable for treating nonordinary states of consciousness. The point is also obscured by Lewis's attempt to portray Ransom after the likeness of Charles Williams. As Lewis said in a letter to Arthur Greeves, "Women find him [Williams] so attractive that if he were a bad man he cd. do what he liked either as a Don Juan or a charlatan."[30] Williams accepted their devotion as a stage in their journey toward God, acted as mentor to them, and eventually sent them back to their husbands or lovers. Thus in portraying Jane's reaction to Ransom as a resolution to "be 'nice' to Mark" (151), Lewis is copying the way several women reacted to Williams. But the life drawing does not quite work; truth is stranger than fiction, and the truth of Williams's nontypical relationships with women clashes with the portrayal of the stages of Jane's reeducation in language and the Tao.

Her next unification of consciousness is blurred for a different reason. It occurs when she, Dimble, and Denniston are sent out to find Merlin, fully expecting that they may die in the attempt: "It was likely, then, that this—this stumbling walk on a wet night across a ploughed field—meant death. Death—the thing one had always heard of (like love), the thing the poets had written about" (233). Just as she had heard of kingship and love and experienced them in her first meeting with Ransom, so now the physical situation of the stumbling walk becomes one with death in clarity of perception. But the point that Jane is being knocked out of her modernistic tendency to live in the analytic stage of language is blurred. Because Lewis is Lewis and not Barfield, he is less interested in Jane's expanded consciousness, the recovery of the meaning of "death" through the image of the stumbling walk, than he is in the recovery of the meaning of life through Christian faith. So instead of showing the importance of the walk as metaphor, he narrates Jane's thoughts about the possibility that Maleldil is the Christian god. His bias—or gift—for Christian apologetic blurs the language theme at this point.

The final stage, in which Jane "tastes," instead of just analyzes, the "triumphant vindication of the body," occurs when she meets Venus, one of the deities who, according to Barfield, arise out of the ancient unity between the spiritual and the material. As Williams's Damaris learned that intellect can be a passion, Jane learns in this meeting that passion can be a passion, for it enables her to imagine what the ancient mythological unity would have been like. Again Lewis's Christian apologetic blurs the language theme. When Jane relates her experience to the Director, he advises her to "agree with your adversary quickly." She responds, somewhat awkwardly, "You mean I shall have to become a Christian?" (316), and after she leaves the Director she has a mystical experience, a direct perception of the Christian God. The dialogue is less than successful, for the artist's task of portraying the extraordinary Director and the ordinary young woman has been absorbed by Lewis's didacticism. Besides blurring the language theme, this sequence is artistically unsatisfying because it mixes levels of verisimilitude. For a protagonist to meet Venus on another planet, or in Narnia, is acceptable fantasy. It is even acceptable to meet her on Earth if the emphasis is on how the uncanny breaks into the ordinary, as in Charles Williams's novels. But here Lewis has juxtaposed two kinds of nonordinary experience: the encounter with the allegorical, literary figure of Venus and the encounter with the deity of the believed religion. It is like putting real Native Americans doing a real tribal dance on the stage with costumed actors; it breaks the illusion of verisimilitude the actors have created.

To complicate the problem even further, Lewis includes in the account of the reeducation of Jane several of his ideas on social issues: the submission of women to their husbands, the submission of both sexes to duly constituted authority, the permanence of marriage, the British class structure, and retributive versus rehabilitative punishment of criminals. The purpose, of course, is to depict the morality of the Tao in action. His mimetic mode is psychological realism, narrated through the third-person, limited viewpoint of Jane. She is alternately disturbed by the Company's courtly deference to the Director, infuriated by his and Mrs. Dimble's remarks on marriage, and surprised that lower-class Ivy associates with the others on an equal footing. To show that feminine submission is not slavery, and perhaps introduce the touch of strangeness we expect in a utopia, Lewis depicts the men and women doing the housework on alternate days. But it is unconvincing because the women (except

Dr. Grace Ironwood) have no other work, such as Dimble's position as a don or MacPhee's gardening, to perform when they are not doing housework. A large segment of the present-day readers also find patronizing the idea that men and women cannot work together. Thus the description of the social system at St. Anne's is relevant to the overall theme of the book, but it is not a complete success.

The parallel account of the reeducation of Mark does not have the same difficulties. Like Jane, Mark is trapped in the language of analysis; his training in sociology has taught him to see the world abstractly. For him, "statistics about agricultural labourers were the substance; any real ditcher, ploughman, or farmer's boy, was the shadow." He avoids using words like "man" and "woman" in favor of entities like "'vocational groups,' 'elements,' 'classes' and 'populations'" (*Strength* 87). When the story opens, he has many of the characteristics of a young man educated on the principles of King and Ketley. He believes in "the preservation of the human race" as "a pretty rock-bottom obligation" (41) without having any settled notion of why humanity ought to be preserved. Therefore he is immediately vulnerable to Feverstone's debunking of the sentiment as a "Busbyism." Like King and Ketley, he believes in bathrooms and personal cleanliness. Also in accordance with their advice, he believes in comparing his conclusions with those of others. In his case, it leads to vacillation and even toadying.

Like Jane's, Mark's scholarship has nothing to do with personal moral choices or carrying on a tradition. (This is in contrast with Denniston of St. Anne's, whose sociological studies have resulted in his advocacy of "Distributivism."[31]) Mark is even more lacking in "ordinate affections" than Jane. His education has done nothing to develop his aesthetic sense, for it did not include either the beauty of literature or the elegance of mathematical or scientific thought. What it has done is amplify a tendency to ignore his emotions, which was already present because of his desire to fit in and to be admitted into the "inner ring." Mark exemplifies Lewis's aphorism, "The head rules the belly through the chest" (*Abolition* 34). He is not yet entirely a Man Without a Chest, but he is consumptive enough to be vulnerable to the pomposities of Wither, the ersatz cordiality of Filostrato, and the twisted sexual appeal of the Fairy. His vulnerability contrasts graphically with the self-possession of Hingest, who rejects Belbury on the sole ground of "taste," saying, "it all depends what a man likes" (*Strength* 70).

Because Mark is a man with a weak chest, his head has little com-munication with his loins, the physical part of his being. Much of his experience with Belbury is a struggle between his natural physical feelings and his trained habitual bias toward abstraction. His moral descent to the point where he is able to write reports of the riots before they happen is largely motivated by his physical reactions to being accepted by the inner ring in the library: "[a] glow of sheer pleasure passed over Mark's whole body. Never had the fire seemed to burn more brightly nor the smell of the drinks to be more attractive" (128). But his physical reactions also support his small steps toward moral behavior. His nausea upon viewing Alcasan's head is what triggers his decision to leave Belbury. Concerning his nausea, Lewis comments, "The virtues he had almost succeeded in banishing from his mind still lived, if only negatively and as weaknesses, in his body" (184–85). His first actual attempt to leave Belbury is powered by "a longing for Jane which was physical without being at all sensual" (189), and his second attempt succeeds because his body, "that body which was in so many ways wiser than his mind" (213), thought for him, so that he struck at the apparition of Wither. His final escape from Belbury and the beginning of his new life are marked by the sensory pleasures of a hot bath and a good meal at the little country hotel, symbolizing the "triumphant vindication of the body" about which Jane planned to write.

In accordance with Barfield's theory of knowledge, which Lewis ac-cepted with some reservations, communication between Mark's head and his loins can only occur through the medium of language. Mark sins against language by his somewhat hysterical journalism (which bears out the contention of Ogden and Richards that literacy without real education leaves the public open to language control through the press), but is then redeemed by the stimulation of his feelings through language, beginning with the confrontation in Dimble's office. Mark experiences Dimble's righteous anger, expressed in concrete terms like "[Jane was] burned with cigars" (218), "Mary Prescott was raped and battered to death" (220), and "you have driven two thousand families from their homes to die of exposure" (221). At Belbury, anger like Dimble's was described as "'whin-ing' and 'yapping,'" but Mark receives an inkling of what such anger really is—the response objectively demanded by the situation, "whether we make it or not" (*Abolition* 29). He also receives the shock treatment of tautology—logical argument—from Dimble: "If you have no power [in the N.I.C.E.], then you cannot protect [Jane]. If you have, then you are identified with its policy. In neither case will I help you to discover where [she] is" (*Strength* 220).

Mark's subsequent arrest by the N.I.C.E. police, which parallels Jane's encounter with death in the plowed field, reveals the true nature of the abstract language that he has previously used to explain his life to himself. He finds that "[h]is 'scientific' outlook had never been a real philosophy believed with blood and heart" (*Strength* 247). In the first chapter of *The Abolition of Man*, Lewis maintains that one way to a heartfelt philosophy is through training in the beautiful, or, as Barfield said more specifically in *Poetic Diction*, through pleasure. In the Objective Room, Frost seeks to deaden Mark's feelings through exposure to badly proportioned, ugly things. Luckily for Mark, the experience only arouses in him a longing for "something he vaguely called the 'Normal'" (299). His refusal to kick and abuse the crucifix amounts to a reversal of his earlier cavalier treatment of symbolism when he wrote propaganda for Belbury.

The other aspect of Mark's development of feeling is his association with the tramp, which draws him away from his sociological abstractions and rubs his nose in the quiddity of sensory life. Mark "had once written a very authoritative article on Vagrancy," but he was "quite ignorant of the life of the roads" (312). The tramp knows nothing but the life of the road, and he is unable to use abstractions in describing it. Since Mark and the tramp have no concepts in common, they cannot communicate in the analytic mode. Nevertheless, "the sort of continual picnic which the two shared carried Mark back into the realm of childhood which we have all enjoyed before nicety began" and "a kind of intimacy grew between them" (313).

Mark's baccalaureate in language as an expression of feeling comes on the way to St. Anne's. First, at the little country hotel he is able to enjoy a children's story (perhaps a good story in rotten English) that, at age ten, he had forced himself to stop reading out of a desire to be grown up. But now he is able to trust his own feelings and follow his pleasure without worrying about whether "the Vigilant school of critics" would look down on him. His response is similar to Jane's desire to read the Curdie stories after she has escaped from Fairy Hardcastle. Mark's new awareness of his feelings leads him to realize that his "laboratory outlook on love" has prevented him from recognizing in Jane "a quality which *demands* a certain response from us whether we make it or not" (*Abolition*

29). He, who had not used "the word *Lady*. . . save as a pure form or else in mockery" (*Strength* 381), comes to realize that Jane is a lady. Now he is ready to meet her in the lodge attached to the enclosed garden of adventure and romantic love.

For both Mark and Jane, reeducation is a process of going past the language of analysis in order to participate in the Tao, the Way Things Are. Jane had analyzed literature as a way of avoiding commitment, of keeping herself to herself. Mark had analyzed human society as a way of reducing it to a playing field for his game of self-advancement. Jane learns the way things are by an experience of the Good, the moral choice of joining the Company and the religious experience of God's presence. Mark learns it aesthetically, by incidents that teach him to pay attention to his likes and dislikes—the Beautiful. But what of the True? How can a correct scientific description of the universe be related to a correct substitute for the "application of science to human affairs" that Haldane (mistakenly) demands?

That Lewis was fully aware of the problem is shown by his 1939 letter to Sister Penelope in which he states that he began writing *Out of the Silent Planet* partly because he realized "that a 'scientific' hope of defeating death is a real rival to Christianity" (*Letters* 167). Similarly, his writing of *The Abolition of Man* arose from his angry perception of a connection between the scientific method and the privileging of referential language over statements of value, which King and Ketley call "only saying something about our own feelings." Since, as Lewis goes on to show, their approach to language abolishes Nature as well as Man, it might be expected that *That Hideous Strength*, the fictional analogue of *The Abolition of Man*, would suggest some kind of imaginative answer to the problem of how "regenerate" scientific research should be conducted. He forcefully states the need in the conclusion to *The Abolition of Man:* "Perhaps I am asking impossibilities. Perhaps, in the nature of things, analytical understanding must always be a basilisk which kills what it sees and only sees by killing. But if the scientists themselves cannot arrest this process before it reaches the common Reason and kills that too, then someone else must arrest it" (90). In *Out of the Silent Planet* he showed that Weston's plan of saving human intelligence by exterminating the equally intelligent Malacandrians was ludicrous; in *Perelandra* he showed Tor and Tinidril preparing to take full charge of their planet in obedience to Maleldil. But his treatment of science in *That Hideous Strength* is disappointing.[32] We see Belbury destroying both humanity and the environment in the name of science; we do not see scientists of good will doing valid research.

In *That Hideous Strength* Lewis does state through Feverstone that Belbury is interested in power rather than knowledge. He appeals to Mark's dream of a better world through science, saying, "If Science is really given a free hand it can now take over the human race and recondition it," but then he shows what he really means in a close paraphrase of Lewis's words in *The Abolition of Man:* "Man has got to take charge of Man. That means, remember, that some men have got to take charge of the rest. . . . You and I want to be the people who do the taking charge, not the ones who are taken charge of" (42). As critics have frequently pointed out, a moderately careful reading reveals that nobody at Belbury is actually doing any experiments. The closest approximation is the work of Filostrato, who is trying to keep the head of Alcasan alive. He is an ironic figure: a fat man who wants to get rid of the body, a physiologist who hates human physiology. He is wrapped up in the technology of keeping the head alive—the tubes, the dials with their flickering needles, the numbers, the sterile white clothes—all the *miranda* of scientific activity. But he has no interest in the ultimate purpose of the experiment. As Frost observes, "What [the Head] says does not really interest [him]" (242).[33] In fact, his experiment is an illusion, since it is not his technology but the Macrobes, or demons, that keep it alive.

The other villains of the N.I.C.E. are not scientists. Fairy Hardcastle is a policewoman interested in social control (i.e., bullying and torture). Straik, a clergyman, sees Filostrato's work as a materialistic validation of the Christian faith, as pouring new meaning into traditional language. Wither and Frost may originally have been psychologists as Haldane speculates, although "even Mr. Lewis did not dare to assign them to any particular branch of science" ("Auld Hornie" 17). The remark about Wither's progress from Hegel to logical positivism makes him sound like a philosopher; but if he and Frost are psychologists, they hate the mind as much as Filostrato hates the body. As Frost tells Mark, "Friendship is a chemical phenomenon; so is hatred," and thought is "merely a by-product of your blood and nervous tissues" (257, 258). In fact, if Frost is actually a behavioral psychologist, then his scientific method is as illusory as Filostrato's technology, since the only mind to which he has access (his own) is being controlled by the Macrobes. Hingest, the chemist, sees through the pretense: "I came here because I thought it had something to do with science. Now that I find it's something more like a political conspiracy, I shall go home" (70). But the conspiracy is able to exist because science has become the model for all knowledge, including the knowledge of language and literature.

Lewis's point is complex and subtle; it might be less frequently misunderstood if he had portrayed the two good scientists, Hingest and MacPhee, more satisfactorily.

He portrays Hingest with the good qualities of common sense, modesty, self-possession, and courage. Hingest's common sense is shown in his evaluation of the College Meeting—"There's nothing extraordinary in the Fellows of Bracton talking all afternoon about an unreal issue" (57–58)—and especially in the way he sees through the N.I.C.E. More importantly, he has a clear idea of what is and what is not a proper object of study by the scientific method. As he tells Mark, "You can't study men; you can only get to know them, which is quite a different thing" (71).[34] His modesty is shown in the way he discounts his own revolutionary discoveries as less important than his aristocratic lineage; there is, after all, a certain innocence in being proud of lineage, since one has neither accomplished nor deserved it. His self-possession is shown in his threat to take up gardening if the pursuit of chemistry becomes unavoidably immoral. Finally, his fight to the finish with his murderers is the courageous stuff of epic, of "The Fight at Finnsburgh" that his name recalls. An admirable old man.

But his very virtues can also be interpreted as evidence that Hingest found his own scientific pursuits uninteresting. When the French scientist visited him at Edgestow, the two spent their time discussing aristocratic lineage rather than science, and this could imply that history is more interesting than scientific research. (After all, Lewis was upset when he met a humanist who did not want to discuss literature [*Letters* 173].) That Hingest seems dispassionate about chemistry is a subtle denigration. His choice of Glossop, the classicist, as his best friend at Bracton is evidence of his broad-minded common sense, but it could also imply that science does not provide as good a basis for *philia* as literature does. Hingest is not a Man Without a Chest; but his strength comes from his heritage rather than his science, and his goodness as a person remains completely unrelated to his work. Thus Lewis leaves his reader with the unavoidable overall impression that science is somehow not as valid as philology and literature.

The portrait of MacPhee is even more unsatisfactory. There is some doubt that Lewis even intended him to be a scientist. In a letter to one correspondent Lewis says, "It is v. important that there are 2 untainted scientists in the book (MacPhee and Hingest)," but less than five months earlier he wrote to another that "the only real disinterested scientist in my book (Hingest) [is] murdered . . . . The next best scientist (Filostrato) is not in the inner circle."[35] MacPhee is described as a scientist in only one passage in the book:

> You could not have done it [combined science and black magic] with Nineteenth-Century scientists. Their firm objective materialism would have excluded it from their minds; and even if they could have been made to believe, their inherited morality would have kept them from touching dirt. MacPhee was a survivor from that tradition. (203)

Has he done what Hingest threatened—given up a corrupt scientific research job to concentrate on gardening? MacPhee is not shown practicing his branch of science, whatever it may be. He does not use science to set up experiments that contribute to the Company's understanding (their chief source of knowledge is Ransom's and Dimble's philological expertise in the Arthurian period and Jane's visions). Nor does he work as a scientist to devise defenses against Belbury or even warn other "untainted" scientists of the danger. Ransom's description of him as a survivor from the nineteenth-century scientific tradition establishes him as a good person, but at the cost of implying that he may be too old-fashioned, too out of touch with his field, to function as a scientist.

There is, to be sure, a passage in which MacPhee helps the Company analyze the significance of Jane's dreams about Alcasan's head, and he does lecture Jane on the importance of unbiased evaluation of evidence. But these passages are not enough to establish him as an educated man of science, especially since his speech and manners suggest that he is not the social equal of Dimble and Denniston. It is hard to see a man as a brilliant scientist when he behaves like a country bumpkin, dipping snuff and mispronouncing "hiatus" (167)—not that such a man might not in fact exist, but that his character does not make for believable fiction, especially science fiction, which requires a preponderance of stereotyped characterizations. Lewis's artistic decision to use MacPhee for comic relief thus inadvertently weakens the possibility of making a point about the way to prevent science from abolishing Man.

On the literal level of the story, there is a plausible reason why we never see MacPhee "doing" science: the Company is virtually in hiding at St. Anne's, and he does not have the necessary equipment. Furthermore, in terms of the technicalities of story construction, the need to connect this story with the two previous novels through the invasion of the Oyéresu prevents the Company from doing much on its own to fight Belbury. MacPhee himself points out this weakness in the plot: "I'd be greatly obliged if any one would tell me what we *have* done" (270). Again, Lewis's decision to emphasize the religious discipline of waiting for guidance prevents MacPhee from modeling licit science.

Despite the good reasons why Lewis does not portray untainted scientists doing research, the result is that only Merlin, the man from the sixth century, is left to represent Lewis's positive ideas of what a regenerate science ought to be. As Dimble says, "In a sense Merlin represents what we've got to get back to in some different way" (286). His characterization, however, is ambiguous. On the one hand he represents the exercise of scientific curiosity within the boundaries of the Tao, for he belongs to "the College," which suggests the kind of teaching Lewis thinks ideal: the master "handed on what [he] had received . . . [and] initiated the young neophyte into the mystery of humanity which over-arched him and them alike" (*Abolition* 74). When Merlin meets the Director, he tests the latter's knowledge by asking him questions from the tradition. The rules of the College forbid Merlin to use an edged tool on any living thing, a far cry from the requirement that the modern biology student must overcome a natural distaste for the dissecting room. In receiving the five heavenly powers and destroying Belbury, Merlin enacts the way modern scientists might wield the enormous forces available to them and still remain in harmony with the ethical system that the whole cosmos obeys. On the other hand, Merlin is not entirely untainted, as is shown by his offer to take from Nature a cure for Ransom's wound. There are two motives for studying Nature—the love of truth and the desire for control. In this offer, and in his proposal to destroy Belbury by his "commerce with field and water" (*Strength* 288), he demonstrates kinship with the controllers, with those for whom "the problem is how to subdue reality to the wishes of men" (*Abolition* 88). Ransom reprimands him, saying, "It never was *very* lawful, even in your day," and "one of the purposes of your reawakening was that your own soul should be saved" (*Strength* 289).

Despite this admitted ambiguity in the portrayal of the scientists, the message of *That Hideous Strength* is, in Haldane's words, "clear enough." Lewis is not saying that a scientific approach to human affairs leads to hell; rather, he is saying that the attempt to divorce language from objective, eternal values leads to Babel—to the destruction of law, scientific inquiry, the environment, and human personality itself. If the "emotive" language that reports feelings is unimportant, then there is no reason to preserve an environment just because it is beautiful and pleasant, so that the N.I.C.E. might as well destroy Cure Hardy, tear up Bragdon Wood, and make all of Edgestow into a quagmire. If the human being is primarily a machine and consciousness a collection of engrams and associations, then law and science are equally useless, for there is no basis for believing that the human race ought to be preserved. If man is no more than an object to be studied by the use of referential language, then there is no need even to believe in human consciousness. As Lewis says in *The Abolition of Man*, those who step "outside the *Tao* . . . [step] into the void" (77).

Because modern people respect science, they tend to respect any group or activity that calls itself scientific. Where an earlier age claimed truth by "the Church teaches" or "the Bible says," twentieth-century man proclaims, "Science has proved." As Feverstone admits, Belbury calls itself the National Institute of Co-ordinated Experiments in order to gain the acceptance that is attached to science. That is why it needs Jules as putative head—he is a popularizer of science. That is why it needs "a sociologist who can write"—until its power is secured, its activities must be explained very carefully. The clues are there; but Mark, the "trained sociologist with a radically realistic outlook" (42) is too used to respecting anything that calls itself scientific to pick them up. Ironically, many readers of *That Hideous Strength* have been gulled along with Mark, and thus they produce a knee-jerk response when it seems that Science is being criticized. There are things that Lewis could have done better, but he is hardly to blame when members of his audience hold the same misconception that he is attacking.

Finally, if Lewis had treated satisfactorily all the side issues that are relevant to the theme of language control, *That Hideous Strength* would be a whole shelf of books instead of a long novel. Aside from the mixture of genres, the best judgment of its faults is found in Lewis's 1955 evaluation of *Nineteen Eighty-Four*. He says that Orwell's novel contains "too much . . . of the author's own psychology: too much indulgence of what he feels as a man, not pruned or mastered by what he intends to make as an artist." He also complains that Orwell's treatment of sex introduces deadwood, that it raises questions that have nothing to do with the main theme "and are all the more distracting for being, in themselves, of interest."[36] *Animal Farm*, he says, is better because "the myth says all the author wants it to say and (equally important) it doesn't say anything else" ("Notes on the Way" 43).

The relationship that Lewis perceives between *Nineteen Eighty-Four* and *Animal Farm* is very similar to the relationship between *That Hideous Strength* and the Chronicles of Narnia. Without the sex, without the distracting side issues, without the lumps of undigested exposition, the Chronicles of Narnia say what Lewis believes about the Tao and about the modern abuse of both feelings and language through a spuriously objective approach to "the meaning of meaning."

· 4 ·

THE CONTEXT

OF CHRISTIAN HUMANISM

A	T FIRST GLANCE, the sparkling stories of Narnia seem far removed from the dull abstractions of language philosophy. However, they do continue the work of *The Abolition of Man* and *That Hideous Strength* in refuting this philosophy. The writing of the Chronicles of Narnia is foreshadowed in both of these books with respect to their concern for children. In *The Abolition of Man* Lewis expresses anger and dismay that young people are being taught a slick cynicism toward the values expressed in traditional literature while supposedly doing "English prep" (16). It is significant, and evidence of his concern for the young, that he attacks the secondary school popularization rather than attacking the ideas of Ogden and Richards directly. In *That Hideous Strength* it is equally significant that the salvation of both Jane and Mark is mediated by children's literature. Jane reads the Curdie books of George MacDonald while recovering from the Fairy's torture, and Mark, after fleeing Belbury, reads a children's serial story before proceeding to St. Anne's; having attained some self-knowledge and sophistication by rejecting Belbury, he is now able to allow himself a simple pleasure.

From stories that appeal to the imagination Jane and Mark receive an antidote to the antihuman implications of a low view of language, a view leading to the treatment of man "as a mere 'natural object'" (*Abolition* 84) and human values as subjective and relatively unimportant. The Chronicles continue Lewis's refutation of this view by showing children who act freely, who think and make decisions within an orderly, God-directed universe, and who thus develop their essential humanity.

But the low view of language is antihumanist as well as antihuman. Ogden and Richards denigrate ancient philosophy in *The Meaning of*

Meaning, attributing the intellectual structures of the Greek philosophers to language superstition:

> The earlier writers are full of the relics of word-magic. . . . Hence the doctrine of the *Logos,* variously conceived as this supreme reality, the divine soul-substance, as the "Meaning" or reason of everything, and as the "Meaning" or essence of a name. (31)

All three of the Ransom books dramatize Lewis's disagreement with this reductive philosophy and his continuing respect for the wisdom of the past. They assert humanism indirectly by presenting an alternative cosmos—one based on Plato's *Timaeus* and enshrined in the works of Dante, Chaucer, Spenser, and Milton—as desirable and significant. The Chronicles continue this humanist tradition and depict a similar cosmos.

Since the word "humanism" has become so broad in meaning as to be almost useless, some definition is in order. A common thread in all uses of the word is an emphasis on knowledge of mankind and this world rather than knowledge about God or the gods. As used in this work, "humanism" refers more specifically to the knowledge of mankind and this world found in the literature and philosophy of the high periods of Greece and Rome. Such knowledge contrasts with both a narrowly focused knowledge of the Bible and also secularism, sometimes called "secular humanism."[1] Christian humanism, as distinguished from humanism in general, consists of the wisdom of Greece and Rome and the interpretation of it in European Christian culture. Christian humanism asserts that the knowledge of non-Christian, even nonreligious, literature and philosophy is compatible with leading a Christian life.

The Christian humanist argues that Christ the Word is Lord of all human culture, and that all human learning is valuable because it contains hints and foreshadowings of the Incarnation. The Christian antihumanist, on the other hand, argues that since Jesus Christ is the Word of God and the Bible is the truth of that Word, it is a waste of time to study anything else. From the beginning, Christianity has experienced tension between these two viewpoints, as evidenced in the Apostle Paul himself, who on the one hand writes to the Corinthians, "I decided to know nothing among you except Jesus Christ and him crucified" (1 Cor. 2:2, RSV), but on the other hand preaches to the Athenians by quoting "some of your own poets" (Acts 17:28). The same tension is found in Augustine of Hippo, who in the *Confessions* blamed his early education because he learned to mourn the death of Dido but not his own sins (Bk. I) but in *On Christian Doctrine* finds truth in pagan authors. He lists the branches of knowledge useful to the Christian teacher or apologist, recommending that literature and philosophy be used as "Egyptian gold": just as the Israelites took precious things from the Egyptians and used them to build the tabernacle for the worship of God, so Christians should do with the wisdom of the classics (II:xl:60). In *The Discarded Image* Lewis describes this perpetual tension as "a Christian 'left,' eager to detect and anxious to banish every Pagan element" and "a Christian 'right,'" including St. Augustine, who saw in Platonism a foreshadowing of the doctrine of the Trinity, and Justin Martyr, who proclaimed that "'whatever things have been well said by all men belong to us Christians'" (48–49).

Lewis, of course, had been a humanist—almost a Christian humanist—before he was a Christian. His formative years at Oxford were spent reading the ancient philosophers and the comparatively less-ancient canon of English poets. He found that his favorite authors tended to be those in the Christian humanist tradition.[2] His first major work of literary scholarship, *The Allegory of Love*, deals with major documents of Christian humanism. In *The Pilgrim's Regress*, the allegorical account of his conversion, he makes it clear that classical literature, which he calls the "pictures" of the Pagans, can be seen as one of God's efforts to get in touch with fallen humanity.

However, some of the tension between humanism and antihumanism that is characteristic of Paul and Augustine also appears in Lewis's writings.[3] On three occasions during 1939–40 Lewis struggled with the role of humanistic learning in relation to religious commitment. In "Learning in Wartime," a sermon preached to the Oxford University community in the autumn of 1939 (after Britain had declared war on September 3), he passionately defends traditional humanistic studies. He says that the desire for knowledge and artistic experience is intrinsic to human nature, and those who try "to suspend [their] whole intellectual and aesthetic activity" until a more propitious time will only succeed in exchanging "a worse cultural life for a better" (*Weight* 46). Human beings never put off their cultural activities until ultimate questions such as salvation or victory are resolved. On the contrary, Lewis says,

> They propound mathematical theorems in beleaguered cities, conduct metaphysical arguments in condemned cells, make jokes on

scaffolds, discuss the last new poem while advancing to the walls of Quebec, and comb their hair at Thermopylae. This is not *panache:* it is our nature. (45)

Lewis implies here that the Christian antihumanist's rejection of secular culture is not even possible. He also asserts that the New Testament encourages Christians to keep on with their normal activities. Those who are born with academic ability should study to the glory of God. The academic profession may not be the best road to God, but it is their road. Furthermore, since a cultural life will exist whether Christians participate or not, it is well that Christians be educated (47–50).

"Christianity and Culture," a collection of short essays published almost at the same time—between March and December of 1940—defends humanistic studies less wholeheartedly. Instead of emphasizing its endorsement of normal human activities, Lewis describes the New Testament as not quite "hostile, yet unmistakably cold to culture" (*Christian Reflections* 15). He says the New Testament does not explicitly condemn the pursuit of literature, but it does not regard literature as important. He quotes Newman's denial that literature can be Christian: "If Literature is . . . a study of human nature, you cannot have a Christian Literature. It is a contradiction in terms to attempt a sinless Literature of sinful man" (16). He adds that literature is a storehouse of human values, but insists that these are *sub-Christian* values (*Christian Reflections* 23).

The contrast between these two positions is largely due to Lewis's different purposes in writing. "Learning in Wartime" is concerned with calming his young audience while "Christianity and Culture" is arguing against the belief of I. A. Richards (and, of course, Matthew Arnold) that literature is destined to replace Christianity, the outworn religion.

In another essay, "Christianity and Literature," published in 1939 but delivered earlier as an address (probably before the outbreak of the war), Lewis denies ultimate importance to humanistic learning while using it against the antihumanist elements of modern literary theory. He finds that the modernist praise of "creativity," "spontaneity," "originality," and "freedom" presents "a disquieting contrast" with New Testament ideas of a Son who copies and obeys the Father and Christians who copy and obey the Son. If the New Testament contains the truth about the fulfillment of true humanity, then modern literary theory must be mistaken. He turns to the classics, with their talk of muses and of efforts "to embody in ... [one's] own art some reflection of eternal Beauty and Wisdom" (*Christian Reflections* 7) for an alternative to this theory that seems to promote true humanity while really undercutting it.

In *A Preface to "Paradise Lost"* Lewis develops further his perception of the antihuman stance of modern literary theory and the Christian humanists' refutation of this stance. He recalls that I. A. Richards praises literature that "produces a wholesome equilibrium of our psychological attitudes" (54) and regards literature that merely pushes our emotional buttons—exploits previously formulated stock responses—as cheap and bad. On the contrary, says Lewis, certain stock responses are "the first necessities of human life"; they come from "a delicate balance of trained habits, laboriously acquired and easily lost." The writers who teach young people "by copying to make the good Stock responses" perform "a service not only of moral and civil, but even of biological, importance" (55, 56, 57). In "the older poetry," by which Lewis means the literature of Greece and Rome and European literature up to Milton, there is a continual reworking of the stock responses: "that love is sweet, death bitter, virtue lovely, and children or gardens delightful" (57).

In *The Abolition of Man,* his angry response to *The Control of Language,* Lewis defends classical literature and philosophy unequivocally.[4] While no substitute for Christian revelation, humanistic studies presuppose traditional ideas of the Beautiful, the Good, and the True—the Tao—and therefore prevent the errors concerning the nature of both language and the universe that lead to the dehumanization of mankind. Although Lewis might still insist, if pressed, that literature is a storehouse of sub-Christian—rather than Christian—values, he has seen in King and Ketley's *The Control of Language* a dangerous tendency to ridicule the sense of wonder, disorganize the stock responses, and doubt all values except personal cleanliness and democracy. He has seen a result of this tendency in modern literature's deliberate cultivation of ugliness—for example, Eliot's image of the sunset as a patient etherized upon a table.[5] More clearly than ever, he sees the need for literature that trains the stock responses: "The little human animal will not at first have the right responses. It must be trained to feel pleasure, liking, disgust, and hatred at those things which really are pleasant, likeable, disgusting, and hateful" (26–27).

What he expressed in cold (or sometimes not so cold) prose in *The Abolition of Man* he also expressed fictionally in *That Hideous Strength.*

The Chronicles provide a profounder and subtler, though simpler, expression of the same convictions.

Thus the context of Christian humanism presents itself as a fruitful one for examining the Chronicles, although it has not been specifically emphasized by previous critics. Some of them, such as R. J. Reilly in *Romantic Religion* (1971), did not comment on the children's stories at all, and those who did were so much more interested in Christian doctrine than in literature that they often turned them into rather dull Sunday School lessons. Notable exceptions are Peter J. Schakel's *Reading with the Heart: The Way into Narnia* (1979) and Paul F. Ford's *Companion to Narnia* (1980). Schakel uses as touchstones to the stories *Mere Christianity*, which Lewis was revising at the time he began to work intensely on the Chronicles, and Jungian archetypes. Ford's book, an encyclopedia in form, uses the context of Catholic theology in the broadest sense and contains much information on Christian humanism, though that is not its main focus. Donald E. Glover, in *C. S. Lewis: The Art of Enchantment* (1981), carefully traces the evolution of Lewis's artistic technique through the series. C. N. Manlove, in *C. S. Lewis: His Literary Achievement* (1987), also treats the Chronicles as art, asserting that "Lewis gave back to children's literature some . . . 'high seriousness'" (120). He does not, however, turn to the resonances of Christian humanism as a source of that high seriousness.

The comparative neglect of Christian humanism as an underlying principle of the Chronicles has perhaps been promoted by Lewis's statements about his motives for writing. In "Sometimes Fairy Stories May Say Best What's to Be Said" (1956) Lewis says "I fell in love with the Form itself: its brevity, its severe restraints on description, its flexible traditionalism, its inflexible hostility to all analysis, digression, reflections and 'gas'" (*On Stories* 46). The title page of *That Hideous Strength* perhaps hints at this love affair, for the subtitle is "a modern fairy-tale for grown-ups." It is not, of course, a fairy story, because the beyond-natural beings do not come from Faery, but from the science fiction process of extrapolation from an existing view of the universe, in this case medieval cosmology and Greek mythology. It has none of the formal characteristics Lewis attributes to the fairy story. Its discursiveness (if not all its analysis, digression, reflection, and "gas") is proper to the novel, and the subtitle tells us less about it than about Lewis's longing for the fairy story form. The Chronicles are fairy stories, but they are not modeled after the traditional tales of the Grimm brothers or even (except superficially) after

Nesbit. Instead, they depict a fairyland that owes the most to Spenser's realm of Faery.

In the same essay Lewis speaks of his desire as a "Man" to promote Christianity "by casting all these things into an imaginary world, stripping them of their stained-glass and Sunday school associations" so as to display them "in their real potency" (47). Here he seems to be inviting a narrowly didactic reading of the stories, one incompatible with Christian humanism. But this statement of didactic purpose must be interpreted in the light of Lewis's view of childhood and premodern literary theory.

Manlove suggests that Lewis decided to write a children's story rather than an adult novel because he believed that "the child has more clarity and directness" and is "more open to experience" than adults (120, 121). But this is not what Lewis says. On the contrary, in "On Three Ways of Writing for Children" (1952) he rejects the idea of treating children as a separate class. He relates how his remark, "I loathe prunes," evoked a "So do I" from the six-year-old at a nearby table and comments that the instant sympathy he and the child felt for each other was an example of "the proper meeting between man and child as independent personalities" (*On Stories* 42). He says he never meant to write something "below adult attention" and insists that "a book worth reading only in childhood is not worth reading then" (*On Stories* 47, 48). That one should not talk down to children is a long-standing conviction of Lewis's, as seen in his offhand remark in *Allegory* (1936): "Those who have least real sympathy with childhood become most laboriously childish when they talk to children" (320).

Because Lewis did not talk down to children, he did not compose the Chronicles by asking himself what children want in terms of plot and incident, or what they need in terms of a moral. He believed that a writer should instead ask what he himself wants and needs, for children and adults are more alike than different.[6] As he wrote to a child, "You see, I don't think age matters so much as people think. Parts of me are still 12 and I think other parts were already 50 when I was 12" (*Letters to Children* 34). Readers who do not sympathize with this point of view find the ages of the children problematic. Manlove says of *The Lion, the Witch, and the Wardrobe*, "[W]e feel the uneasy juxtaposition of children and child-adults: . . . what are we doing except in wish-fulfillment with a child who leads an army into battle?" (123); and Crouch calls it "a fundamental weakness of the 'Narnia' books" that schoolchildren should become "kings and queens in a magical world" (*The Nesbit Tradition* 124). For readers who are aware that they have felt about the same age all their lives, on the other hand, here at last are books that feel natural. That people do not have specific ages on Aslan's Mountain, that they rise to adult behavior and sink back into childishness simply contributes to such readers' underlying awareness that a previously unfelt need for being treated as a person instead of an age category is being met.

As for what Lewis himself needed, the fact that he was working on his autobiography, *Surprised by Joy,* while writing the Narnian books is significant.[7] The theme of *Surprised by Joy* is the role of Joy in bringing him to a philosophical acceptance of theism. The last chapter, entitled "The Beginning," briefly recounts how theism led to an acceptance of traditional Christianity's view of Jesus as the Son of God. It was inevitable that the frozen, unemotional conversion he describes (237)[8] would need to be reordered according to the principle stated in *The Abolition of Man:* the head rules the belly through the heart. In order to live according to the belief system his head told him to be correct, the unpredictable rushes of Joy had to be replaced by stable, trained sentiments. When he states that "the subject [Joy] has lost nearly all interest for me since I became a Christian" (238), he is not ruling out the training of the heart. Such training is not only a major component of spiritual growth, but also a constant task for a Christian who lives, as Lewis did, in contact with the modern reductionist philosophies of behaviorism and linguistic analysis.

Furthermore, Lewis began both the Chronicles and the autobiography in middle age, the time of life when one readjusts the inner balance achieved as a young adult. Both the autobiography and the fairy stories may be seen as artistic reflexes of that internal process.[9] *Surprised by Joy* is Lewis's attempt to express directly what his experience has taught him about the sources of health for the soul;[10] the Narnia stories are a parallel attempt to enact this health in fiction. Both are a strengthening of the Chest, which the children who read or hear the stories need as much as Lewis does. After all, the children also live in the modern atmosphere of reductionist language philosophy, and one day they will study King and Ketley's *The Control of Language* (or a text like it) in secondary school.

Lewis's remark that he hoped to make Christianity attractive, to display it in its "real potency," must also be seen in terms of the theory of literature set forth in Sidney's *Defense of Poesie* (1597) and discussed by

Lewis in *English Literature in the Sixteenth Century*. It is not a narrow didacticism, but a comprehensive one, closely related to a deep love of classical literature and directed toward the training of the emotions rather than the mastery of cognitive concepts.[11] Sidney assumes the existence of the Platonic forms of virtue, which are "out there" even though we cannot physically see them. He says that literature gives us "speaking pictures," a concrete understanding of these moral concepts, just as a painting (a nonspeaking picture) provides an understanding of an animal one has never seen. Lewis says it would not have occurred to Sidney to argue that "the ethical is the aesthetic *par excellence*. . . . He thought we would know." Sidney believes, says Lewis, that the literary artist portrays for us "images of virtue" and "the final sweetness of that sweet world, 'the form of goodness, which seen we cannot but love.'" Although we smile at Sidney's idea that fiction can help people be good, says Lewis, we worry about the movies' contribution to juvenile delinquency; and he asks, "Why should fiction be potent to corrupt and powerless to edify?" (*English Literature* 346). The implied conclusion is that literature can teach the attractiveness of virtue.

Richards's theories of language and literature do not allow for this kind of didacticism, which promotes goodness by showing its beauty. Richards holds that the words for various virtues are nonreferential—that there is nothing "out there" to be the subject of a "speaking picture." Thus literature can "adjust the attitudes" by using emotive language well, but to present instructional portrayals of specific virtues would entail a cheap reliance on stock responses. Ironically, Lewis's goal of training the emotions in the Chronicles is very similar to Richards's goal of adjusting attitudes.[12] In *The Abolition of Man* Lewis emphasizes the need for love, for emotional commitment, if a person is to behave virtuously: "No justification of virtue will enable a man to be virtuous. Without the aid of trained emotions the intellect is powerless against the animal organism" (33–34). But since Lewis believes that the virtues are something more than nonreferential, emotion-arousing words, he portrays specific virtues in the Chronicles and works at directing the emotions toward the love of these virtues. The stories do teach Christian doctrine and behavior, but with the kind of didacticism Lewis praises in *A Preface to "Paradise Lost"*: "when the old poets made some virtue their theme they were not teaching but adoring, and . . . what we take for the didactic is often the enchanted" (v).

Early in life, Lewis had found this enchantment in Spenser's *Faerie Queene,* and in a very real sense that gargantuan work is a model for the Chronicles.[13] Spenser's Fairyland is an alternate world, and so is Narnia. The natives of Fairyland, whom Spenser calls elves, are not physically distinguishable from the human beings who enter it; there is no evidence that they are immortals, like Tolkien's elves, or even particularly numinous. In the same way, the human Narnians are "sons of Adam and daughters of Eve." People from our world, such as Prince Arthur and Britomartis, go into Spenser's Fairyland to have adventures and receive moral training. Similarly, in *The Voyage of the Dawn Treader* Aslan tells Lucy, "This was the very reason why you were brought to Narnia, that by knowing me here for a little, you may know me better there" (216). Spenser's stated purpose was "to fashion a gentleman or noble person in vertuous and gentle discipline" (136). At least one of Lewis's stated purposes was to encourage "a generation which is born to the Ogpu and the atomic bomb," and he adds, "Since it is so likely that they will meet cruel enemies, let them at least have heard of brave knights and heroic courage"(*On Stories* 39). Finally, the Narnian series resembles *The Faerie Queene* in its Christian humanism, its use of classical literature and philosophy as "Egyptian gold." By asking what Lewis praised in *The Faerie Queene,* we find new keys to what he was doing in the Chronicles.

First, Lewis praises *The Faerie Queene* for its Sidneyan didacticism, the way it teaches the virtues by making them concrete, "speaking pictures." Spenser's "business," says Lewis, "was to embody in moving [emotionally powerful] images the common wisdom" (*English Literature* 386). *The Faerie Queene* shows Guyon struggling to maintain the middle way of temperance, Britomartis fighting for her chastity, and Una surviving in the wilderness, faithful to the Red Cross Knight. The Chronicles show the children and the Narnians struggling to act in accordance with truthfulness, bravery, and fairness.

If, as Lewis believes, the essence of becoming truly human involves learning to make the good stock responses, then didactic literature that teaches such responses will be full of archetypal imagery. Lewis admires Spenser for his handling of major archetypal oppositions such as Light and Dark, Spring and Autumn, Life and Death. He points out that Spenser depicts evil as lifeless and inert, good as vital and fertile (*Allegory* 315). The Chronicles have this same archetypal quality, as is shown by Schakel's insightful analysis of them according to Jungian archetypes. Lewis also praises Spenser for showing "the primitive or instinctive mind, with all its terrors and ecstasies" (*Allegory* 312); in the stories he includes such instinctive terrors as the fear of falling and such instinctive ecstasies as the love of warmth and furriness.

Lewis also praises Spenser for his syncretism, his amalgamation of classical mythology with the popular mythology of witches and goblins. This quality is also basic to the Chronicles. Tolkien, who disliked *The Faerie Queene* for its philologically incorrect archaic diction, also disliked the amalgamation of mythologies in the Chronicles.[14] But Lewis defends Spenser's syncretism as an outgrowth of his assumption that "the truth about the universe was knowable and in fact known." Naturally, great teachers of different traditions and great poets of different mythologies would agree on many points. Modern people, in contrast, begin by assuming that objective truth is unattainable and therefore "regard diverse philosophies as historical phenomena, 'period pieces'" to be enjoyed for their unique flavor (*English Literature* 387, 386). The syncretism of the Chronicles is likewise a result of Lewis's life-affirming desire to find truth and virtue in various traditions, an attitude that is also very suitable to children's literature. He also believes that the central fact about the universe, the Incarnation of Christ, is "knowable, and in fact known," and makes it the center of the Chronicles.

Finally, Lewis says that *The Faerie Queene* is not true to life, "but the experience of reading it is like living." He praises Spenser's resolution of antitheses, the radiance of "the great allegorical *foci*" which manifest themselves in the various adventures, "the constant re-appearance of certain basic ideas, . . . the unwearied variety and seamless continuity of the whole." Spenser depicts "inner realities so vast and simple that they ordinarily escape us," as the biggest names on a map escape us—wisdom of a kind "which rarely penetrates into literature because it exists most often in inarticulate people," and, Lewis adds, "To read him is to grow in mental health" (*Allegory* 358–59).

Above all, Lewis values Spenser for his portrayal of processes working themselves out. He is, Lewis says, "not the poet of passions, but of moods," and explains, "not of falling in love but of being in love, . . . not of our sudden surrenders to temptation but of our habitual vices; not of religious conversion but of the religious life" (*English Literature* 391). This quality is what Lewis sought, perhaps unconsciously, in his fairy stories.[15] Each of the Chronicles depicts a particular mood, a stage of life, or sometimes contrasting attitudes. Lewis believes that the "school story," with its surface realism, is likely to mislead children, while the fairy story shows them the true nature of experience. In writing the stories he depicts a process working itself out—perhaps the same process that he is experiencing as he simultaneously deals with his urge to write fairy stories, his meditation on the workings of *Sehnsucht* in his early life, and his need to strengthen his own love of "the final sweetness of that sweet world." The choice of Spenser as a model almost makes itself.

These, then, are the Spenserian characteristics of the Chronicles: concrete examples of virtuous behavior modeled by the characters; stock responses stimulated by an amalgamation of mythologies and by the use of archetypal oppositions; and an experience of reading that is like the process of living. Most importantly, we find a concentration on pleasure, as Lewis finds in *The Faerie Queene* an "ordered exuberance" and "an invigorating refreshment" (*English Literature* 393). He praises Spenser for portraying good as "unconscious, unspoiled and humble . . . accompanied by gaiety and fun" and speaks of a certain episode as "an important one, because it shows good as fun, as a romp" (*Spenser's Images* 86, 84). In the same way the Chronicles, though thoroughly Christian and thoroughly didactic, have pleasure as their chief goal, and the goal of pleasure precludes all doctrinal hairsplitting. As Lewis said of Spenser, the religion is nothing "narrower than Platonised Protestantism" (*English Literature* 385); his own stories may be even more religiously comprehensive than Spenser, since Lewis's twentieth-century Anglicanism is far removed from the doctrinal struggles of the sixteenth century. Within the context of Christian humanism, the Chronicles are eminently humane.

The two epic poems of the English Renaissance most saturated with Christian humanism are, of course, *Paradise Lost* and *The Faerie Queene*. Lewis's use of *Paradise Lost* as the basis for *Perelandra* is indisputable. His use of *The Faerie Queene* in the Chronicles is less obvious; the resemblances are not found primarily in verbal echoes, plot situations, and characters (although there are a few borrowings) but in the concept of structure and the method of creating "speaking pictures."

Lewis's description of the structure of *The Faerie Queene* applies to the Chronicles. In Spenser's Fairyland, the various states of mind "become people or places." Each book has a central "'allegorical core'" expressed in a place, such as the House of Holiness in Book 1 and the House of Alma in Book 2 (*English Literature* 380–81). Each of the Chronicles has a central mood and, secondarily, a theme, and several of these are centered in a place: the Stone Table in *The Lion, the Witch, and the Wardrobe*, the contrast between Aslan's Mountain and the enchanted underground in *The Silver Chair*, and the Stable in *The Last Battle*. A third characteristic, the existence of a main quest surrounded by lesser stories, is not possible in the Narnian books because Lewis is working in miniature. However, the way the various books fit together to create "the sympathy of moods, the careful arrangement of different degrees of allegory and different degrees of seriousness" (*English Literature* 381) is Spenserian.

The *Faerie Queene* is organized around six virtues: holiness, temperance, chastity, friendship, justice, and courtesy. The seven Chronicles are not explicitly named for these virtues, although each of the six is presented in at least one of the books.[16] (As might be expected in children's books, courage and obedience are emphasized more than chastity.) The six books of *The Faerie Queene* can be divided into three groups of two: the first two books, Holiness and Temperance, deal with aspects of sanctity; the middle two books deal with various aspects of love and friendship; and the final two deal with the societal virtues of justice and courtesy.

Although, it must be emphasized, Lewis did not plan the Chronicles as a unit, they can be divided into three similar groups.[17] The first group, consisting of the first three books, is analogous to the first group of *The Faerie Queene* in that it deals with the process of sanctification (or, more specifically, the role of Joy in sanctification) and temperance, exercised by rejecting greed for money and power. The second group deals primarily with the right use of language—with the relationship of knowledge and language in *The Silver Chair* and with rhetoric as a moral discipline in *The Horse and His Boy*. One secondary topic in both books of the second group is love and friendship (as in the middle books of *The Faerie Queene*) and another is the workings of God's Providence. On the story level, the last group recounts the beginning and end of Narnia; thematically, it enacts a summation, a coming to terms with a lifetime. *The Magician's Nephew* is set in the first decade of the twentieth century, the time of Lewis's childhood, and *The Last Battle* is set in the postwar England of his old age. Together they depict the forces seeking the abolition of man; and, like Spenser's last two books, they deal with justice and courtesy (although courtesy is treated more fully and from a different perspective in *The Horse and His Boy*).

Finally, the Chronicles resemble Spenser (or at least Lewis's interpretation of Spenser) in that reading them is like living—specifically, like living a Christian life. The first book, *The Lion, the Witch, and the Wardrobe*, depicts the state of very early childhood, when all a person knows of Christianity is the celebration of Christmas and Easter. The second, *Prince Caspian*, depicts an age, perhaps just before puberty, when the child must decide for itself whether to accept the Faith, and *The Voyage of the Dawn Treader* depicts a more communal aspect of this age. The two middle Chronicles depict young adulthood, the time of university training and marriage. The sixth book, *The Magician's Nephew*, depicts middle-aged thoughts about youth and beginnings, while the final book presents the feelings that accompany old age and death. These "ages" of Narnia are purely a matter of mood, of emotional coloring, not allegory. As the first reader of each story, Lewis interacted with his own artistic creation in a pattern of emotional growth.

The objection may be raised that while *The Faerie Queene* is classified as allegory, Lewis insisted vehemently that the Chronicles are not. Apparently what Lewis meant was that the Narnian stories are not allegories in the sense that *The Pilgrim's Regress*, for example, is allegory; that is, they do not present a configuration of symbols and personified abstractions to be decoded by studying their relationships, the way one works a crossword puzzle. Even *The Faerie Queene* is not totally allegorical in that sense. Instead, the six books are a mixture of what Lewis calls "different degrees of allegory." Various passages range from the allegory based on wordplay, like that which Lewis uses in *The Pilgrim's Regress*, to completely realized symbolic images that are so polysemic as to defy analysis (and, as we have seen, even *The Pilgrim's Regress* contains a few of those). Some of Spenser's narratives present literal examples for the reader to follow, while others require a mental exercise of application to one's own life. The same range is found in the Chronicles.

The actions of the English children and human Narnians such as Caspian and Rilian are not allegorical but exemplary; they do not symbolize good and bad behavior but model it. The talking beasts, the giants and witches, the fauns and centaurs are what Lewis has called "hieroglyphs," characters who wear their personality on the outside, like an insect's exoskeleton. They are types, symbols of various aspects of complex human attitudes and emotions. For instance, Mrs. Beaver typifies domesticity and motherliness, the Badger in *Prince Caspian* loyalty and persistence, Puzzle the Donkey in *The Last Battle* good-hearted stupidity. Aslan is not a hieroglyph; he is not a symbol of Christ, not "a Christ-figure," as the misshapen critical jargon has it. He *is* Christ, incarnate in the body that Christ might have in a parallel universe. Lewis called him "a supposal"— that is, an extrapolation. The choice of the lion is dictated, obviously, by the fact that the lion is conventionally the King of the Beasts and because of the association of lions with strength and courage. Nevertheless, he is not simply a type but a complex character. Lewis remarks that Spenser used "mythological forms to hint at theological truths" because this is the best way to write a story which is "religious" without being devotional and to allow God to appear "frequently, but always *incognito*" (*Allegory* 355–56). That is what he himself did in his miniature *Faerie Queene*.

Abolishing the Controllers: The First Three Chronicles

It cannot be overemphasized that the didacticism of the Chronicles consists in the education of moral and aesthetic feelings rather than the cognitive presentation of doctrine.[18] The goal is not to fictionalize a catechism, but to prevent children from growing up without Chests. For example, the desired response to *The Lion, the Witch, and the Wardrobe* is not to believe in the vicarious suffering of Christ but to *taste* it, as Jane tasted kingship in *That Hideous Strength*. In each one of the stories a particular virtue or configuration of virtues is presented, and the reader is brought to love it through participating in the artistry of the tale. By concentrating on Christian doctrine as formulated confessionally, previous commentators have often treated the books as mere religious rhetoric and brought back the "watchful dragons" of inhibited feelings that Lewis was trying to avoid. To correct this tendency, it is necessary to place artistry above Christian doctrine, to look for patterns of imagery and tone as well as concepts.

The first three Chronicles comprise a unit in that all deal specifically with the nature of Joy and the search for it. *The Lion, the Witch, and the Wardrobe* enacts the early emotional response toward mythological beings that Lewis describes in *Surprised by Joy. Prince Caspian* enacts the recovery of Joy after it has been lost in the course of growing older. Wordsworth, whose phrase "surprised by joy" furnished the title to the autobiography Lewis was working on, also provides an insight into the first two Narnian books in his "Intimations of Immortality." In *The Lion, the Witch, and the Wardrobe* the children are "glorious in the might / Of heaven-born freedom" (Wordsworth, "Intimations" ll. 123–24), while in *Prince Caspian* the "clouds of glory" have "fade[d] into the light of common day" (ll. 65, 78) and must be restored by Aslan. *The Voyage of the Dawn Treader* concludes this subgrouping by presenting the paradigmatic journey of the Christian life, in which the original search for Joy is balanced within a larger pattern. It works out Lewis's remark in *Surprised by Joy* that he was no longer much interested in Joy. It is also the Narnian equivalent of Jane's "You mean I shall have to become a Christian?" (*Strength* 316), though perhaps more artistically successful than the analogous passage in the adult novel.

The Lion, the Witch, and the Wardrobe

Just as Lewis began his first venture into writing science fiction by using H. G. Wells's *First Men in the Moon* as a model, so his first venture into writing children's stories begins with E. Nesbit (Christopher, *C. S. Lewis* 110). The age/sex arrangement of the explorers of Narnia is the same as in Nesbit's *Five Children and It:* older boy, older girl, younger boy, younger girl. He omitted the baby, who really plays little part in Nesbit's stories. Lewis also uses Nesbit's opening situation: the children are separated from their parents and must rely on their own resources for entertainment.

But just as the addition of Ransom the philologist and the concern with language philosophy changed Lewis's handling of Wells, so his concern about the effect of "the control of language" on children and his love of Spenser changed his handling of Nesbit. The Chronicles show a tighter, surer artistry and a greater philosophical depth. The children in Nesbit's story spend their time rescuing themselves from the scrapes they get into because of their thoughtlessness. In contrast, the Pevensie children find their way into Narnia by what seems like chance, only to learn that they have really come to assume their destiny as kings and queens of Narnia. The resulting story is both more serious and more fun.

The tighter artistry is shown in the way Lewis begins individualizing the children in the seemingly random conversation of the first chapter. Peter, who is destined to be High King, is jovial, saying, "We've fallen on our feet and no mistake." Susan, who is never perfectly sincere and who ceases to be a "friend of Narnia" in *The Last Battle,*[19] speaks affectedly, calling the Professor "an old dear." Edmund, the sinner, says crossly, "Who are you to say when I'm to go to bed? Go to bed yourself." Lucy, the saint, is conciliatory: "Hadn't we all better go to bed?" When the children think of exploring the surroundings, Peter imagines royal creatures like eagles, stags, and hawks. Lucy thinks of the homely badger, and Edmund of the clever, lurking snake (fox in the British edition). Susan thinks of foxes in the American edition and rabbits in the British edition, neither of which are common symbols of courage and nobility.

The philosophical depth is shown in the immediate introduction of the issues raised by Richards and others. In their first conversation with the Professor, Peter tries to apply the scientific criterion of repeatability to determine whether Narnia is factual:

> "Well, Sir, if things are real, they're there all the time."
> "Are they?" said the Professor; and Peter did not know quite what to say. (45–46)

This conversation also introduces the issue of whether logic is mere tautology. The Professor sets up a syllogism: since Lucy is not mad and does not tell lies, then her report of Narnia must be the truth. His muttered comment, "I wonder what they *do* teach them at these schools" could be a veiled reference to King and Ketley's *The Control of Language*.

Unlike Nesbit, who generally keeps her children in one place, Lewis follows Spenser by weaving together two lines of action. In *The Lion, the Witch, and the Wardrobe* there is the story of Lucy, Peter, and Susan, who are taken by the Beavers to meet Aslan at the Stone Table, and the story of Edmund, who becomes involved with the evil White Witch and accompanies her on a journey toward the Stone Table. The two story lines come together when the three children meet Aslan and he sends his forces to rescue Edmund. Then the action divides again. The girls witness Aslan's death and resurrection and then accompany him to the White Witch's castle to rescue those who have been turned into stone. The boys fight the Battle of Beruna.

The divided plot serves to "strengthen the Chest" by setting up contrasting images. Lewis uses images of cosiness, nourishment, and furriness to produce an emotional affirmation of courage, honor, and kindness. He uses images of cold, hunger, and stoniness to produce an emotional rejection of cowardice and treachery.

The children experience coziness, the pleasure of being in a warm confined place, and the pleasure of wholesome nourishment when they are with creatures who are brave, honorable, and kind. Mr. Tumnus the Faun lives in "a little, dry, clean cave of reddish stone" (11) and serves an excellent meal. Mr. Beaver takes the children to his "very snug little home" in the beavers' dam (69). Its compactness suggests a boat or, for a modern child, a camper. Again the pleasure of snugness, which Lewis noted in Book 6 of *The Faerie Queene*,[20] is combined with the enjoyment of a meal, especially the steaminess of a small, warm room in winter. Mr. Beaver's remark, "It's snowing again" (61), reminds us that one of the joys of winter is the feeling of isolation from the outside world, of being free to eat and drink in comfort while the snow piles up outside. Finally, "the old hiding place for beavers in bad times" is so snug that "they were all a bundle of fur and clothes together" (99).

Edmund's experiences are just the opposite. He eats the addictive Turkish Delight outdoors, sitting at the Witch's feet and bundled up in her mantle. He does not enjoy the nourishing meal at the Beavers' home because he is thinking of Turkish Delight, and the name of Aslan so repels him that he sneaks out of the cosy shelter to stumble through the storm without his coat. At the Witch's castle—a large, drafty place filled with the deadness of creatures turned to stone—his treachery is rewarded with dry bread.

The images of furriness are not unambiguously good or bad, for fur is much more basic to the tone and theme of *The Lion, the Witch, and the Wardrobe* than a black-hat/white-hat morality. The images suggest very young childhood, when we make furry toys the center of our imaginative life and the object of our love. Furriness is important to the theme because Narnia is a land of Joy, the romantic Joy that surprised Lewis and Wordsworth alike, a Joy closely connected with Nature. The very entrance to Narnia is furry, through a wardrobe filled with fur coats; inside, the children find the heart's desire, the ability to communicate with Nature as symbolized by talking beasts and mythological creatures such as fauns and satyrs, dryads and naiads, giants and centaurs.

Lewis is seeking to train the emotions, to implant the sense of awe and wonder in the presence of Nature. He wants to inoculate his young readers against the attitude toward Nature that he hates in *The Abolition of Man*, that Nature is a machine for us to "understand analytically and then dominate and use . . . for our own convenience . . . [while] we suspend our judgements of value about it, ignore its final cause (if any), and treat it in terms of quantity" (81). Furriness is thus a symbol for Nature, which in one sense is neither good nor bad. Lewis, however, uses it to express emotional responses to moral values. It is an image of good when Aslan frees a lion from its enchantment: the lion "shook his mane and all the heavy, stony folds rippled into living hair" (165). It is an image of evil when the wolf attacks Susan: its hair bristles in anger, and when Peter stabs it, "everything was blood and heat and hair" (128) as it dies.

In Spenser, furry beings are sometimes neither good nor bad, but at other times they suggest an opposition between the artificiality of evil and the "natural spontaneity" of good (*Allegory* 325). For example, Lewis says the lion, the satyrs, and Satyrane, who come to the rescue of Una, or Truth, in Book 1 of *The Faerie Queene*, "represent the world of unspoiled nature" (*Allegory* 335). In *The Lion, the Witch, and the Wardrobe* both the White Witch and Father Christmas wear fur, but the Witch's face is an unnatural white accented with an unnaturally red mouth, her reindeer are an unnatural white, and her expression is "proud and cold and stern" (27), the opposite of natural spontaneity. Father Christmas's robe is red, with fur inside the hood, and his beard is white; his reindeer are a natural brown, and he is "big" and "glad" and "real" (103).

Because of the subtle emphasis on furriness, Lewis's creatures of Nature are not merely human beings in disguise. Instead, they fall into a kind of spectrum of animality. Mrs. Beaver, with her sewing machine and her motherly fussing, comes closest to being a dressed animal of the sort we find in *The Wind in the Willows*. The stone lion, who expresses catly relaxation in being restored to life—first yawning, then scratching, then bounding after Aslan—is the most purely animal. Fenris Ulf, the Witch's chief security guard, falls somewhere in between. Readers thus exercise their emotional need to accept their own animality, to get away from the disastrous Cartesian image of the soul as the ghost in the machine.

Similarly, the emotional power of Aslan's furriness gets away from the overly spiritualized, prissy denial of the Incarnation that is a common misconception of Christianity among nonbelievers and even some believers. When the children first meet Aslan, all they see is "the golden mane and the great, royal, solemn, overwhelming eyes" (123). Then they see him contrasted with the Witch: "those two faces—the golden face and the dead-white face— . . . together" (138). The girls experience his passion in the shearing of his mane and feel his resurrection in the restored mane flying backward in the wind.

Lewis apparently did not think out consciously the manifold significance of furriness. In a letter quoted by Glover, Lewis sees so little of its importance that he even offers to get rid of the fur coats: "The fur coats can be altered easily. . . . I don't know why Morrel shd. feel let down: fur *is* nice, otherwise there wd. be no temptation to trapping and one *does* find it in wardrobes. But that will be altered" (35). Fortunately, it was not. Far from being a minor detail, it is part of the whole emotional experience of entering Fairyland and being trained in Joy.

The subtlety of this deceptively simple story has given rise to other criticism. Schakel has called the Father Christmas episode a "basic inconsistency" because "Christmas celebrates the birth of Christ in his earthly incarnation" and suggests that "Lewis should perhaps have created a Narnian equivalent to our Christmas instead of taking it into Narnia."[21] On the contrary, Lewis is following Spenserian techniques. He uses Father Christmas as an easily recognized, popular symbol, just as Spenser used the iconology of popular pageants, and he uses a mythological form which is not part of the believed religion to hint at a theological truth.

Lewis also uses the Spenserian method of centering the story around an allegorical core, in this case the Stone Table. It is truly "the place of the Lion," the scene of Aslan's passion, death, and resurrection. It is the place of loss and helplessness, but it is also the place of the last courtesy of the mice in ministering to Aslan's body and of the joy beyond hope of Aslan's victory. Combined with the information that quite ordinary children are called to be kings and queens of Narnia, the mixture of sorrow and joy presents an image of life far more powerful than the prudential democracy of King and Ketley's *The Control of Language*.

It is very easy to read *The Lion, the Witch, and the Wardrobe* as theological instruction, but Lewis is "not teaching but adoring" and his "enchanted" artistry is directed toward moving children and adults alike toward learning to love Aslan. His readers know that the children get Christmas presents because Aslan is on the move; they welcome the conquest of spring over winter; they see the statues regain movement and color as Aslan breathes on them; and they see Aslan as the source of parties and laughter. The Witch is like the Conditioners in the way she freezes feelings, and like modern life itself in the way she yells "Faster, faster." Aslan brings back the innocent past that Mr. Tumnus describes, the time when "the whole forest would give itself up to jollification for weeks on end" (12). He is cheerful and fun-loving as well as solemn and powerful. On the night before his suffering, he deliberately puts away sadness: "It came into [Lucy's] head that he looked sad as well. But the next minute that expression was quite gone. The Lion shook his mane and clapped his paws together . . . and said, 'Meanwhile, let the feast be prepared'" (124–25). After his resurrection he stands, "his eyes very bright, his limbs quivering, lashing himself with his tail" and then leads the girls in "such a romp as no one has ever had except in Narnia" (160–61). In the Witch's courtyard he "whisked around" like "a cat chasing its tail," "pounced," and "rushed" (164–65). Thus Lewis succeeds in removing from Aslan the stained-glass associations with the Christ of our world.

It is a mark of the delicacy of the emotional training that Lewis treats wrongdoing very lightly. He is writing for children who need to accept the good things that come to them without the tortured guilt of trying to deserve them. Aslan receives Peter's confession that he was partly responsible for Edmund's treachery without reassurance, but also without reproach, and it is not clear that Edmund is ever told that Aslan died for him. His behavior has an important consequence—he does not receive a Christmas present—but he is restored to his rightful place as a King of Narnia.[22] The children love Aslan not because they owe a debt of gratitude, but because he is beautiful. Narnia teaches them to love beauty so that later they may embrace truth and goodness.

Prince Caspian

At the end of *The Lion, the Witch, and the Wardrobe* the Professor advises the children about getting back into Narnia. He says, "Don't go trying to use the same route twice. Indeed, don't *try* to get there at all" (186). His words echo John's experience in *The Pilgrim's Regress;* every time the young man tried to see his Island again, he attained only a substitute or a corrupted form of it. The theme of *The Lion, the Witch, and the Wardrobe,* the attainment of Joy through the love of Aslan, is also the theme of *Prince Caspian.*

The second Chronicle is a reprise of the first, but it depicts the recovery of Joy rather than its original attainment. The central image is plant life— the trees and tree spirits, and the vines of Bacchus. When the Pevensie children return to Narnia, they find themselves surrounded by overgrown trees and hampered by thickets. (The trackless forest of Spenser's Fairyland has its fullest Narnian realization in *Prince Caspian*.) The image of frozen-ness in *The Lion, the Witch, and the Wardrobe* has its analogue in the contrast between the way the Telmarines "silenced the beasts and the trees and the fountains, [and] . . . killed and drove away the dwarfs and fauns" (47) and the joy of Nature under the right rule of a son of Adam. This begins to occur when Lucy wakes out of sleep to meet Aslan and to dance with the trees and culminates in parties provided by Bacchus and the other Nature deities under the supervision of Aslan. It treats in more detail the topics of good education, man's relationship to Nature, proper rulership, and the Chest virtues of fidelity and constancy. Peter Pevensie models proper rulership, and Trumpkin models fidelity and constancy.

The plot structure repeats that of *The Lion, the Witch, and the Wardrobe* except for the addition of a story-within-a-story. The four children are at a railway station on their way to boarding school when they find themselves in a thicket close to a beach. They come to realize that they have entered Narnia hundreds of years after their first adventure, then meet Trumpkin the Dwarf by rescuing him from his captors. He narrates the story-within-a-story of Prince Caspian and the effort to restore Narnia to its original inhabitants by putting down Telmarine rule.

Just as in *The Lion, the Witch, and the Wardrobe* the children set out for the Stone Table, in *Prince Caspian* they set out for the same place, now called Aslan's How. But lacking the kind of guidance provided by the Beavers in *The Lion, the Witch, and the Wardrobe*, they become lost in the deep forests. Aslan comes to lead them, though at first only Lucy can see him. The division of the party occurs close to the How, with the boys and Trumpkin going to help Caspian and the girls accompanying Aslan. Instead of his resurrection, they witness Aslan calling to life the forces of Nature, and then they participate in his bacchanalian romp. Meanwhile, just as Peter led the fight against the Witch's forces in their first adventure, he instructs Caspian in the art of kingship and offers himself in single combat against the usurper, Caspian's Uncle Miraz. As in *Macbeth*, Aslan's party, especially the trees, come to augment Caspian's forces, and they win. There follows a wonderful feast. *Prince Caspian* differs from *The Lion, the Witch, and the Wardrobe* in that the English children do not stay after the victory is won, because Caspian is now the human ruler of Narnia. The morning after the battle, Aslan leads them to a doorway "from nowhere into nowhere" (208) and they return to our world, along with all the Telmarines who are unwilling to share Narnia with the beasts and spirits of Nature.

Although the second Chronicle virtually repeats the plot of the first, the overall impression is that it deals with a later stage of childhood. In *The Lion, the Witch, and the Wardrobe* the children are "glorious in the might / Of heaven-born freedom"; they are close to Nature without any effort to be so. In *Prince Caspian* they are older, somewhat conscious of the "shades of the prison-house," and indeed at the end Aslan tells Peter and Susan that they are too old to return to Narnia again. In the first Chronicle the children's thrones are prepared for them; their destiny is fixed. In the second they must choose to follow Lucy, who at first is the only one who can see Aslan.

Prince Caspian is a much more practical book than *The Lion, the Witch, and the Wardrobe.* When the children feel the magic beginning in the railway station, they sensibly and quick-wittedly join hands so that they won't be separated. When they find themselves on the beach, they briefly enjoy wading and splashing but then begin to cope with the practical problem of getting food and water. They plan ahead and even keep track of their coats and shoes—a mark of maturity obvious to any mother— where before, they lost the fur coats. Their maturity is also demonstrated when the boat containing Trumpkin and his captors first appears: Lucy's "How excited they'll be to see us" (28) is the book's last expression of guileless childhood, for the others shush her, and they all take cover with an unchildlike but well-founded caution.

Their new self-reliance is in sharp contrast to their first entries into Narnia, where they were always met (by Mr. Tumnus, by the White Witch, by Mr. Beaver), guided, and given food. In *Prince Caspian* they are responsible for their own survival and, more importantly, for discovering the meaning of their experiences. With no Mr. Beaver to tell them their destiny, they must reason it out. And Trumpkin can tell them the story of Caspian, but it is up to them to deduce that they have been called into Narnia to help the young prince.

The Pevensie children also seem older because they have already gone through the stages of education that Caspian experiences. The story-within-a-story begins when Caspian is a very young child—Wordsworth's six-year-old who lives in a world of pretend—and brings him up to youth in stages parallel to theirs. Just as the Pevensie children learned of Narnia by means of the magic wardrobe, Caspian learns of it by another kind of magic—the magic of story. Like them, he learns that he is the true king of Narnia. Just as the Pevensies are jerked into Narnia for their second visit, Caspian is thrust into Old Narnia by the fall from his horse.

Another reason that the children seem older is the existence of other human beings in Narnia. *The Lion, the Witch, and the Wardrobe* depicts the psychological age just beyond infancy when a child is involved in its own feelings and responsive to the spiritual significance of the environment but is oblivious to other people. *Prince Caspian* deals with a later stage, a stage when the child becomes a social and political being; thus, the story raises issues of choice and obedience that were glossed over in the first Chronicle. Edmund's choice to follow the White Witch is obviously wrong; in *Prince Caspian* the choices are not so black and white. In *The Lion, the Witch, and the Wardrobe* we are told that the four children ruled Narnia, but we never see them at work. In *Prince Caspian* the story-within-a-story gives a detailed account of the prince's training in the art of kingship, and he learns even more from Peter's example. We see him making difficult decisions and growing in responsibility.

Making the children seem older and introducing more complex issues contribute to the working out of a larger theme, the relationship between Joy and a right attitude toward Nature. Not only must Prince Caspian learn to rule himself and to obey Aslan, but he must also learn to serve and protect the natural order. The Telmarines have "reduce[d] things to mere Nature *in order that* [they might] 'conquer' them" (*Abolition* 82–83). Thus, the unnaturalness of the evil White Witch in *The Lion, the Witch, and the Wardrobe* is here shown in a more complex way.

The didactic purposes and the artistic coherence of *Prince Caspian* require that there be large numbers of humans, enough to dominate and destroy Old Narnia. The result is that there are many inconsistencies between the first story and the second. There is no use in asking questions like "Since there were no other humans, who ruled Narnia after the Pevensies returned to our world?" and "Since Caspian the First gained Narnia through conquest and unjustly destroyed Nature, under what law is Prince Caspian the rightful king?" The training in emotions that Lewis purposed for the second Chronicle required men, so he provided men. The explanation of how they got there is complex and lacking in artistic inevitability, but the story is sufficiently powerful that we do not question the lame explanation while reading it.

Lewis's Narnia, like Spenser's Fairyland, is a stage setting, not a "sub-creation." To look for the kind of consistency that Tolkien gave his works leads away from the emotional impact of the stories, for Lewis's method of working was quite different from Tolkien's. All the doors on Tolkien's stage open; Lewis's doors do not open unless the story requires that someone go through them. Each of the Chronicles presents a new situation; like Spenser's, their unity is a unity of overall thematic patterns and didactic purposes rather than a consistency of literal detail. In *The Lion, the Witch, and the Wardrobe* the primary didactic purpose was to inspire the love of Aslan; in *Prince Caspian* it is to show Joy in the context of self-control—by example in the actions of Caspian and by allegorical image in the trees, the actions of Bacchus, and Aslan's banquet.

The education in kingship that Caspian receives is completely opposite from the training of Controllers implied by King and Ketley's *The Control of Language*. It is based on medieval political philosophy, the Law that Bracton College had ceased to study. It begins in earnest when Caspian's tutor, Dr. Cornelius, takes the young prince up on the roof to view the conjunction of the two planets, Victory and Peace. This expresses the medieval idea that the king must study divine law and then convey it to his people as positive law. The orderly movement of the "great lords of the upper sky" symbolizes the law of God, and the king must imitate the order of Heaven in wise laws to govern the movements and relationships of his subjects. Thus Dr. Cornelius charges Caspian to do what he can to bring back "the long-lost days of freedom" (48).

Those who rule must also know how to obey. The medieval principle that the king himself is under the law, an important issue in *That Hideous Strength*, is dramatized in the actions of both Caspian and Peter. The king cannot please himself, for he is bound by custom. Thus Caspian follows custom by turning his eyes away from Pattertwig the Squirrel's hiding place for nuts instead of satisfying his curiosity. Similarly, in appointing the marshal of the lists, Peter is bound to recognize the Bulgy Bear's customary, hereditary right, even though he might prefer to have someone more competent in the position. Even Nikabrik, the enemy of the king, must be given honorable burial according to the customs of his own people. (The fact that real medieval rulers often violated this principle is irrelevant to Lewis's story.)

The king is bound by the laws of courtesy as well as justice, and Lewis shows both Caspian and Peter behaving courteously. Caspian accepts honey from the Bulgy Bears, though he would prefer to refuse, and Peter tactfully answers Reepicheep's request that a mouse be marshal of the lists: "Some humans are afraid of mice . . . and it would not be quite fair to Miraz" (182). Peter also shows courtesy in using the "proper" inflated language in the challenge to Miraz, for to use casual language would insult Miraz's position and lower the importance of the occasion.[23]

Just as Caspian and Peter model the obedience and courtesy of a king, Trumpkin models the obedience and courtesy of a subject. If there is to be an orderly society, people must often obey duly constituted authorities, whether they agree or not. Trumpkin exemplifies this sort of obedience when he volunteers to go to Cair Paravel even though he does not believe in the horn. He says, "You are my King. I know the difference between giving advice and taking orders. You've had my advice, and now it's the time for orders" (92). The point is further emphasized when the Pevensie children are disagreeing about whether to go with Lucy as she follows Aslan. Trumpkin thinks Lucy's story of seeing Aslan is "all bilge and beanstalks" but says, "If you all go, of course I'll go with you; and if your party splits up, I'll go with the High King" (142). Like a soldier who is taught to respect the office rather than the individual who happens to be the officer, Trumpkin follows the line of command, not his personal preference.

The medieval king ruled by the grace of God (at least theoretically), and the point is made that Caspian is not to be king because he is someone special but because it is his destiny. When he first finds himself among the Old Narnians, Trufflehunter the Badger sees him as king because "Narnia was never right except when a Son of Adam was King" (65). His acknowledgment is confirmed by Glenstorm the Centaur, who has interpreted the conjunction of Tarva and Alambil: "I watch the skies, Badger, for it is mine to watch, as it is yours to remember" (74). And Caspian responds to having been chosen: "he began already to harden and his face wore a kinglier look" (79). Then he begins to show that he is ruler indeed by bringing order to his motley supporters.

The positive examples of the just society are balanced by negative ones. Trumpkin's obedience is contrasted with Nikabrik's factionalism, his preference for the dwarfs over the whole company. Caspian's submission to courtesy and customary law is contrasted with King Miraz's subjection to his passions. Glozelle and Sopesian, Miraz's counselors, are able to play on his anger and his fear of being called a coward to trick him into accepting the challenge to single combat. They have no commitment to Miraz because of his office, and indeed his discourtesy in calling Glozelle a coward leads to his downfall as Glozelle kills him. In this way Lewis depicts the virtues of kingship and makes them lovable through the examples of Caspian and Peter.

These virtues, however, can only be practiced in freedom of spirit and within a context of right feelings toward Nature. In *The Lion, the Witch, and the Wardrobe* Lewis uses beings from classical mythology along with the talking animals to express the autonomy, the otherness of Nature and the respect that human beings should have for it. In *Prince Caspian* he depicts this configuration of feelings in the celebration led by Bacchus, or Dionysus, an allegorical figure after the method of Spenser.

The traditions surrounding Bacchus are complex. He is best known, of course, as the god of wine, but he is also the father of civilization and the first one to plow the earth with oxen (Sandys 197). Coleridge describes him as "the symbol of that power which acts without our consciousness from the vital energies of nature" (in Bush 72). He symbolizes freedom; according to Seneca, one of his names is Liber because wine frees the mind "from the servitude of cares, assures, and makes it more lively and confident" (Sandys 196). Edmund's comment, "There's a chap who might do anything—absolutely anything," recalls the words of a renaissance translator of Ovid: "in himselve [Bacchus is] made up of all contrarieties; valiant and effeminate, industrious and riotous, a seducer to vice, and an example of virtue: so variously good and bad are the effects of wine according to the use or abuse thereof" (Sandys 161).

Lewis's young readers could not be expected to be aware of this tradition, but, like Spenser, Lewis provides the clues to the meanings with the story itself. The description of the romp—the wild girls, the luxuriant growth of grapevines, the eating with "sticky and stained fingers" and "no table manners at all"—expresses "the vital energies of nature" and the human being's unconscious response to them. The next morning, Bacchus acts as Liber. He breaks the bridge that "chained" the river and inspires dogs to break their chains; he interrupts boring school sessions and invites those who will to join the dance; he turns water into wine and heals Caspian's old nurse. These are actions of the forces of Nature. Wind and weather as well as the growth of vines will break a bridge; setting children at school work is unnatural; and, as Lewis pointed out in *Miracles*, the forces of Nature annually turn water into grape juice. The relationship between these forces and wine is that the intoxication of wine frees human beings to get in touch with the natural energies within themselves.

As god of both freedom and civilization, Bacchus mediates between the just kingdom, which Peter works to restore, and the wildness, the otherness, the vitality of Nature that the Telmarines fear. The rationality of justice and the energy of physical being come together in the Chest and heal the "dissociation of sensibility." Like Father Christmas in *The Lion, the Witch, and the Wardrobe,* Bacchus expresses the laughter and conviviality that is one of the bases of civilization, yet so impossible to Men Without Chests. But the Dionysian side of humanity can create balance and joy only under God. Thus Susan says, "I wouldn't have felt very safe with Bacchus and all his wild girls if we'd met them without Aslan" (154). As in *The Lion, the Witch, and the Wardrobe,* the revelry trains the feelings by showing that Aslan is on the side of freedom, celebration, and plenteousness rather than uncomfortable Sunday clothes, long-faced piety, and self-denial.

Far from being a Sunday school lesson, most of *Prince Caspian* is concerned with two aspects of the Tao understood by all peoples—justice and the proper release of inhibition. The central Christian image of the book, the passage in which Lucy meets Aslan and then the others have to follow her by faith, must not be isolated from the example of kingship and the allegory of the bacchanal. In this passage Lewis is not modeling a simple level of faith, but rather a complex relationship between the Tao and Christian revelation. Trumpkin must obey Caspian and Peter even when he does not agree with them because he has nothing else to go on than his private judgment, so that the principle of obedience to duly constituted authority applies. Lucy must *disobey* Peter because she has a direct revelation of Aslan's will, for Christians are told, "We ought to obey God rather than men" (Acts 5:29).

In summary, the intellectual and moral relationships in *Prince Caspian* are far beyond those of the first book. Aslan is "bigger" because the children are older, and the joy of knowing him, like the geography and population of Narnia, is more complex. Whether it is artistically better, or even as good, is debatable. Most readers do not have enough classical learning to appreciate the nuances of the bacchanal, and it is not as immediately accessible to those without a classical background as the passion and resurrection of Aslan is to those without a Christian background. Whether Lewis realized the problem is unclear;[24] however, in the subsequent books, he did not use a classical figure as the keystone of the allegory again.

The Voyage of the Dawn Treader

The third Chronicle, *The Voyage of the Dawn Treader,* is surprisingly different from the first two in both plot structure and imagery; nevertheless, it, too, trains the emotions against the reductive view of humanness espoused by the Controllers. More closely than the first two books, it follows Spenser, whom Lewis calls "the poet of ordinary life" (*English Literature* 391), in creating a feeling that to read it is to participate in *ordinary* life. There is an overall absence of tension. The English children are called into the Narnian world merely to share Caspian's *Wanderjahr,* not to accomplish a royal task. If Lucy and Edmund had not been aboard, the only incident that would have had a different outcome is the recovery of visibility by the Dufflepuds. In the first two books there was suspense arising from the need to reach the Stone Table in time, but *The Voyage of the Dawn Treader* lacks such a deadline. Just as most people live from day to day as if they had forever, the travelers move from point to point at a natural pace.

In contrast with the first two Chronicles and their quest for Joy, there is an ordinariness about *The Voyage of the Dawn Treader.* Eustace, the main character, is not royalty, is not destined to be set on a throne like Caspian and the Pevensies. In *Prince Caspian* the distinction between the king who commands and the citizen who obeys is introduced; in *The Voyage of the Dawn Treader* we learn that Eustace, who is neither royal nor special, has the same duty to become brave and honorable as "their majesties." He is set upon the ordinary path to wholeness, thereby denying the modern tendency to reduce the ordinary man to a tool of the Controllers.

The most striking feature of *The Voyage of the Dawn Treader* is the almost complete absence of the panoply of mythological characters in the first two books—the fauns and satyrs, the dryads and naiads, Bacchus and Silenus, the centaurs from classical literature; the dwarfs, witches, giants, and werewolves from Northern literature; and the talking animals from children's stories. On the literal level, one would not expect to find classical Nature deities on board, since they are the spirits of particular localities. Dwarfs, inhabitants of the underground, are out of place at sea, and the ship is not large enough to carry a good giant. One would expect talking animals, however. In *The Last Battle* there are water rats with navigational skills, and cats are traditional seafarers. But Reepicheep the Mouse is the only talking animal on the ship.

Again Lewis has adjusted his stage setting in accordance with his artistic purpose. Since the story is a journey to strange places with strange inhabitants, the travelers should be as ordinary as possible. The otherness of Narnia in relation to England must be deemphasized in this book, because the ship is the normal place that contrasts with the strangeness of travel. Moreover, Reepicheep's character is more striking than it would be if he had to share the stage with other talking animals.

Instead of the romance/interlace structure of the first two books, the plot is episodic, with a simple line of narrative broken only by excerpts from Eustace's diary. Edmund and Lucy and their cousin Eustace are drawn into the sea east of Narnia by looking at a picture of a Narnian ship. They find that King Caspian has undertaken a voyage to recover the seven lords who had been exiled by his Uncle Miraz. As the voyagers sail eastward, they land on various islands and have adventures until they finally account for all seven of the lords. Then they continue to sail eastward because Reepicheep's destiny is to enter Aslan's country. At last they come to the end of the world, where the water flows over the edge— the Narnian world is (naturally) flat—and go their separate ways. Reepicheep goes over the falls in a coracle, Caspian and his sailors turn back toward Narnia, and Aslan appears to the English children and sends them back into our world.

This third book is like Book 1 of *The Faerie Queene* in that it deals specifically with sanctification and the disciplines of the Christian life. It is like Book 2 in that it provides images of moderation (what Spenser means by "temperance"). An important aspect of moderation is the handling of money and power, and this is also a thread in *The Voyage of the Dawn Treader*. Finally, the voyage itself is somewhat reminiscent of Guyon's voyage in Book 2 in which he encounters tests of moderation, although there are no obvious parallels on the literal level. As for the fictional mode of *The Voyage of the Dawn Treader*, it is exemplary in the training of Eustace's attitudes and in the travelers' responses to some of the trials they encounter. It is allegorical in the imagery connected with the ship and in adventures like the encounter with the Dark Island. Eustace's imprisonment in the body of a dragon is allegorical in providing an image of sinfulness and exemplary in depicting his shipmates' kindness toward him.

The Voyage of the Dawn Treader could be subtitled "The Book of the Church," for on the allegorical level the voyage is an image of ordinary Christian life. First, the Church is commonly pictured as a ship. Traditional church architecture produces a structure that looks like the keel of a ship upside down, and indeed the main section of the interior is called the "nave." Medieval *artes praedicandi,* manuals for preachers, quoted James 1:6, "a heaving sea ruffled by the wind," and applied it to the instability of this world, for which the Church offers the only security.[25] Second, the ship has a double mission, to sail toward Aslan's country and to seek the lost—the double mission of the Church. Like the Church, shipboard society is organized hierarchically, and the passage of time is marked in an orderly fashion, as it is by Church calendars and horaria.

As in Spenser, not all details have allegorical significance. Such things as the cross shape formed by the mast and yardarm and the wind of the Holy Spirit as a mover of the Church are irrelevant. The resemblance between the *Dawn Treader* and the Church is an image, a resonance of language, rather than a carefully worked out set of correspondences. It allows young readers to taste the emotional quality of ordinary life inside the Church, the stock responses involved in being a member of the Church, and the Church's role in preventing the abolition of man.

The beginning and end of the story resonate with the qualities of the sacraments of Baptism and Holy Communion,[26] which the Church of England (and despite his claim to be a "mere Christian," Lewis was an Anglican rather than a Roman or a member of a free church) recognizes as "generally necessary to salvation." The children's arrival on the *Dawn Treader* is like baptism as practiced in the Church of England. The children are drawn into the picture and fall into the water without choice, without understanding, without any question of whether they are worthy. Like the newly baptized infant, they join fellow travelers on a journey that is already in progress, just as the children board the *Dawn Treader* after it has been "nearly thirty days at sea" (18). One becomes a member of a specific parish, one that may or may not be congenial.[27] Edmund and Lucy find the company congenial; Eustace most emphatically does not, but there is nothing he can do about it.

The adventure ends with the Breakfast of the Lamb, which is like Holy Communion as Anglicans experienced it in Lewis's day. Although basically the incident is a retelling of Christ's meeting with his disciples in John 22, the details have an Anglican flavor. In Lewis's day, the main Sunday service in most parishes was Matins, or Morning Prayer (Neill, *Anglicanism* 403); Holy Communion was called "Early Service" and was a quiet, sparsely attended affair. The Lamb's change of form, so that he is seen as Aslan, enacts the Anglican belief in the Real Presence of Christ, which is not quite as well defined as the Roman Catholic doctrine of Transubstantiation (see Myers, "Compleat Anglican" 153). In imagery and tone the meeting resembles Lewis's description of his reaction to MacDonald's *Phantastes:* "it was homely and humble" and "had about it a sort of cool, morning innocence."[28] And just as the cool, morning innocence of *Phantastes* affected Lewis's nonliterary life, the meeting with the Lamb affects the life the children will lead in England.

Because the story depicts ordinary spiritual experience, the direct presence of Aslan is confined to the Breakfast of the Lamb episode, except for Lucy's brief conversation with him on the island of the Dufflepuds. He appears in images rather than in his own person: in the dream (if it was a dream) sequence of Eustace's undragoning; as a picture in the magic book; and speaking from the small image of himself in Caspian's cabin. On Deathwater Island, when the travelers are about to succumb to the gold lust, he appears on the hill and at some distance above them; the sight of him restores them to normality, but he does not speak. Lucy sees him as the albatross with the "strong sweet voice" (160) when the sailors are struggling desperately to get the ship away from the Dark Island,[29] but not in his own form.

On the exemplary level, *The Voyage of the Dawn Treader* continues the theme of just rulership established in *Prince Caspian,* with especial emphasis on moderation (Spenser's Temperance) in the handling of money and power. The first major episode is a continuation of Caspian's education in kingship with the Lord Bern as mentor. It contrasts the bureaucratic justice of our modern world with the justice of the king under the law. Lewis provides a concrete image of this abstract idea: the desk at which Gumpus sits, "muddling and messing about with accounts and forms and rules and regulations" (42–43), is overturned and Caspian sits royally in the chair without a desk to separate him from his suppliants and with the naked sword of justice across his knees. Caspian makes Bern ruler of the Lone Islands— not the absolute rule of the bureaucrat with his petty but irresistable regulations, but the conditional rule of a feudal lord under the Tao, hedged about with the "customs, rights, usages and laws of Narnia" (48).

In Book 2 of *The Faerie Queene,* Guyon visits the Cave of Mammon. Eustace visits the cave of the dragon, a traditional embodiment of avarice, and himself becomes a dragon. Because he is wearing a diamond bracelet at the time, he finds that it has "sunk deeply into his scaly flesh," causing him incessant pain. He becomes thoroughly sick of it, and after his undragoning he manifests his new freedom from avarice by allowing Caspian to toss it away. The dangers of avarice are also depicted in the adventure on Goldwater Island, where the greed for gold causes a momentary quarrel between Caspian and Edmund.

Another major episode, the landing on the island of the Dufflepuds, exemplifies the need for moderation in dealing with power as well as money itself. Lucy models the practice of proper restraints on magic (or, by extension, the near-magic powers of science and technology). In the process of carrying out her task of reading the spell that makes invisible things visible, she resists the temptation to use the spell that will make her the most beautiful woman in the world, although she succumbs to the temptation to find out what her friend thinks of her. Beauty is power for a woman, and the ability to know another's thoughts is power for anyone. But when the visibility spell makes Aslan appear, he tells Lucy that the moral principles of the Tao are not changed by technique: "'Spying on people by magic is the same as spying on them in any other way'" (135).

While Lucy is upstairs exercising magical power, the Dufflepuds are below practicing the follies of Mass Man. They have expressed their independence by disobeying rules made for their own good and by turning themselves invisible, which has had the unforeseen side effect of making them even more vulnerable to the completely nonexistent danger from the magician. Their constant rejection of their natural lord, Coriakin, does not free them; instead, it puts them completely under the power of the Chief. They exemplify Screwtape's words: "What with the weekly press . . . . your man has been accustomed, ever since he was a boy, to have a dozen incompatible philosophies dancing about together inside his head" (*Screwtape* 8).

Although the main interest of this episode is the rollicking satire of the follies of Mass Man, it makes the same point as traditional fairy stories such as "The Three Wishes"—that the real issues of life cannot be solved by manipulating outward circumstances. It is also the point that Lewis made in *The Abolition of Man:* "For the wise . . . the cardinal problem [is] how to conform the soul to reality . . . [by] knowledge, self-discipline, and virtue. For magic and applied science alike the problem is how to subdue reality to the wishes of men" (88). Thus Lucy, who is sometimes wise, resists one of the two temptations to manipulate outward circumstances. The spell "'for the refreshment of the spirit'" (133) is licit, because it creates its effect inwardly by acting on the imagination rather than changing circumstances.

The transformations of Eustace, first into a dragon and then back into a boy, occupy a middle ground between the allegorical churchly element and the exemplary lessons in rulership and moderation. Eustace begins the voyage as the Boy Without a Chest. He is too young to have studied the Green Book, which was intended for the upper forms, but otherwise he is the victim of a thoroughly modern education. The fact that he likes only nonfiction books implies that he has been taught that statements of fact are verifiable and important, while statements about value are "only" saying something about the speaker's feelings. The fact that he calls his mother and father "Harold" and "Alberta" implies that he knows nothing of the respect for parents and elders that is such an important part of the Tao. His preference for health food implies that he has been taught to regard the body as a machine and follows an overintellectualized life-style that has no place for Dionysian celebration. As a thoroughly modern boy, he is thoroughly serious. His characterization, like that of Jane in *That Hideous Strength,* is a gentle satire of the self-centered solemnity of the intellectuals of his time.

The endragoning of Eustace allows him to see his character and behavior as others experience it. As in the other Chronicles, the treatment of his sinfulness is lightly handled, devoid of a crushing sense of guilt. His gradual realization that he has turned into a dragon brings about his own moral judgment that "he was a monster cut off from the human race," but this somber sentence is tempered with the light irony of "A powerful dragon crying its eyes out under the moon in a deserted valley is a sight and sound hardly to be imagined" (76).

There is also a mixture of seriousness and humor in the paradox that the endragoning causes Eustace to behave for the first time as a member of the company. He receives their charity—Lucy's attempts to heal his foreleg, Reepicheep's companionship, and the whole company's efforts to devise a way to carry him along—and in return contributes what he can to the life of the group. With a child's gusto, Lewis enumerates the advantages of camping out with your personal dragon: he can kill game, start a campfire with his breath, take people for rides, and warm their backs with his hot sides. The mixture of fictional modes is pleasurable: the endragoning is fantastic and symbolic, the acts of kindness literal and exemplary, and the camping details simply fun.

The same mixture characterizes the account of Eustace's friendship with Reepicheep during his dragon period. It is a measure of Lewis's light, humorous approach that the most spiritually mature person on the Church ship is Reepicheep the Mouse. He is the gentleman who models all the virtues of the Chest that Eustace lacks. Like Chaucer's Knight, he "loved chivalrie, / Trouthe and honour, fredom and curteisie" (*Canterbury Tales* 1:45–46). Eustace, who knows nothing of these knightly virtues, at first sees Reepicheep as a performing animal, "silly and vulgar and—and sentimental" (12). (The accusation of sentimentality, of course, bespeaks Eustace's modernity more than any quality of the Mouse.) He swings Reepicheep by the tail, masking his cruelty as a joke and displaying the contrast between his own vulgarity and Reepicheep's honor. But Reepicheep, because of his "fredom" (generosity), forgets his previous wrongs and comforts Eustace the dragon.

What he does is both humorous and noble. He passes on to Eustace the medieval-renaissance tradition of Boethian philosophy. Boethius taught that one should seek permanent good rather than the transient happiness of worldly honors and comforts. He describes the wheel of fortune, which carries some people down to adversity and lifts others to prosperity. This blind operation of necessity was traditionally illustrated by stories of the fall of great men from prosperity into adversity, to teach rulers that the fragility of their glory should lead them to be humble and kind to the less fortunate. Reepicheep displays this nobility toward Eustace, setting before the dragon the ideal of detachment from worldly happiness. It is not his fault that the stories about the lives of rulers seem irrelevant to Eustace's situation; "it was kindly meant and Eustace never forgot it" (85).

Eustace's restoration to human form combines the imagery of the springs of baptism that refresh Spenser's Red Cross Knight, the medieval setpiece of the well or fountain in the enclosed garden, and Dante's plunge in the river of Lethe in the *Purgatorio*. Lewis artistically distances it by presenting it as Eustace's confession to Edmund rather than narrating it directly. It depicts the inner meaning of baptism, conversion of life, rather than the Church's performance of the sacrament. It does not make Eustace a member of the company, since he already is a member (though a very unprofitable one), but it does give him a new set of clothes and a new outlook.[30] In the subsequent fight with the sea serpent he is able to manifest the bravery of a very miniature Red Cross Knight.

In addition to presenting the two sacraments, *The Voyage of the Dawn Treader* images forth the two phases of the Christian life, the active and the contemplative. The stay at Ramandu's Island provides the transition between the two phases. It rounds off the search for the lost lords and shows Caspian's maturity in kingship. Here he rules the sailors by cleverness rather than force, putting down the incipient mutiny by making it a privilege to accompany him further. The magic feast at Aslan's Table, which many critics have allegorized as a Narnian Holy Communion,[31] is best seen as an attempt to set forth the numinous quality of Celtic horns of plenty and the feasts of Arthurian knights on their way to fulfilling a magic quest. Another preparation for contemplation is the conversation with Ramandu, in which he turns their thoughts to the great dance of the stars and suggests to them that the universe is larger and stranger than they can know. He also corrects Eustace's "modern" belief that the scientific account of a phenomenon is the whole story. When Eustace says, "In our world a star is a huge ball of flaming gas," Ramandu gently corrects his reductionism: "Even in your world, my son, that is not what a star is but only what it is made of" (180).

The last stage of the voyage, the contemplative experience, begins with a description of the lands under the sea. Here Lewis repeats his assertion of plentitude, that the world is full of things completely irrelevant to man, existing only for themselves. He combines traditional imagery with some of his own. The shipmates' eyes become "as strong as eagles'" (206) because medieval people thought eagles could look at the sun without blinking and thus used the eagle as a symbol of contemplation. The silence and whiteness, along with effortlessness of motion, may be found in Dante's *Paradiso*. To these traditional images Lewis adds his own Silver Sea of lilies and the description of the water that is "wetter, more liquid, than ordinary water" (204).

Only Reepicheep, the chosen one and the most spiritually mature, actually achieves the contemplative state of union. For the others, contemplation is a prelude to further action. Just as the Red Cross Knight's visit to the House of Holiness prepares him for the final task of killing the dragon, so Caspian is called to return to Narnia. His desire to abdicate is overruled first by his shipmates and then by Aslan himself, repeating the lesson that the king rules under the law. Like Caspian, Edmund and Lucy are called "to come close to [their] own world now" (215), "to do [their] duty in that state of life, unto which it shall please God to call [them]."[32] This call is answered in the beginning of *The Silver Chair* where Eustace lives out his contemplative experience by fighting for justice at his school, Experiment House.

It would not have been surprising if *The Voyage of the Dawn Treader* had been the concluding volume of the Chronicles of Narnia. These first three books present a complete course in the training of the Chest needed to block the abolition of human responses by the Controllers. They provide a compendium of Christian doctrine: in *The Lion, the Witch, and the Wardrobe,* the love of God Incarnate and the major Christian holidays of Christmas and Easter; in *Prince Caspian,* the experience of personal faith and of following Aslan, obeying him both in battle and celebration; and in *The Voyage of the Dawn Treader,* the two sacraments and a life of action and contemplation in the Church. Lewis must have recognized that the series would have to take a different direction if it was to continue.

Language North and South: The Middle Chronicles

Spenser's middle books form a unit because the virtues of Chastity (including married love) and Friendship (an aspect of marriage) are so closely related and because the characters of the Book of Chastity carry over into the Book of Friendship. In fact, Spenser revised the ending of the third book to postpone the resolution of Amoret's story into the fourth book. But at first it is not obvious that Lewis's middle Chronicles even form a unit. *The Silver Chair* and *The Horse and His Boy* deal with entirely different characters and even different portions of the Narnian history. *The Silver Chair* is a close sequel to *The Voyage of the Dawn Treader,* while *The Horse and His Boy* recounts events that occurred in the Golden Age when the four Pevensies were ruling Narnia as grownups, a time barely mentioned at the end of *The Lion, the Witch, and the Wardrobe.*

Nevertheless, several features of the middle Chronicles make it useful to treat them as a unit. In their own way, both, like Spenser's middle group, also deal with marriage and friendship. In *The Horse and His Boy* Aravis leaves Calormen to escape a marriage arranged for her on purely mercenary grounds and later marries Shasta, who has become her friend, so that they can quarrel and make up "more conveniently." She is like Spenser's Britomartis in that she is both feminine and tomboyish. In *The Silver Chair* Eustace Scrubb and Jill Pole become friends because they are allies against the school bullies, and they treat each other as equals during the Narnian adventure. When they think death is imminent, they shake hands, apologize for having hurt the other, and call each other by their Christian names for the first time. Furthermore, both the two middle Chronicles depict a stage of life older than the early childhood and prepuberty stages of the first three. The life tasks they depict are those of young adults. The witch in *The Silver Chair* actually subjects them to the "enchantment" of modern language philosophy, which most people encounter as late-secondary or university students. *The Horse and His Boy* deals symbolically with the life problem of separating from parents, from their values and life-style, in order to discover oneself. The children's greater maturity and autonomy are suggested by the fact that in both books the children are consciously trying to get into Narnia, whereas in the first three books it happens by accident or by magic.

If the experience of reading the Chronicles is to be like living, then the fullest effect comes from reading them in order; but since *The Horse and His Boy* and *The Silver Chair* deal with the same stage of life, it does not much matter whether they are read in the order of composition or the order of publication. Lewis wrote *The Horse and His Boy* first, but publication of it was delayed so as to keep the three books of Caspian's reign together. This allows Lewis to plant references to the fifth book in *The Silver Chair* and thus tie the two stories together more closely.

The Silver Chair and *The Horse and His Boy* complement each other in that they deal with the spiritual landscape north and south of Narnia, the land that is analogous to the Middle Way of *The Pilgrim's Regress*. Both stories are about the humanistic disciplines of rhetoric and logic, for both present images of civilized debate and its opposite. *The Silver Chair* is "northern" in that it deals with the intellect, the relationship of knowledge to moral character. *The Horse and His Boy* is "southern," for it deals with feelings: rhetoric as a reflection of good and bad character, the effect of freedom on motivation, and natural versus artificial behavior. In Spenserian terms, *The Silver Chair* is the book of Knowledge, or perhaps Prudence, and *The Horse and His Boy* is a miniature book of Courtesy.

Finally, both books are Spenserian in that they contain actual references to episodes in *The Faerie Queene,* which is not true of every Chronicle.

The Silver Chair

The third sentence of *The Silver Chair* promises, "This is not going to be a school story." But it is. Two casual similes suggest that education is the central theme: Trumpkin the Dwarf is compared to "some crusty teacher, whom everyone is a little afraid of and everyone makes fun of and nobody really dislikes" (47); and when Prince Rilian emerges from the hillside, the Narnians fall into "dead silence," like the silence "in a rowdy dormitory if the Headmaster opens the door" (199). Whereas the first three Chronicles enact the education of the feelings, *The Silver Chair* is *about* education, especially the conflict between the modern education represented by *The Control of Language* and the traditional education of Christian humanism, which, as Sidney pointed out, was meant to produce moral virtue.

The story begins and ends at Experiment House, a school apparently based on the premise that children must not be taught traditional values or disciplined by instruction in basic subjects but simply be "allowed to do what they liked." Even when the Head finds out about an instance of bullying, she does not appeal to an objective code of behavior or use the authority given her by the Tao. Instead, she tries to analyze them psychologically, to treat them as "mere 'natural object[s]'" rather than persons (*Abolition* 84). In contrast, when the bullies are beaten by Caspian, Jill, and Eustace at the end of the book, the wrongdoers are (in Lewis's view) at last being treated as persons, for they are at last being confronted with the just demands of the Tao.

In between, the story is a straight quest to defeat a witch, like *The Lion, the Witch, and the Wardrobe* and *Prince Caspian;* and also like them, it is told in an omniscient voice, though primarily from the viewpoint of a little girl. Unlike these other quests, the plot is simple. The characters are separated only briefly, and there is no interlacing. The source of narrative variety is the places: the children go from Experiment House to Aslan's Mountain to Narnia to Underland, and then the steps are reversed until they are back at Experiment House.

The various places form the allegorical core of the book, depicting various kinds and degrees of knowledge. Experiment House, of course, represents modern ignorance. Jill and Eustace are trapped there between the bullies and the stone wall that closes in the school grounds. Aslan's Mountain, which is beyond all created worlds, is the place of absolute Truth—and like Spenser's, the truth is a Platonized Christianity. The civilized world of Narnia, which is ruled by King Caspian, is a very pleasant place indeed, but Truth is not self-evident there as it is on Aslan's Mountain. North of Narnia, as in *The Pilgrim's Regress,* there is the irrationality and savagery of the giants, and under it, the realm enchanted by the Green Witch, an image of the closed universe produced by modernism. There Prince Rilian is trapped in the Silver Chair, the principle that assertions about value are purely subjective, "only saying something about our own feelings."[33] Significantly, when he kills the Green Witch, the scene is parallel to the Red Cross Knight's killing of Error in Book 1 of *The Faerie Queene* (Cox 161). Bism, which the children and the Narnians look into but do not visit, is another instance of Lewis's idea that the universe is full of wonders having nothing to do with mankind, things human beings cannot and need not know.

Just as Lewis included fauns and satyrs, Bacchus and Silenus, in the first two Chronicles when he wanted to center the books on Joy and kinship with Nature, so in *The Silver Chair* he includes nonhuman inhabitants that have something to do with knowledge. Instead of beavers and badgers, the children first meet an owl, the bird of Athena and a symbol of rationality. They ride on owls at the beginning of their quest and on centaurs, famous for their scientific and medical knowledge and their ability to read destiny in the stars, at the end of it. Puddleglum the Marshwiggle, the children's tall, spindly guide and companion, is something like a tutor. His skepticism and precision in saying that he saw a suit of armor, not a knight, perhaps owes something to Lewis's tutor, W. T. Kirkpatrick, who was also quite tall.[34]

The giants symbolize the opposite of knowledge, arrogant stupidity. The ones that line up in the ravine to play cockshies and argue in meaningless, polysyllabic roars are like the giants in the ninth circle of Dante's *Inferno,* whose heads and shoulders protrude from the ditch where they stand and who also bellow meaningless insults (Cox 163–64). (The Inferno is the eternal prison of those who have lost the good of the intellect.) The "gentle" giants of Harfang, though seemingly less stupid, are sentimental and silly. They have no respect for rationality and thus are perfectly willing to eat other rational beings—a talking stag, a marshwiggle, or humans—

when they can get them. The combination of strength and silliness in them forces their guests to act flirtatious and childish.

The exemplifications, somewhat less prominent than the allegorical places and animals, are chosen to show character traits that turn out to be the foundation of knowledge. Jill and Eustace provide examples of wrong behavior in their quarreling and lack of discipline; Puddleglum's actions are prudent and courageous, despite his doleful conversation. While he is enchanted, Prince Rilian is boorish and given to inappropriate humor; but when he becomes himself again, he is courteous and brave.

The allegorical images display in visible form three kinds of knowledge: principles, which are revealed to us; facts, which are gained through sensory experience; and logic, which enables us to process principles and facts.

The four Signs that Aslan gives Jill on the mountain symbolize revelation. Like the Ten Commandments, they prescribe certain behaviors and are an aspect of the children's calling by Aslan. When Jill says, "Nobody called me and Scrubb, you know. It was we who asked to come here," Aslan replies, "You would not have called to me unless I had been calling to you" (19). Like the Hebrews who were called by God, Jill is to learn the Signs by heart and reinforce them by constant repetition. The Ten Commandments are one expression of the Tao, or "the First Principles of Practical Reason" (*Abolition* 56). They are not to be analyzed, but rather turned into stock responses by repetition and discipline.

But the allegory of the Signs is powerfully polysemic. The Signs also symbolize the rudiments of a subject, which are revealed by teachers to their pupils and which, like the Signs, must be learned by heart instead of questioned and analyzed. This educational theory is not modern, but it is Lewis's. For example, in "The Parthenon and the Optative" (1944) Lewis recommends beginning education "with hard, dry things" like grammar and prosody so as to teach pupils "what knowledge is like" (*On Stories* 109). The purpose of learning Greek grammar and prosody is to enable one to enjoy reading the poetry with ease and precision. Similarly, the purpose of knowing the Signs is suggested in the Snow Dance at the end of the book, a Narnian celebration in which musicians, dancers, and snowball throwers all know their places and act in perfect harmony to mirror the order and beauty of the Cosmic Dance.[35]

In addition to basic principles acquired by revelation, there are empirical facts acquired from sensory experiences. Contrary to those who believe facts to be the only reliable knowledge, the story dramatizes the way facts are affected by the limitations of the senses and the passions of the experiencer. For example, Glimfeather the Owl observes the children's arrival, but his difficulty in thinking clearly during the daylight hours at first keeps him from making the correct decision about their arrival. The sensory information Trumpkin gets from speech is almost all false because of his deafness; thus he draws an incorrect generalization from it: the talking animals do not talk plainly. The passion of fear causes Jill to mistake the giant torsos for piles of rock, a foreshadowing of the error the travelers make later when their passionate desire to reach Harfang prevents them from observing the message in the ruined city. Jill's physical ability to tolerate heights causes her to underestimate the danger of falling off the cliff on Aslan's Mountain, while her fear of closed-in places causes her to overestimate the danger of crawling through a narrow underground space. By showing that sensory experience is so vulnerable to extraneous influences, Lewis is vaccinating his child readers against the language philosophers' assertion that only factual statements are significant.

Finally, there is the knowledge derived from logical reasoning, which helps a person see the implications of information derived from sensory experience and the testimony of others. Since the language philosophers were at that time denigrating logic as mere tautology, Lewis demonstrates Prince Rilian's mental imprisonment by showing him committing errors in logic. Rilian claims to *know* that his lady is "a nosegay of all virtues" because she has been kind to him; yet later he admits that this kindness is merely an assumption, because he cannot remember any other life: "my thought is that she saved me from some evil enchantment." On the other hand, he says, "Even now I am bound by a spell" (132, 136). Since being saved and being bound are logical contradictories, how can he assert both simultaneously? He claims to *know* that he turns into a serpent—"So they tell me, and they certainly speak the truth, for my Lady says the same" (137)—though he handles this testimony by assuming that "What my Lady says is true," a premise for which there is absolutely no evidence.

The key scene with the Green Witch, which represents Platonized Christianity's encounter with language philosophy, tests all three kinds of knowledge.[36] The witch begins by denying the existence of Narnia, and because they are underground, Rilian, Puddleglum, and the children have no way to prove its existence through sensory perception. The claim that Narnia exists becomes, in effect, a metaphysical statement—one that is not factually significant because it is not empirically verifiable. The witch's patronizing response is a paraphrase of Ayer's opinion that metaphysical statements may have "considerable value . . . as works of art" (*Language* 44). That is, she tells Rilian soothingly that he shall "be king of many imagined lands in [his] fancies" (*Silver Chair* 153). Since she denies having the same sensory perceptions that they have had, they turn to metaphor, explaining that the sun is like a lamp and Aslan is something like a cat. She is able to dismiss these explanations as mere metaphor, ignoring the possibility of the logical refutation that the virgin Reason had set forth in *The Pilgrim's Regress:* "By what rule do you tell a copy from an original?" (64). Because the witch has dulled their minds by the smell of the green powder and the sound of her mandolin-like instrument, her opponents are not able to use logic to refute her.

But through courage Puddleglum stamps on the fire. The bad smell restores the sharpness and credibility of the senses, and his pain restores the keenness of his logic. He is able to assert that there is something beyond both sensation and logic—his value judgment that if the witch's world is the only real one, it is not worth living in. His solution reasserts the validity of revelation and the existence of knowledge beyond empiricism. He accomplishes what Cox has called "epistemological release." Here Lewis presents in story form one of the most important points of *Abolition,* that true knowledge is related to character—to courage, self-control, and discipline.[37] It is for this reason that Aslan gave Jill the task of memorizing—learning by heart—and repeating the Signs.

Another facet of the relationship between character and knowledge is depicted in Prince Rilian. The fact that he is dressed like Hamlet symbolizes his doubt and uncertainty (Cox 160–61), the inevitable result of being imprisoned underground, away from the knowledge of his true place in life as prince of Narnia. He shows us what it is like to be ignorant of metaphysical concepts and statements of value, subjected to the kind of education that produces Men Without Chests. Since such education also involves a narrow focus on some branch of factual knowledge, it is significant that Prince Rilian became vulnerable to enchantment because he narrowed his perceptions, spent all his time hunting down the serpent who killed his mother, just as Hamlet was trapped by the need for revenge.

The imagery of the story is chosen to encourage children to reject narrow empiricism and to choose the kind of knowledge received by revelation, practiced through character, and celebrated in harmony with the true nature of the universe. The imagery forms an interesting counter-point to that of *The Lion, the Witch, and the Wardrobe,* where the winter air was threatening and warm coziness was associated with the good. In *The Silver Chair* warmth and coziness quickly turn into feelings of im-prisonment, while heights, coolness, and floating through the air are images of the good. Jill is warm and comfortable in her room at Cair Paravel, but she must leave it to begin the quest. The children must also leave the cozy tower where the Parliament of Owls is held, which is fairly neutral, since the Parliament does no harm, even though it accomplishes little. The rooms at Harfang are unpleasantly large rather than cozy, but they are at least warm and comfortable enough until the travelers realize that they are prisoners who must escape into the cold air.

The Underland is warm and crowded, but not cozy and comfortable. The description of it owes much to Spenser's episode of Guyon's descent into the Cave of Mammon in Book 2 of *The Faerie Queene.*[38] The Silver Chair on which Prince Rilian is restrained is found in Mammon's Garden of Proserpine (2.7.53), though Guyon refuses to sit in it. Spenser also speaks of the darkness, the "faint shadow of uncertain light" (stanza 29), and the busy "deformed creatures, horrible in sight" (stanza 35). There are also reminders of Wells's underground scenes in *First Men in the Moon* and *The Time Machine:* the blue lights, being forcibly escorted by the Selenites, the deformity and grim toil of the Morlocks. Unlike its literary forebears, however, Lewis's Underland is not really evil, and when the enchantment is broken the closed-in place becomes a fine underground lake, a pleasure resort for the Narnians.

The imagery of spaciousness is associated with good, with being in the care of Aslan in this book. Trapped at Experiment House, the children escape to Aslan's Mountain, where the trees grow so far apart that one can see into the forest and the air is exceptionally fresh. Jill finds being blown into Narnia very comfortable. The Marshwiggles live in wigwams "on a great flat plain which was cut into countless little islands by countless channels of water," for they "are people who like privacy" (57). The regained freedom of the gnomes is expressed by the way they throw themselves into the canyon of Bism and float downward on the thermals. When Rilian and the others regain freedom, they feel "as if all their dangers in the dark and heat and general smotheriness of the earth must have been only a dream. Out here, in the cold, with the moon and the huge stars overhead . . . and with kind, merry faces all around them, one couldn't quite believe in Underland" (197). Though the children become "sore and jolted" as they ride on the centaurs, they are learning about Narnia, and the image is one of freedom and spaciousness: seeing "those glades and slopes sparkling with last night's snow," being wished good morning by talking animals, breathing "the air of Narnia," and hearing the voices of the trees (207).

Some critics see in *The Silver Chair* a lessening of the creative energy in the first three Chronicles (Ford xxxiii). However, the animals and mythological beings are more closely and artistically integrated with the thematic pattern than the ones in the first two stories. The giant in *The Lion, the Witch, and the Wardrobe,* for example, seems to function only as comic relief, and the significance of Bacchus in *Prince Caspian* is never quite felt. It is difficult to render exciting the relationship between intellect and character, but Lewis makes "speaking pictures" of freedom and disciplined detachment by showing them to us as spaciousness and flight. Through all their travels and puzzlements the children learn that only Aslan is completely real, for his "wild breath" blows away Narnia "like wreathes of smoke" (211). And in his reality, for Lewis, is real knowledge.

The Horse and His Boy

The fifth Chronicle focuses on the tasks of social maturation: learning how to behave as an adult, coming to terms with parents, and choosing a spouse. On the literal, chronological level it takes place during the reign of the four Pevensies over Narnia, but in theme and tone it deals with the issues of young adulthood. In a sense Lewis himself was coming to terms with a parent in that "Minto," his surrogate mother, had to be put in a nursing home in April of 1950, the year *The Horse and His Boy* was being written (*Letters to Arthur Greeves,* 517–18). The biographical background is not of great importance, except as evidence that Lewis was continuing to write for his child audience the stories that he needed for himself, just as most people deal with issues of behaving as an adult, understanding parents, and forming intimate relationships over and over as they grow in mental health. Artistically, *The Horse and His Boy* is a departure from the previous stories in that it is the first to be told from the viewpoint of the male protagonist. It returns to the technique of the double plot, separating the boy and girl in the city of Tashbaan and again after they reach Narnia. It also includes the complexity of the story-within-a-story.

The story is Spenserian both in fictional mode and in the presentation of theme. Concerning Spenser's Book of Courtesy, Lewis remarked that it is more exemplary than allegorical (*Allegory* 353); the same is true of his miniature book of courtesy. In Spenser, courtesy is not the observance of outward rules of etiquette but the grace of an inward and spiritual attitude. It springs from the ability to see beneath appearances—to choose real and lasting values instead of surface glitter. It involves humility, honor (being too proud to lie or cheat), and the consciousness of being a free moral agent. Furthermore, true courtesy is found among the shepherds, not in the court (350–52). Lewis's miniature book of courtesy provides examples of all these principles. His Hermit exemplifies the spiritual aspect of courtesy; the mare, Hwin, behaves with humility, honor, and freedom; and the other main characters learn to see beneath appearances. Like Spenser, Lewis depicts true courtesy in the pastoral settings of Archenland and Narnia and a false imitation of courtesy in the court of Calormen.[39] In fact, Prince Rabadash and the courtier Ahoshta are Lewis's versions of Spenser's Turpine and Blandina, "the boor and the flatterer" (*Allegory* 352).

The plot construction repeatedly hints at the theme of courtesy. For example, hospitality is an aspect of courtesy, and the story opens with a Calormene lord demanding hospitality from Shasta's foster father, a poor fisherman. Shasta, who has had no training in etiquette, learns by eavesdropping that the fisherman is not really his father and that the lord wants to buy him. Then he learns that the lord's horse, Bree, is a talking horse. Captured by the Calormenes as a colt, Bree sees partnership with Shasta as an opportunity to escape to Narnia, even though it wounds his pride to be seen with such a poor rider. On the way Shasta and Bree meet Aravis, a high-born Calormene girl who is running away from home to escape marriage to the elderly, misshapen Ahoshta, and her Narnian horse, Hwin.

The only practical route northward takes them through Tashbaan, the capital city. There Shasta is mistaken for his real twin brother by the Narnians who are visiting the city and is separated from his fellow travelers. Meanwhile, Aravis is recognized by her friend, Lasaraleen, a snob married to an elderly courtier. The contrast between Lasaraleen's hospitality to Aravis and the way the Narnians treat Shasta is an undercurrent of the two sequences, in which each child learns half of the information needed to complete the adventure. By eavesdropping on the Narnians' conversation, Shasta learns their plan to steal away from Tashbaan because they fear the anger of Prince Rabadash when Queen Susan rejects his hand in marriage. He also learns the best route through the desert. Meanwhile Aravis learns Prince Rabadash's plans to attack Archenland and then conquer Narnia so that he may possess Queen Susan. When Shasta's twin brother, Corin, reappears at the Narnian residence, Shasta is able to escape and meet the others on the far side of the city, as they had originally planned. By this time he has learned enough of Narnian ways to regret the discourtesy of his escape.

The children and horses meet on the far side of the city and trek through the desert. In Archenland they find a hermitage; Aravis and the horses stay there to experience the simple hospitality of the Hermit, who directs Shasta to run on foot to find King Lune and warn him of Rabadash's attack. King Lune meets Shasta with courtesy and provides him with a horse so that he can ride to Narnia with the Archenlanders; but as they ride through the night Shasta becomes separated from the others. During the night he meets Aslan and comes to know him as guard and guide, the moving force of all the events of his life and indeed of the various courtesies he has received. The next morning, Shasta finds himself in Narnia, where he receives rustic hospitality from the dwarfs.

The contrast between Calormen and Narnia with respect to hospitality is very close to Spenser, who demonstrates that the two greatest hindrances to hospitality are pride and cruelty.[40] All the Calormenes in the story are either proud or cruel, or both, and their hospitality shows it. The Calormene lord forces the fisherman to offer hospitality and then receives it with scorn. Prince Rabadash's hospitality toward the Narnians becomes a threat to make guests into prisoners as soon as Queen Susan refuses his offer of marriage. Because of her pride in her clothes and social position, Lasaraleen is more interested in showing off than in making Aravis comfortable. But once the travelers reach the North, they receive good hospitality. Aravis and the horses are entertained, like Spenser's Serena, by a hermit "with entire affection and appearaunce plaine" (*Faerie Queene* 6.5.38), whose kindness and humility approaches, according to Lewis, "the sterner or more awful forms of the good" (*Allegory* 352), and Shasta receives similar treatment from the dwarfs.

When the Narnians march by the dwarfs' home on the way to battle, Shasta joins them and participates in the battle at Anvard. At this point the thematic emphasis shifts away from hospitality to chivalry, which is another kind of courtesy. The aristocratic, courageous behavior of the military Narnians and Archenlanders is astonishing to Shasta, who has been reared by a fisherman. After the Calormene army is routed, Rabadash demands a single combat with King Edward, but King Lune points out that the Prince, "by attacking our castle of Anvard in time of peace without defiance sent" (187), has forfeited his claim to be treated as a knight. Even so, hospitable King Lune treats Rabadash with all possible generosity, but Rabadash responds churlishly. Aslan appears and gives him the outward form of an ass to match his behavior. Meanwhile, Shasta has been recognized as Cor, the heir to the throne of Archenland instead of Corin. His destiny is to be a just and chivalric king and to marry the aristocratic Aravis after they both grow up.

The story is a variation of "The Ugly Duckling," and despite its awkward complexities and improbability, the plot is admirably fitted to model the principles of courtesy. When young people leave home, they need to have a thorough knowledge of the customs of their own community, but they also need a sense of basic morality so that they will be able to evaluate the new customs they encounter. The children and the horses experience the contrast between Calormen and the Northern lands, and they work at finding their place in the new environment. The plot complications allow Lewis to set positive and negative examples side by side without doing it too obviously.

First, there is the negative example of the Calormene parents—the fisherman who beats and starves Shasta, the stepmother who persecutes Aravis, and the Tisroc who coolly sends Rabadash to possible death. They depict the toxic home life that children must escape in order to grow. King Lune, in contrast, is the positive example of the nurturing parent who is proud of his children and continues to feel kindly toward them even when he threatens a punishment. Similarly, there is the negative example of Calormene marriage—the superficiality of Lasaraleen's union with a courtier, which is based on money and social position, and the cruel domination of the marriage Rabadash desires to contract with Susan. He lusts for her beauty, even though he calls her a "false, proud, black-hearted daughter of a dog" (106), and declares, "I must have her as my wife, though she shall learn a sharp lesson first" (107). In contrast, the future marriage of Aravis and Shasta-Cor will be based on friendship and shared values: "Both were still and solemn for a moment as each saw that the other knew about Aslan" (197).

The children and the horses also provide positive and negative examples as they struggle with courtesy. Shasta, having grown up in a fisherman's hut, does not know how to behave: "And he tried to put on what he thought very grand and stiff manners, but . . . the result was dreadful" (32). Such sulky, awkward behavior is common in young adults, stemming from having a low opinion of oneself combined with an almost total self-centeredness. Shasta suffers intensely when Aravis and Bree seem to be leaving him out of the conversation, though his suffering is partly self-inflicted. But his character is basically good, and at the end of the book he is beginning to learn the manners of the North: "The Prince bowed, and a very clumsy bow for a Prince it was" (195).

Like Shasta, the two horses do not know the rules of etiquette. Because they left Narnia as foals, they do not know what talking horses do. Bree, whose fear of being ridiculous is even greater than Shasta's, suffers even more than Shasta because of his pride. He has an exaggerated sense of self-worth because of having compared himself with the non-speaking horses of Calormen. He thinks himself too good to carry Shasta and twits the boy for his riding. His pride prevents him from fully enjoying the Hermit's hospitality because he is so ashamed at having run from danger, and with the dramatic exaggeration of the young adult he says, "I've lost everything." He loves to roll but is afraid other talking horses do not do it, and because he "can't bear to give it up," he enters Narnia looking "more like a horse going to a funeral than a long-lost captive returning to home and freedom" (202). In contrast, Hwin understands that these social deficiencies, however painful, really matter very little in the long run. Unlike Bree, and unlike most young adults, she realizes that she is not the center of everyone's attention, so that if she wants to roll and look ridiculous, other Narnian horses won't care "two lumps of sugar" (201). She displays the humility that Lewis praises as the outstanding characteristic of Spenser's Book of Courtesy.[41]

To complete the pattern, Aravis understands the outward forms of courteous behavior but lacks the concern for other people that a true lady should have. She has no qualms about drugging her maid and thus setting her up for a beating. As far as she is concerned, Shasta is a peasant unworthy of her attention, and as they travel together, she "never [speaks] to [him] at all if she [can] help it" (42). In Tashbaan she begins to appreciate him a little because she becomes "so tired of Lasaraleen's silliness" (99). When the lion attacks them and Shasta, empty-handed, nevertheless tries to save her, she is humbled by his courage. Her cure is complete when she realizes the justice with which Aslan punishes her: he has clawed her back with stripes like the ones her maid must have received.

The details of the plot show how courtesy stems from an awareness of God's Providence. If God is arranging all one's circumstances, it is possible to relax and be courteous, for it is not necessary to push neighbors aside in order to survive. Julian of Norwich, one of Lewis's favorite spiritual writers, refers to Christ as "homely and courteous" and advises Christians to respond courteously to Christ's care by taking their troubles "lightly." Shasta's first opinion is "that I must be the most unfortunate boy . . . in the world" (156), but Aslan tells him a different version of his life, revealing the providential care underlying the misfortunes. Later, when it is learned that Shasta is really Prince Cor, King Lune instructs him in the courtesy with which he must respond to providential care. Providence has made Shasta the crown prince, and it is his duty to accept his place and set an example of courtesy, even when he is not getting what he wants: "When there's hunger in the land . . . [the king must] wear finer clothes and laugh louder over a scantier meal than any man in [the] land" (215). Rabadash, who has no sense of Providence, is discourteous and also believes that he must have exactly what he wants at all costs. Thus when Queen Susan rejects his proposal of marriage, he displaces his anger by kicking the Grand Vizier.[42]

The primary symbol of discourtesy in Spenser's Book 6 is the Blatant Beast, who embodies infamy and slander. Instead of using an allegorical monster, Lewis provides examples of how good and evil characters are revealed in different ways of speaking. He shows that the verbal forms of courtesy are not empty, nonreferential, "emotive" language but are woven into the soul of what it means to be human. In the writing, Lewis makes use of the traditional assumption that rhetoric is a moral discipline, that the trained rhetorician is a good man speaking well.[43] Thus he is careful to include a greater variety of literary styles in The Horse and His Boy than in any of the other Chronicles.

However, these shifts of style sometimes seem awkward, and they do not always fulfill their purpose. The most unsuccessful style is school English, which perhaps owes more to E. Nesbit than the conversation of real schoolchildren and which is meant to express the shyness that Aravis and Shasta-Cor feel toward each other. Shasta says, "I do hope you won't think I'm got up like this . . . to try to impress you . . . or any rot of that sort," and Aravis says, "No, shut up. There's something I've got to say at once. I'm sorry I've been such a pig" (196). Lasaraleen's version of school-girl English is more successful, contributing to the overall contrast between the true courtesy of the North and the phony courtesy of the city. She uses numerous adjectives and emphatic adverbs to express her scatter-brained triviality—"how perfectly thrilling" and "madly in love." Because she knows nothing of her own she is constantly quoting: "my husband says," "they say," "I'm told."

In general, the contrast between the "grave and mysterious" Calormenes and the free, friendly Northerners is well portrayed. The Calormenes are verbose, sententious, and indirect. Lewis slyly undercuts their gravity and mystery by making their proverbs ridiculous. For example, Shasta's foster father says, "Natural affection is stronger than soup and offspring more precious than carbuncles" (4). Soup, of course, varies greatly in its strength; "carbuncle" means "a red jewel" in medieval romances, but its modern meaning is "a red sore." Other proverbs are ridiculous because of their verbosity and indirectness. Instead of "Visitors and fish stink after three days," the Tisroc says, "For the departure of guests makes a wound that is easily healed in the heart of a judicious host" (106).

The verbosity is achieved partly by the "and synonym" disease. Instead of saying a thing once, the Calormenes say it twice or more, with the synonyms joined by "and." For instance, the Tisroc says to Rabadash, "Tell us what you desire and propose" (107). The Vizier praises the Tisroc for his "prudence and circumspection" and calls him "irrefutable and sapient" (109). Rabadash says that "the High King Peter is a man of prudence and understanding" who will desire "the high honour and advantage of being allied to our House" (112).

In addition, the Calormene habit of prefacing every noun in direct address with "O" turns every conversation into a series of poetic apos-trophes. Shasta, like Rabadash, says "O my Father" to the fisherman, but when he gets to the North he adopts Northern style, calling his real father, King Lune, simply "Father." The empty compliments like "O the delight of my eyes" and the Vizier's "O Tisroc, whose reign must and shall be interminable" (114) show that the Calormenes' gravity and mystery are a mere covering for emptiness, hypocrisy, and cruelty.

Of course, elaborate forms of speech are not inevitably associated with character defects. Aravis uses all these tricks of speech in telling the story of her escape, but her deliberate use of a high style in storytelling is justified as an exercise of artistic method. And Lewis, as author, makes the point that Hwin's speech in the story is reworded "in the grand Calormene manner" (35) and that the order of telling is artfully manipulated to arouse suspense (37). He comments that Calormene children are taught storytelling instead of essay writing, adding, "The difference is that people want to hear the stories, whereas I never heard of anyone who wanted to read the essays."

The courtly Narnians also speak in a highly elaborate style, but one that contrasts with Calormene style at several points. Their proverbs are direct, homely, and intentionally humorous, as befits the speakers, the Raven and a dwarf: "See a bear in his own den before you judge of his conditions," "Come, live with me and you'll know me," "Easily in but not easily out, as the lobster said in the lobster pot," and "nests before eggs" (62, 63, 70). When the Narnian king and queen give an order, they preface it with "of your courtesy." Their nouns of address are names—Susan, Queen Susan, or (Edmund's intimate address to her) Su—or titles such as Your Majesty, Madam, and Sister,[44] without impossible compliments such as "O eternal Tisroc" (112). In contrast, the Tisroc calls Rabadash by name only twice, and one of those includes a threat to his life.

One feature of Narnian style is deliberate archaism. They say "naught" instead of "naughty" and "hastilude" instead of "spear contest." Instead of the group genitive, "the king of Archenland's son," they use the older form, "the king's son of Archenland." The archaism is meant to indicate the courtesy of better days. In *Prince Caspian* High King Peter used archaic forms in composing the challenge to King Miraz, but in *The Voyage of the Dawn Treader* all their majesties spoke normally. Perhaps, too, Lewis was following Spenser's deliberate archaism.

King Lune's speech is courtly, like that of the Narnians, but just a little more rural and therefore more conservative. The implication is that he is bluff, hearty, and honest. He says "'tis" instead of "it is," "nay" instead of "no"; he also uses the Shakespearean word "pajock," which is thought to be a form of "peacock."[45] One of his tricks of speech is to omit the subject of a sentence when it is "thou": for example, "Sit down, Corin, or shalt leave the table"(207). Like the Narnians, he is courteous to his subordinates, though simply addressing them as "friend" instead of framing his request with "of your courtesy."

One important indication of King Lune's conservatism is his use of both "you" and "thou." He makes a clear distinction between the plural "you" of formality and the singular "thou," which at least through the seventeenth century was used when speaking to intimates and inferiors.[46] For instance, before he knows who Shasta is, he addresses him with the polite "you"—"You can ride fast, friend?" (149)—but when he learns that Shasta is his son he says, "Thou art my heir" (214). So courteous and noble is he that he continues to address Rabadash as "you" and "your Highness" even though Rabadash calls him "a barbarian dog" (207) and no one could have blamed Lune for switching to the "thou" of contempt.

These special styles of the Calormenes, the Narnians, and King Lune stand out against a background of ordinary English, which is used when the four travelers speak with each other or when Aslan speaks to them. Aslan's ordinary English is heightened by rhetorical figures at times of extreme emotion. For instance, in speaking to Shasta he uses anaphora, the repetition of a phrase at the beginning of each sentence: "I was the lion," "I was the lion," "I was the cat" (150). In speaking to Bree he uses antimetabole, "Do not dare not to dare," and anaphora again, "Here are," "here is," "these are" (193). The Hermit speaks a terse, undescriptive version of ordinary English: "Here is water and there is grass. You shall have a hot mash when I have milked my other cousins, the goats." This terseness is just enough like Aslan's style to express his contemplative contact with utter reality.

The juxtaposition of behaviors, heightened by the juxtaposition of styles, then, is the essence of Lewis's Book of Courtesy. There is little allegory. The training of stock responses through imagery largely comes about through the contrast of two environments. Narnia is "the happy land of Narnia—Narnia of the heathery mountains and the thymy downs, Narnia of the many rivers, the plashing glens, the mossy caverns and the deep forests ringing with the hammers of the Dwarfs" (9). From the stinking hut of the fisherman to the desert's killing heat, Calormen is an unhappy land. Just as Spenser contrasts pastoral courtesy with the false courtesy of the court, Lewis contrasts rural Archenland with Tashbaan—its crowded narrow streets, its "smells . . . [of] unwashed people, unwashed dogs, scent, garlic, onions, and the piles of refuse which lay everywhere," its statues which are "impressive rather than agreeable to look at" (52).

All the senses are engaged to influence the reader to hate Calormen and love Narnia. Even after the travelers have successfully escaped from Calormen, its hatefulness continues in the hardships of the desperate race through the desert: "trot and walk and trot, jingle-jingle-jingle, squeak-squeak-squeak, smell of hot horse, smell of hot self, blinding glare, headache" (125). In the latter half of the twentieth century, the contrasts between Calormen and the North seem to reflect an insensitive "cultural blindness" (Ford 95n), but this too is partly due to the influence of Spenser, for whom "Paynims and Saracens" were symbols of evil.

The comparative paucity of allegorical imagery in *The Horse and His Boy*, like that of Spenser's Book 6,[47] results in a work that is less lyrical than *The Voyage of the Dawn Treader* or even *The Silver Chair*, and far less lyrical than the first two Chronicles. On a realism/fantasy continuum, the story of Shasta and Aravis is closer to *Pride and Prejudice* than to *Phantastes*. But it is good of its kind, and it renews the longing for Narnia, for honesty, humility, and simplicity, in readers who have followed the Chronicles thus far.

Mutability: The Last Two Chronicles

The most obvious feature of the last two Chronicles is their biblical overtones. In *The Magician's Nephew*, Lewis narrates the creation of Narnia, paralleling Genesis, and in *The Last Battle* he recounts the last judgment and destruction of Narnia, paralleling Revelation. Unfortunately, these parallels have encouraged some readers to focus on a close comparison of the stories and their biblical sources with the intent to determine whether, if at all, Lewis departs from orthodox theology. But to treat the Chronicles in this way is (to paraphrase *The Abolition of Man*) to reduce them to the level of "Doctrine" in the sense that we suspend our judgments of literary value about them, ignore their artistic cause (if any), and analyze them as a set of cognitive propositions.[48] Moreover, reading the last two Chronicles in this way precludes the more fruitful approach of Christian humanism. Writers in the tradition of Christian humanism specialize in twice-told tales, in applying well-known stories in new ways. Thus the more important question is not how the recycled material is related to the original, but how it is related to the new context in which it appears—

not which theory of original sin underlies *The Magician's Nephew,* but what the creation story means in the Narnian setting.

The second most obvious feature of the last two books is that in them Lewis attempts to resolve the inconsistencies which cropped up when he placed the first five stories in a Lewisian stage setting rather than a Tolkienian subcreation. Even so, minor errors of detail remain, such as the confusion of temporal sequence in *The Magician's Nephew.* At their first meeting, Digory tells Polly that he heard Uncle Andrew yell "last night." Then the book continues, "That was how Polly and Digory got to know one another; and as it was just the beginning of the summer holidays and neither of them was going away to the sea that year, they met nearly every day" (4). The next paragraph describes how they began "to do . . . indoor exploration" (5). All this implies that some time elapsed between their first meeting and the beginning of the exploration. But in the second chapter, when the exploration leads into Uncle Andrew's study, Digory finds that his uncle screamed when the guinea pig disappeared "last night" (4, 15), which implies that they began their exploration on the first day they met. If they did, then the description of how they met every day is misleading and irrelevant. However, avoiding minor discontinuities in the flats of his stage setting simply was not one of Lewis's priorities. Even with these occasional confusions, he succeeds so well in connecting the stories that Huttar believes "it is these last two books that make of the whole collection a unified literary work." He sees the seven Chronicles as constituting a new literary genre, which he calls "scripture," "a sort of Bible for a Bibleless age" (Schakel, *Longing* 123).

One of the undeniable pleasures of reading the last two books is the pleasure of recognition—of seeing Genesis and Revelation in a new form and of remembering places and persons from the earlier books. But it is neither the retelling of biblical stories nor the resolving of inconsistencies that gives the Chronicles their artistic unity. Instead, the last two books are part of the artistic unity of the Chronicles primarily because they continue to be part of Lewis's miniature *Faerie Queene.* The need to unify what he had already written accounts for the rather frenetic journeys between worlds in *The Magician's Nephew* and the narrative-slowing excursions into Narnian history in *The Last Battle,* but it does not eliminate the overall Spenserian purposes of training stock responses, giving examples of virtue, and growing in mental health through literary pleasure. Although on one level Lewis was creating a Narnian Genesis and Reve-

lation, as an artist and a man he was coming to terms with the p
of time.

In addition to the literal level—the narration of the beginning a
of Narnia—and the allusive resonances provided by the biblical background, the last two Chronicles have an emotional tone arising from the
issue of mutability—the changes that an individual must endure in the
later stages of life. *The Magician's Nephew* presents the emotional experience of middle age, of evaluating the choices one has made; *The Last
Battle* presents old age's fight for life that can end only in death. The two
stories also present a contrast between the pre–World War I world of
Lewis's childhood and the post–World War II world of his maturity. And,
finally, these last two Chronicles continue the battle against "the abolition
of man," by reasserting the values of Christian humanism.

The Magician's Nephew

The major issue of *The Magician's Nephew*, like that of Genesis 2, is the
relationship between illicit knowledge and the control of Nature. Although
from one viewpoint the tension between knowledge and blessed innocence,
between control and trust, has existed in the world since Genesis, and
from another viewpoint it has existed since Kepler and Newton, for Lewis
(since every man is the center of his own universe) it began in his
childhood, before the Great War. Thus *The Magician's Nephew* is set in
1900, before the war-motivated explosion of science and technology had
occurred in our world. In *The Abolition of Man* Lewis calls magic the
"twin" of science, especially applied science, and contrasts the "knowledge"
of magic and science with the "wisdom" of the past (87–88). It is not
surprising, then, that in *The Magician's Nephew* the evil characters, Jadis
and Uncle Andrew, are both magicians, and the good adults, Frank and
Helen, are simple rural folk.

The book feels middle-aged in its nostalgia for a simpler world. Middle
age is a time to look toward the inevitable end, but also a time to make
a new beginning. *The Magician's Nephew* takes us to Charn, a world
ending, and to Narnia, a world beginning. It shows Digory's mother
receiving a new life that leads to joy, and Jadis a new life that leads to
despair. Middle age, too, is the time for nurturing and admiring the young,
and one of the central pleasures of the book is rejoicing in the freshness
of Narnia. On a more personal level, the book allows Lewis to go back

to the time when he was a child, tolerantly view both the good and bad aspects of prewar life, and, in fantasy, rewrite his own history by telling about a sick mother who got well instead of dying (Ford 69).

Because middle age is the time when one goes back over life and considers the possibilities of having made different choices, the emotional tone of middle age fits beautifully with the story line, a retelling of the primal choice of Eden. In connecting the creation of Narnia with the previous books, Lewis introduces a new pair of child explorers and tells us that the boy, Digory, is Professor Kirke of *The Lion, the Witch, and the Wardrobe* and, suitably enough, "the sort of person who wants to know everything" (36). In this Digory is like his Uncle Andrew, a magician who also wants to know things. Digory's inordinate curiosity leads him to choose evil; he strikes the bell in Charn and awakens Jadis, the evil ruler of Charn, allowing her to enter the new, unspoiled Narnia. But Aslan forgives him and commissions him to bring an apple from a magic garden to form a tree of protection for Narnia and undo the consequences of his first choice. The quest gives him an opportunity to make a better choice, for when he arrives at the garden, he finds that Jadis is already there and has eaten an apple, which turned her face "white as salt," for she is the White Witch of the first book. She tempts Digory with control, telling him to take the apple to his mother instead of Aslan, but he resists temptation and returns the apple to Aslan, who plants it. In the newness of Narnia it grows quickly, and Aslan allows Digory to take an apple from the new tree back to his mother. It does cure her, and a seed from the apple grows into the tree that provided the lumber for the magic wardrobe of *The Lion, the Witch, and the Wardrobe*. In later life Digory's curiosity, rightly directed, leads him to become the wise professor of the first Chronicle who knows that "it's all in Plato."

In accordance with the middle-aged life task of reevaluating one's choices, Aslan tells Digory what would have happened if he had succumbed to temptation. This is inconsistent with Digory's literal age and also with previous Chronicles, where Aslan says that nobody is ever told what *would* have happened, but it is consistent with the mood and developmental tasks of middle age. In Uncle Andrew the book depicts the sins of middle age instead of the childish faults of disobedience and craving candy or the young adult faults of laziness and lack of discipline. Uncle Andrew's sins are lust, self-indulgence, and the desire for power and financial security: he lusts for Jadis, indulges his appetite for brandy, and plans to

become rich through the economic development of Narnia. It is noteworthy that *The Magician's Nephew* is the only one of the Chronicles that
describes the journey of a middle-aged person, or even an adult, into
Narnia. (In *Prince Caspian* we are told that the pirates and their women
came into Narnia, but we do not see it happening.)

Whereas coming to terms with middle age provides the book with an
important emotional coloring, the training of stock responses that is most
basic to the artistic structure of the book is learning to love Aslan as
creator and hate the life-defying development of knowledge apart from
the Tao. Thus, the center of the book is the account of the creation of
Narnia and the resultant contrast between the two kinds of magic—the
witchcraft of Uncle Andrew and Jadis, by which human beings learn to
manipulate the forces of Nature for their own purposes, versus the magic
of Aslan's Narnia, creation itself, to which human beings must respond
with wonder and submission to the moral law.

The account of the creation of Narnia shows that Nature is worthy of
existence in itself. Jadis and Uncle Andrew, who see it only as raw material
for their exercise of power, are shown to be deluded as well as evil. The
fact that the efficient cause of the creation is music symbolizes the underlying harmony of Nature. The sudden appearance of the stars, singing,
recaptures for the reader the wonder of the night sky, so often ignored
or blotted out by artificial lights. The cabby's reaction, "Glory be! I'd ha'
been a better man all my life if I'd known there were things like this"
(100), reproduces the juxtaposition of the beauty of the natural order
with moral purity in Psalm 19.

Once the stars sing and the sun comes up, the rest of creation occurs
in the order dictated by the Great Chain of Being: first the land, then
plants, and then animals. The music that brings forth the animals "made
you want to rush at other people and either hug them or fight them"
(113), a description of the concupiscible and irascible passions that motivate
animals—and people insofar as they are animals. In people, of course,
these passions must be governed by reason, and in *The Abolition of Man*
Lewis suggests that the values of the Tao are to man what the instinctual
passions are to animals (90).

The calling forth some of the creatures to be talking beasts enacts a
private theory of Lewis's that perhaps the original Adam and Eve were
called from the already existing race of hominids and given speech and
self-consciousness (*Letters* 237). When the Narnian beasts are touched,

they "instantly [leave] their own kinds and [follow Aslan]" (*Nephew* 115). It also extends the pattern of being chosen that is found in sacred history, from Abraham to the Apostles. In creating the talking beasts as another link in the Great Chain of Being and then giving man dominion over them, Lewis suggests the true nature and duty of man with respect to his animal heritage.

Aslan also gives speech to inanimate Nature—to the waters by naiads, the earth by dwarfs, the trees and fields by dryads and fauns and satyrs— thus portraying an attitude, a complex of emotions, that would prevent the exploitation of Nature by the magic of science and reasserting Lewis's often expressed conviction that all Nature exists for its own purposes as well as for providing man with food and comforts. In his 1947 pamphlet "Vivisection," Lewis made the point that contempt for Nature is the victory "of ruthless, non-moral utilitarianism over the old world of ethical law . . . of which Dachau and Hiroshima mark the more recent achievements" (*God in the Dock* 228). Scientific experimentation with a view to increasing control over Nature is the attitude that leads to the discovery of the Deplorable Word in Charn, obviously a counterpart of the atom bomb.

As Huttar has pointed out, the details of the creation, such as the way the animals spring out of the ground and shake the dirt from their flanks, are suggested by Milton's *Paradise Lost* (in Schakel, *Longing* 124). But *The Faerie Queene* is also important. The Mutability Cantos, the surviving fragment of Spenser's seventh book, describe the natural processes: the changes in the four elements, day and night, the hours, the procession of seasons, the pageant of the months, life and death, and the motion of the planets in their spheres. Nature is the "great grandmother of all creatures bred, . . . ever young yet full of eld" (7.7.13), and Mutability comes before this "veiled and numinous"[49] personage to be judged. Although there are no close verbal echoes, *The Magician's Nephew* resembles this Spenserian fragment in its rejoicing in Nature. Furthermore, the characterization of Jadis is reminiscent of Spenser's villainess Mutability, who is the daughter of a Titan who rebels against Jove and a "bad seed" from the race who "sought to assaile the heavens eternall towers." Like Mutability, Jadis in her own way conquers her own world; alters "the worlds faire frame"; breaks the laws of Nature, Justice, and "Policie"; and threatens to strike Cynthia, the Moon, with her "golden wand" (7.6.2–21). This connection between Mutability the Titaness and Jadis is hinted at even in the first Chronicle, when Mr. Beaver says that the White Witch "comes of the giants" (*Lion* 77). Jadis is nearly seven feet tall; she rebels against Aslan by her reaction to his singing, standing with mouth shut tight and fists clenched; and later (chronologically), in the first story, she alters the "faire frame" of Narnia by imprisoning it in perpetual winter. Finally, just as Mutability is so fair that her beauty moves Jove from his first stern judgment of her (7.6.31), Jadis has power over both Digory and Uncle Andrew because of her beauty.

Mutability's life-denying alteration of Nature is similar to the manipulation of magicians (or scientists who deny the Tao) in that both oppose the spirit of Aslan's creativity. *The Magician's Nephew* thus repeats the message of the Ransom trilogy, and Lewis repeats some of its effects. The characterization of Uncle Andrew combines features of Weston and Devine. Like Weston, Uncle Andrew does not believe that ordinary considerations of morality apply to him: "Men like me who possess hidden wisdom, are freed from common rules just as we are cut off from common pleasures. Ours . . . is a high and lonely destiny" (18). Just as Weston regarded Ransom as expendable, so Uncle Andrew has no scruples about sending the children into a different universe. And just as Weston was punished by being drenched with cold water, so was Uncle Andrew. He learns what it feels like to be a caged animal when the young, naive Narnians try to make a pet of him. He lacks Weston's scientific detachment, however, and is more like Devine in his desire to make money out of Narnia and his devotion to the pleasures of the flesh. His career as a man of the world is not as successful as Devine's, for in the final analysis he retains only a highly edited memory of Jadis: "dem fine woman, sir, a dem fine woman" (186).

The description of the Wood Between the Worlds is so powerful that it might be described as a second allegorical core. It is connected with the description of creation in that it symbolizes the mysterious emptiness that underlies all *natural* phenomena—not the spiritual world of the Platonic Forms, but matter itself. Like some modern physicists, Lewis suggests that the All consists of many parallel universes. He differs from the physicists in that the foundation of his universes is not the emptiness of the atom, but a place that is itself full and fecund. It is similar to Ransom's discovery in *Out of the Silent Planet* that empty space is not really empty. Like Ransom's space, the Wood Between the Worlds owes much to the *Cosmographia* of Bernardus Silvestris. The idea of portraying the place between the parallel universes as a wood was probably suggested to Lewis by the fact that the Greek *hyle* means both "material" and "wood," and that the allegorical characterization of chaos in the *Cosmographia* is called "Silva," the Latin word for "wood" or "forest."[50]

The Wood resembles the Garden of Adonis in Book 3 of *The Faerie Queene* in that each one is the passageway to other worlds. In the Garden of Adonis, Nature has placed "the first seminary / Of all things that are borne to live and dye" (3.6.30). The Wood is also like the Garden in its extreme fertility. Because it represents pure materiality, the absence of form, things have no names there. As Lewis told a correspondent, "What goes easily into words is precisely the abstract—thought about 'matter' (not apples or snuff), about 'population' (not actual babies) and so on."[51]

On another level, the passivity of the Wood Between the Worlds is the opposite of the itch to know, to manipulate, and to control that motivates the magicians. But it means a great deal more than that; there is almost no limit to its evocative spell. As Lewis said concerning the kinds of love in Book 3 of *The Faerie Queene*, "The more concrete and vital the poetry is, the more hopelessly complicated it will become in analysis: but the imagination receives it as a simple—in both senses of the word. Oddly enough, it is the chief duty of the interpreter to begin analyses and leave them unfinished" (*Allegory* 345).

The numinous quality of creation and the human response of wonder and submission is expressed, of course, in taboos, first against striking the bell in Charn and then against entering the garden. Described with the imagery of the Garden of the Hesperides, Milton's Garden of Eden, and any number of medieval enclosed gardens, Lewis's garden is marked by a verse taboo inscribed on the gate and guarded by a wonderful bird. It is a visible form of the moral law, mysterious and sacrosanct. The temptation that Digory experiences there is the temptation to achieve control over his mother's death at the expense of violating the moral law. Later Aslan tells the children that the apple will work "according to [its] nature," like the scientific magic that we manipulate. But scientific control outside the universal value system cannot bring happiness, and Aslan warns that "length of days with an evil heart is only length of misery" (174).

In keeping with the central image of scientific magic versus the moral law, the exemplary element of *The Magician's Nephew* has to do with the four cardinal virtues—justice, prudence, temperance, and courage—that are known to all people, completely aside from Christian revelation. The one most emphasized is justice. Uncle Andrew and Jadis are negative examples of justice: they break promises, appropriate the goods of others to their own uses, and ignore the rights of other creatures. A positive example of justice occurs when Digory tells the whole truth about how Jadis got into Narnia, even though he fears it will destroy his chance to get help for his mother from Aslan. The cab driver who becomes King Frank exemplifies justice when he promises to "rule these creatures kindly and fairly, remembering that they are . . . Talking Beasts and free subjects" (139). His justice contrasts with the rulership of Jadis, who regarded her subjects only as units of power to be expended for her pride. Concerning Spenser's Book of Justice, Lewis comments that "[J]ustice [is] the art of allotting carefully-graded shares of honour, power, liberty and the like to the various ranks of a fixed social hierarchy, and when justice succeeds, she produces a harmony of differences" (*Allegory* 347). In the portrayal of the talking beasts discussing what to do with Uncle Andrew and the Dwarfs and Moles preparing for the coronation, Lewis shows the gaiety and merriment of "a harmony of differences."

Digory sins against prudence when he is so eager to explore a new world that he does not consider how to get back to Earth and again when he strikes the bell in Charn without considering the consequences of his action. Uncle Andrew sins against prudence (not to mention the scientific method) when he is so reluctant to believe in talking animals that he cannot hear their speech.

Medieval moral theology often presented the eating of the fruit in the Garden of Eden as gluttony, a sin against temperance. This is suggested in the description of how the smell of the apple affected Digory, but the clearest negative example of temperance is Uncle Andrew's slavery to alcohol.

Finally, Digory exemplifies courage when he consents to go into an unknown universe after Polly without knowing whether he can get back and when he pushes in close to the rearing horse while trying to send Jadis out of our world. It is less dramatic, but equally courageous, when he tells Uncle Andrew that he is a coward and a wicked magician rather than a noble adept. Frank the cabby exemplifies courage in trying to calm the horse and in behaving calmly when the group lands in the nothingness of yet-uncreated Narnia. It is partly his courage that makes him fit to rule.

The symbolic oppositions between Nature and antinatural experimentation, the examples of good and bad behavior, and the cross-references to previous books all contribute to an emotional coloring of middle age in *The Magician's Nephew*. In keeping with the development of middle-aged detachment when looking at an earlier and simpler time, *The Magician's Nephew* is lighter and more humorous than the other Chronicles. The asides about life in the old days (schools were nastier but food was nicer) and the helplessness of childhood in being "given dinner with all the nice parts left out and sent to bed for two solid hours" (84) are worth a chuckle. The argument among the Narnian talking animals with the repeated "I object to that remark very strongly" is not quite as funny as the Dufflepuds in *The Voyage of the Dawn Treader*, but it does very well in context. The account of Jadis's attempt to take over London could have been frightening, but it is not. Her vanity in imagining that Uncle Andrew is a "great Enchanter" who "for the love of my beauty . . . has made a potent spell which shook your world to its foundations" (65) is only slightly less ridiculous than Uncle Andrew's vanity in seeing himself as "a devilish well preserved fellow for [his] age" (76). The old-fashioned politeness of Uncle Andrew is ludicrous in relation to Jadis's bloodthirsty, tyrannous commands, and her commands are ludicrous in relation to Aunt Letty's Edwardian primness.

By recalling E. Nesbit, the light touch in the handling of all these elements helps to place the action at the turn of the century. Furthermore, the light touch harmonizes with the rejoicing in creation that is the most important stock response of this book. And it helps to make the absurd, improbable plot acceptable. Its jovial humor provides a striking contrast to the very different tone of the last Chronicle.

The Last Battle

The last Chronicle is usually treated as Lewis's Apocalypse. Certainly the descriptions of the stars being called home, the last judgment, and the shutting of the door on Narnia are vivid and memorable. It is less often remarked that *The Last Battle*, like Orwell's *Nineteen Eighty-Four* and the return to the Shire in *The Lord of the Rings*, is a picture of England after World War II. After two devastating wars, the loss of dominion over the seas, and the rise of socialism, England was no longer merry. In *The Magician's Nephew* it is just circumstances that are wrong, not everything: the tree of protection flourishes in Narnia, and there is happiness in England once Digory's mother is healed. In *The Last Battle* everything in Narnia is wrong, and efforts to stop the decline just make things worse.

Lewis is showing that countries do not last forever. Neither do people. The emotional quality of the book communicates mortality and mutability, and paying too much attention to the biblical parallels blurs the other levels of meaning.

The plot shows how things get worse and worse until the end, and after the end there is a new beginning. The story begins when Shift, an old ape who lives near the waterfall in western Narnia, finds a lion skin and uses it to dress Puzzle, his donkey companion. He uses Puzzle, thus disguised, to pretend that Aslan has come back to Narnia and installs the donkey in a stable to become the recipient of goods and services for his own benefit. He soon becomes allied with the Calormenes, helping them to infiltrate Narnia, exploit its timber, enslave the talking animals, and prepare to dominate it. Meanwhile, Tirian, the last king of Narnia, at first believes that the great lion of Narnia has really returned, but when he sees all the destruction ordered by "Aslan" he loses faith in the lion's goodness and gives himself up to the Calormenes, who tie him to a tree. In his desperation he calls out to the Friends of Narnia and finds himself in England as a phantom. Almost immediately he is back in Narnia, and a few seconds later Jill and Eustace appear beside him. The three of them make repeated unsuccessful efforts to rescue the enslaved Narnians, stop the destruction of trees, and expose the false Aslan. They capture Puzzle from the stable and prove to the dwarfs that he is not really Aslan, but the strategy backfires; having been fooled once, the dwarfs refuse to believe in the real Aslan and reject the kingship of Tirian as well.

The final conflict takes place in front of the stable, where Tirian, the children, and a few loyal Narnians prepare to die fighting. Tash, the god of the Calormenes, is in the stable (although the Calormenes have introduced him as a syncretistic deity they call Tashlan), and anyone who is defeated is put into the stable (a form of death). The Narnians must decide whether to believe Shift or Tirian. A few more Narnians rally to Tirian, but they are betrayed by others. One by one the opponents of Tashlan and the Calormenes are forced into the stable. As Tirian is forced into the stable, he takes the chief Calormene with him. He finds that he has entered another world, and he is in the presence of the Narnian travelers from our world.

Then Aslan himself appears. He presides over the destruction of Narnia and performs the last judgment, in which bad Narnians cease to be talking beasts and go off into nothingness. The children learn that they have actually died in a train wreck in England as well as being forced into the stable in Narnia, and that indeed the real Narnia and the real England have not been lost but exist in Aslan's Country. They meet all their friends from the previous books and live happily ever after.

On the plot level, Lewis is describing the end of Narnia as analogous to the Christian view of the end of our world, but that is not the main point of the story. Instead, he is allowing his child readers (and himself) to taste human mortality. In the exemplary mode, the surface details communicate what it feels like to see the decline of the nation one loves, what it feels like to become old and helpless. The actions of Tirian, the children, and other good Narnians exemplify the proper response to defeat and death. The allegorical core of the story is the stable, which becomes a sort of stage; in this most philosophical of the Chronicles, Lewis shows in exactly what sense a "real stage setting" is and is not real.

The way the surface details contribute to the emotional quality of the book is subtle. On the literal level Tirian is between twenty and twenty-five, but as he talks with Jewel the Unicorn, they both seem elderly. Theirs is an old, tested friendship; "each had saved the other's life in the wars" (13). Like old people, they see the world they knew breaking up—the spirits of the trees killed by indiscriminate lumbering, the talking horses harnessed—and feel that they have lived too long. When Shift forces Puzzle to dress in the lion skin, the pathos of it suggests the way old people are puzzled by changes in the world they once understood and are often exploited by so-called friends. The imprisonment of Tirian feels like an old person's loss of freedom, and like an old person recalling happier days, he remembers the stories of Caspian and Rilian and the Golden Age of Narnia. Like an elderly person fighting for health and independence, Tirian finds that his battle can only end in defeat.

The surface details also capture the despair of patriots over the desolation of England. Just as the Narnian trees are cut down and their spirits destroyed, the trees of England were cut down during World War I to be used in the construction of trenches. Just as Shift, without hereditary lordship or a traditional code of behavior, can take over Narnia, with the dwarfs responding by rejecting both him and Tirian's legitimate kingship, so the class system of England broke down during the early twentieth century. Just as Aslan has not been seen for years, so that Tirian cannot say with surety that he would not do the horrible things attributed to him, so in England knowledge of the traditional religion broke down.

And just as the Narnians gather before the stable to receive news and orders, so mass man is controlled by those who have access to the communications media.

The cynicism of the dwarfs mirrors the situation described by Ogden and Richards in *The Meaning of Meaning:* the media have created a mass of people who are educated in the sense that they are minimally literate but untrained in critical thinking and unable to evaluate what they read or hear. It is as if the dwarfs had attended a secondary school where *The Control of Language* was taught. They react to eternal verities and traditional sentiments with scoffing, but they have nothing to believe instead. Their determination to look out for their own interests reflects the disillusionment of the working classes after World War I, which led to the great coal-mining strike. In addition, their pathetic determination never to be taken in again echoes Lewis's own post–World War "new look" described in *Surprised by Joy* (204).

The depiction of both personal and national decline is enhanced by Lewis's use of animals and mythological beings. Lewis very much admired George Orwell's *Animal Farm* (1945), and *The Last Battle* makes so much use of the "hieroglyphic" properties of such creatures that it could almost be called Lewis's *Animal Farm*. Orwell's tyrannical animals are pigs because of their fatness and the scientific fact that they are more intelligent than other animals. Lewis's choice of the ape as the bad animal is governed by traditional learning rather than science, for in medieval literature the ape (Latin, *simius*) was a symbol of hypocrisy or unintelligent imitation (Curtius 538–40). Incidentally, Shift has a weak chest.

The other animals in *The Last Battle* have attributes and personalities commonly assigned to their species. The donkey, of course, is stupid; the horses who gallop to their death intending to support the king are spirited and noble; the dogs are loyal and eager; they bark excitedly, and when they come to support Tirian "they all [stand] up and put their front paws on the shoulders of the humans" and talk in barks, saying, "We'll help, we'll help, help, help" (116). The cat has no interest in the religious question of whether Aslan or Tash is the real deity. It is concerned with nothing but profit; it symbolizes hypocrisy as it walks toward the stable "primly and daintily, with its tail in the air" (107). The lamb is meek, but Lewis adds to the proverbial attribution the biblical idea that the meek are able to be more outspoken than others, so that it is only the lamb who dares to ask, "How could Aslan be friends with [Tash]?" (31). The mice, rabbits, and squirrels are the "little people" of society—compassionate but helpless.

Lewis calls attention to the importance of the various animal natures by the composition of the Seven gathered for the last defense of Narnia: Tirian, the Narnian human; the two English children; Jewel the Unicorn, a mythical animal; Farsight the Eagle, a Narnian bird; Puzzle, a Narnian animal; and Poggin the dwarf, a representative of the earth and the inanimate forces of Nature. A fox, a bull, and a satyr are among those on the other side, but the fact that Poggin fights for the king demonstrates that these aspects of human nature are not evil in themselves.

Thus, the emotional tone of old age and the "hieroglyphic" creatures combine to form a background for the exemplary actions of Tirian and his followers as they show how to respond to personal and societal desolation. Their actions show that without physical resources and without hope, it is still possible to die on the right side. No doctrine about an afterlife, no suggestion that death is unreal, sustains them as they go into the last battle. Their heroism is modeled not on the Bible but on Northern literature. In "A Cliche Came Out of Its Cage" (1950), Lewis wrote,

> The weary gods,
> Scarred with old wounds, the one-eyed Odin, Tyr who has lost a hand,
> Will limp to their stations for the last defence.
>   Make it your hope
> To be counted worthy on that day to stand beside them;
> For the end of man is to partake of their defeat and die
> His second, final death in good company. The stupid, strong
> Unteachable monsters are certain to be victorious at last,
> And every man of decent blood is on the losing side. (*Poems* 4)

The friendship of Jewel and Tirian shows what it is to die in good company; Jewel says, "We have known great joys together. If Aslan gave me my choice I would choose no other life than the life I have had and no other death than the one we go to" (*Battle* 99). Textbooks like *The Control of Language* debunked the "sweet and fitting" death for one's country as "mere irrational sentiments" (*Abolition* 42), but Tirian and his friends find them true. Lewis puts a classical epigram in the mouth of Roonwit the Centaur: "Noble death is a treasure which no one is too poor to buy" (91).

In the actual face of death, most people find the hope of an afterlife—
no matter how firmly they believe in it—not so much untrue as simply
irrelevant. According to the Gospel of Matthew, Jesus himself cried, "My
God, my God, why hast Thou forsaken me?" (27:46). In contrast with the
relatives of Uncle George in *The Pilgrim's Regress,* who all put on masks
and pretended not to see how dreadful Uncle George's face looked without
one, Lewis is honest with his young readers. He spares them the physical
horrors by symbolizing death as the forced entry into the stable, but he
does not spare them the sadness. The slaughter of the horses, the death
of the bear with the final words, "I don't understand" (119) are almost
unendurable.

Nevertheless, he shows them that even the hopeless situation is not
devoid of all joy. At the tower, Tirian and his friends enjoy their sleep,
their stew, and their bath. They learn the happiness of focusing on the
present moment. As they turn their steps toward Stable Hill, they become
less miserable "because they [are] now thinking of what was to be done
this very night" (97). Even after they retreat to the white rock knowing
that the Calormene reinforcements have arrived and there is absolutely
no hope, pleasure is still possible—and even magnified by their desperation. They find a trickle of water, and "such was their thirst that . . .
while they were drinking they were perfectly happy and could not think
of anything else"(128). Finally, Lewis makes the point that Tirian's death
"wasn't quite so bad as you might think" because he was so busy that he
didn't have time "to feel either frightened or sad" (130).

Also exemplary are the efforts of the characters to distinguish truth
from falsehood, reality from appearance. When scientific developments
throw doubt on the factual validity of Christian beliefs, one response has
been to reject thought in favor of Christianity. Lewis shows that the refusal
to think leads only to superstition. When Shift says Puzzle should pretend
to be Aslan, there is a loud thunderclap and a small earthquake. Puzzle
interprets it as a sign that Aslan disapproves of the pretense, but Shift
argues that it is a sign of approval. He does not know the principle set
forth in *The Abolition of Man:* "From propositions about fact alone no
practical conclusion can ever be drawn" (43).

Similarly, Tirian's first actions are unwise and ineffective because his
knowledge of traditional principles is faulty. His anger at the destruction
of the trees leads him, like Moses, who had also been separated from the
traditions of his people, to attack the slave-driving Calormenes. Then his

shame, combined with sorrow that Aslan is apparently not what he expected, leads him to abdicate. He has forgotten, if he ever knew, the principle from Bracton that King Lune told Cor: "The King's under the law, for it's the law makes him a king" (*Horse* 215). He had no more right to give himself up to the Calormenes than Caspian did to leave his kingdom in *The Voyage of the Dawn Treader* or Rilian to explore the land of Bism in *The Silver Chair*. And one expression of his confusion is the proposal that he and the children disguise themselves as Calormenes.

Moreover, the Narnians are unable to discern whether any specific command is from the true Aslan because they have lost their knowledge of the Tao. They are vulnerable to the ape, who interprets the phrase "not a tame lion" as he pleases. But people who have read *The Lion, the Witch, and the Wardrobe* remember that in it Aslan refuses to disobey the High Emperor's law, even though that law leads to his death. If they have read *The Voyage of the Dawn Treader,* they remember that Aslan appeared when Lucy read the anti-invisibility spell and that he promised to obey his own rules. Thus Roonwit correctly argues, "The stars never lie, but Men and Beasts do," but Jewel counters by wondering if Aslan might contradict the stars, since "[h]e is not [their] slave . . . but their Maker" (15, 16). The *characters* are confused, but readers of the previous books know that Aslan's commands are given because they are right, not that something is right because he commands it.

The Narnians' inability to discern the truth comes to a showdown at the stable, the allegorical core of the book in accordance with Lewis's use of Spenser's poetic structure. With a sure touch, Lewis describes the location as like a theater: the Narnians are the audience, the stable is the backdrop, the grass before the stable is the stage, and the bonfire serves as footlights. The essence of a theatrical performance is that the viewers see an appearance, the shadow (in the Platonic sense) of reality. The Narnians who watch the play are dependent on the interpretations of Shift and the Calormene, who function as a sort of chorus. But Tirian and his friends, who now know the truth, are situated behind the scenery. They see that the ape is a puppet of the Calormenes. They see that the exchange between Ginger the cat and Shift has been rehearsed. They see that it is not Emeth, but another Calormene, whose body is thrown out of the stable.

But it is a real stage setting after all, and when Tirian enters the stable, he finds the Seven Friends of Narnia, crowned and at ease, and learns that they are in Narnia, "the real Narnia, which has always been here and always will be here" (169). But to say the new Narnia is real is not to say that the old Narnia was only an illusion.[52] When they have watched the destruction of it and Peter has closed the door, they weep, even "[w]ith Aslan ahead, and all of us here." And Tirian says, "I have seen my mother's death. . . . It were no virtue, but great discourtesy, if we did not mourn" (158).

By showing Tirian and his friends fighting for the old Narnia as if there was no afterlife, Lewis teaches the importance of the here and now. By showing that much of what they did was futile and doomed to failure, he teaches that the here and now is only a shadow of the real. But it is only through taking the old Narnia seriously that one can attain the new Narnia. The old Narnia is a shadow, but it is a real shadow, and the way to reach it is through heroism rather than the cynicism taught in *The Control of Language*. The dwarfs missed the new Narnia; they adopted "Vanity of vanities, all is vanity" as their motto, but instead of making them realize the need to accept and enjoy, as Qoholeth teaches (Eccl. 9:7, 8), it set them on the way to distrusting everything about life. They so shut their senses to the simple enjoyments of life, to everything that might be "Humbug," that they were unable to respond to the real Aslan when he appeared. Similarly, Queen Susan is "no longer a friend of Narnia" because she refuses to take seriously the real shadow of Narnia and the Joy it affords.

In *Surprised by Joy* Lewis says that he began his search for Joy by loving the old pagan stories; the Gospel story did not seem nearly as compelling to him. Happily, he found that in one sense he did not need to choose between classical lore and Christianity. In the great poets of Christian humanism such as Dante, Spenser, and Milton he found the pagan stories, augmented and spiritualized by Platonism and its offshoots, being used to enhance the truths of Christianity. Taking Spenser as his primary model and using Spenser's combination of allegorical and exemplary modes of fiction, Lewis created the stories of Narnia to speak to his own deepest needs. In the process he preserved the absolutes of the Tao, the classics of Western culture, and the most striking elements of the Gospel story in one place and in simplified form. But the most important thing he got from Spenser and the other Christian humanists was the overwhelming importance of pleasure in literature, even children's literature. For children and adults who are friends of Narnia, their favorite Chronicle is always the one they are reading at the moment.

· 5 ·

THE CONTEXT

OF MYTH & HISTORY

L EWIS BEGAN his fiction-writing career with an allegory, *The Pilgrim's Regress*, in which John (or Jack) seeks the island of Joy. The turning point of the story comes when John finds that the island ahead of him, which he has sought all his life, is the same as the mountain behind him, which he has tried all his life to escape. Similarly, in the Chronicles of Narnia, Lewis created an island of story, and in *The Last Battle* the children find that Narnia is not an island but a peninsula "jutting out from the great mountains of Aslan," and that the same is true of "all the *real* countries" (182). The myth of Cupid and Psyche was an island-story that had long occupied Lewis's mind, and when he next turned to fiction, he wrote a novel showing how that story is another spur of Aslan's (Christ's) mountain. In so doing he confronted again the low view of language, this time dealing with its implications concerning the truth of history and the relationship of fact to myth.

As Lewis wrote *through* his life in the Spenserian mode of the Chronicles of Narnia and *about* his life in the autobiographical mode of *Surprised by Joy*, he must have found history to be a singularly slippery rascal. What he learned about himself in struggling with the past perhaps influenced his decision to make his last work of fiction, *Till We Have Faces*, an autobiography—a book about a woman writing a book about her life.[1] In *The Magician's Nephew* the authorial voice says, "What you see and hear depends a good deal on where you are standing [and] what sort of person you are" (125). Orual, the heroine of *Till We Have Faces*, might have said, "What you see and hear depends on what you have written," for the process of writing changes the sort of person she is. Her experience, and Lewis's experience in creating her, may be best appreciated in the context of the relationship of myth and history.

By the time Lewis set out to write *Till We Have Faces,* the low view of language had become more precisely expressed than it had been in Ogden and Richards's *The Meaning of Meaning.* For example, A. J. Ayer said in *Language, Truth and Logic* (1936) that "The criterion which we use to test the genuineness of apparent statements of fact is the criterion of verifiability." A statement is "factually significant" if a person can lay out the test conditions that would lead to the conclusion that it was either true or false (35). Ethical propositions, such as "it is wrong to steal," and propositions about God are not statements because they are unverifiable in this sense.[2]

This approach, if strictly followed, would mean the end of history, since there is no way to verify that the testimony of those who witnessed the past is factual. In practice, historians who were influenced by the linguistic philosophers considered testimony that is plausible according to the known laws of the physical universe as factual and rejected testimony about supernatural events as nonfactual. R. G. Collingwood, a philosopher and don of Magdalen College, criticized Ayer in his *Essay on Metaphysics* (1940), saying that he confuses propositions, which are statements to be verified by an appeal to facts, with suppositions, which are axioms that the mind must have in order to manipulate experience (Patrick 103). There is a sense, he says, in which every scientific or historical fact is known by faith, since it is based on axioms that must be accepted (Patrick 97). Thus, historians who automatically reject the miracles of Jesus, for example, as unhistorical, are merely failing to recognize and criticize their own suppositions. But Collingwood's refutation did not meet with much acceptance. In 1954 Lewis wrote to his friend Dom Bede Griffiths that "the Logical Positivist menace" was making Christian apologetics very difficult, adding, "At the Socratic [Club] the enemy often wipe the floor with us."[3] But theologians, philosophers, and biblical critics had begun much earlier to raise doubts about a major tenet of Christianity, the historicity of Jesus, especially in Germany.[4] Neill, for example, begins his account of the subject with references to Kant, Hamann, Lessing, Goethe, and Hegel. Coleridge, about whom both Barfield and Richards wrote books, brought these views to England in 1789 (2–3). A pioneer contribution to the question was Strauss's *Leben Jesu,* published in 1836 but not available in England until it was translated by George Eliot in 1846. Strauss denied historicity to the supernatural elements of the Gospels; he believed that there was a historical substratum, but that everything abnormal or supernatural was the result of man's myth-making propensities (13–16).

Meanwhile, the study of the New Testament was being affected by the rise of comparative philology. J. J. Griesbach (1745–1812) classified the existing manuscripts into families by comparing textual variants, just as the Indo-Europeanists classified languages into families (66, 81). As the scholars began to apply to the New Testament the same scientific methods they used with other ancient documents, new questions about its meaning arose. Neill notes that they also recognized the problems arising from the increasing focus on natural science and a mechanistic worldview (96), the worldview for which the linguistic philosophers found such strong justifications in the period between the wars.

There followed a number of "lives" of Jesus in which, as Neill puts it, the Gospels were "reduced to the level of what scholars in the middle of the nineteenth century regarded as possible and suitable" (112). (In other words, they were applying the criterion of verifiability in a loose way before A. J. Ayer had promulgated it.) Albert Schweitzer summarized all the "possible and suitable lives of Jesus" in The Quest for the Historical Jesus (1906), concluding that we simply do not have the materials for a biography of Jesus in the modern sense (192–94).

A further complicating issue concerned the distinction between truth and fact, myth and history. Just as A. J. Ayer maintains that "there is no opposition between the natural scientist and the theist who believes in a transcendent god [because] the religious utterances of the theist are not genuine propositions at all" (Ayer 117), so Rudolf Bultmann (1884–1976) began to maintain that it is unnecessary to establish the historicity of the Gospels. The acceptance of their content is strictly a matter of faith; it has nothing to do with being convinced that certain alleged historical events took place. Bultmann denies that the Resurrection actually happened; however, Jesus's disciples thought it did, so that Jesus was alive for them, and he can be alive for modern disciples in the same way (232–33). In effect, Bultmann removes the truth of literal historicity and substitutes the truth of myth.

In separating "the essential message" from traditional belief, Bultmann can be compared with his contemporary, Karl Barth (1886–1968). Like many other Europeans, Barth found his faith, which was theologically liberal, devastated by the outbreak of World War I. The mainline churches had committed themselves to the evolutionary doctrine of steady progress, a doctrine quickly refuted by the horror of the war. Barth found, as Neill puts it, that "moral platitudes and optimistic vistas now had nothing to say to people." He turned to his Bible, however, and found that it was inspired—not because it provided historical fact, but because it spoke to the contemporary condition. The result was his *Epistle to the Romans,* published in 1918 (203–07).

Another attack on the historicity of the Gospels came from form criticism. Neill mentions K. L. Schmidt, who shows that the first part of the Gospel of Mark consists of unrelated single episodes pasted together by bridge passages, a structure very different from the connected narrative of the Passion. Another form critic, Martin Dibelius, contrasts the popular style of the Gospels with the high style of the Greek classics (240–45). The work of the form critics cast doubt on the belief of some Christians that the Bible was dictated to its authors by the Holy Spirit.

If the events related in the Bible were written, rewritten, and edited as a normal human activity, then they could not possess a dictated-by-God accuracy. Thus the form critics turned their efforts to determining the *Sitz im Leben* of various Gospel stories—the situation of the early Christians which made a particular story especially relevant to them and motivated them to preserve and modify it. An understanding of the *Sitz im Leben* would furnish clues to the story's deviation from historical reliability.

Form criticism, like Bultmann's divorce of myth from fact, seems as much an expression of the times as anything else. Like the New Criticism, it tries to pin down a text and make reading more like a scientific experiment. Also, like New Criticism, it involves close reading of the text, speculation about how the words represent an adjustment of needs and emotions (Richards's "attitudes"), and a tendency to focus on short passages rather than approaching a literary text as a whole.

This, then, was the biblical and historical paradigm in which the priests of the Church of England were being trained at the time that C. S. Lewis was converted to Christianity and became a practicing member of the Church. People fascinated with the story of Lewis's conversion as it is dramatically related in *Surprised by Joy* tend to ignore the gradualness of it. When Lewis became a theist, he did not immediately tackle the problem of the historicity of the Gospel. Although no longer a prisoner of the Spirit of the Age, the remnants of intellectual chains still clung to him, and he tended to assume that the articles of the Christian creed were not to be taken with complete literalness. His earliest attitude is perhaps expressed in the conversation between John and Christ in *The Pilgrim's Regress*. Christ says, "Your life has been saved all this day by crying out to something which you call by many names, and you have said to yourself that you used metaphors." John asks if he acted wrongly. And Christ replies, "*Perhaps not.* But you must play fair. If its help is not a metaphor, neither are its commands. If it can answer when you call, then it can speak without your asking" (146; emphasis added). Christ's "perhaps not" seems to imply that John need not believe in the literal, factual salvation history, even though God is in some sense real.

Another indication of Lewis's own lack of certainty occurs in the episode of the journey under the mountain, after John has dived into the water of baptism. The episode raises a question about the distinction between factual statements and religious language. Wisdom, or philosophic idealism, appears to John and tells him "that no man could really come where he had come and that all his adventures were [mere] . . . mythology" (170). But the voice of God replies, "Child, if you will, it *is* mythology. It is but truth, not fact: an image, not the very real. But then it is My mythology. . . . This is the veil under which I have chosen to appear even from the first until now" (171). The phrase "It is but truth, not fact" surely suggests some sort of Bultmannian dichotomy. Since *The Pilgrim's Regress* is in some sense Lewis's own story, Lewis must have held the attitude expressed by the voice of God at some point in his own conversion process. The letter to Arthur Greeves concerning Lewis's formulation of the relationship of myth and fact bears out this inference.

Aficionados of Lewis tend to assume that he solved his problem about the historicity of the Gospels in the famous conversation about myth with Hugo Dyson and J. R. R. Tolkien in September 1931. This conversation has been vividly reconstructed by Humphrey Carpenter from a letter to Arthur Greeves and other sources—reconstructed so vividly that many readers have accepted it as having the factual accuracy of a stenographic transcription. But we do not know precisely what was said on that occasion, and while Lewis writes to Greeves that "the story of Christ is simply a true myth," he concludes the letter with "I am also *nearly* certain that it really happened."[5] Apparently his convictions were not as firm then as they later came to be. Furthermore, Lewis had striking evidence that just as one could accept Christianity without being completely sure of the historicity of the Gospels, one could also accept the historicity without becoming a Christian. In *Surprised by Joy* he reports,

Early in 1926 the hardest boiled of all the atheists I ever knew sat in my room on the other side of the fire and remarked that the evidence for the historicity of the Gospels was really surprisingly good. "Rum thing," he went on. "All that stuff of Frazer's about the Dying God. Rum thing. It almost looks as if it had really happened once." (223–24)

Just when Lewis began asserting unequivocally the historicity of the Gospels is uncertain. In "What Christians Believe," his second series of Broadcast Talks (in 1942), he set up this argument: "Either this man [Jesus] was, and is, the Son of God: or else a madman or something worse" (*Mere Christianity* 41). Since Jesus was obviously not "a madman or something worse," he must have been the Son of God. Lewis ignores another possibility, raised by Bultmann and by Wilhelm Wrede before Bultmann (*Interpretation* 249), that Jesus never claimed to be the Son of God, that his deity was a myth created by the Christian community. Lewis probably did so because he was addressing a mass audience under the severe time constraints of a radio broadcast. On the other hand, he may have omitted mentioning it because he had decided to be "certain that it really happened" but had not yet adopted a defense of the Gospels' historicity.

Lewis's most definite statement on this historicity comes very late, in an address to Cambridge theological students on May 11, 1959. It was published by Walter Hooper as "Modern Theology and Biblical Criticism" in *Christian Reflections* (1967) and again as "Fern-seed and Elephants" in a book by that name in 1975. In it Lewis takes on Bultmann and the form critics and incidentally presents a refutation of the linguistic philosophers' definition of a factual statement. This address, presented some three years after the publication of *Till We Have Faces,* is an explicit statement of the attitude toward myth and history implied in the novel.

One of its main points is that the ordinary person's life looks mythical and extremely unlikely from the outside, and anyone trying to apply the *Sitz im Leben* method of analysis to his works and those of his friends is invariably wrong. For example, critics attempting to reconstruct the situation that influenced J. R. R. Tolkien in writing *The Lord of the Rings* concluded, quite plausibly, that the Ring of Doom was a symbol for the atom bomb. After all, the work was published at the time when people had just learned of the existence of such a weapon and were reeling from the shock. However, Lewis knows that the Ring was conceived much earlier, long before the beginning of World War II (*Reflections* 160). The same thing is true of the *Quellenforschungen* (source study) method as practiced by form critics Schmidt and Dibelius. A critic using this method would assume, quite reasonably, that an important source of Richard Lancelyn Green's fairy story *Land of the Lord High Tiger* was Lewis's Chronicles of Narnia with Aslan the lordly lion. But in fact, says Lewis, "I know the genesis of that Tiger and that Lion and they are quite independent" (160). He also says, "Reflection on the extreme improbability of his own life—by historical standards—seems to me a profitable exercise for everyone. It encourages a due agnosticism" (164).

Lewis also argues that Bultmann and the other demythologizers lack literary judgment, that they are "imperceptive about the very quality of the texts they are reading." Lewis was unimpressed by the quasi-scientific method of close analysis stemming from Richards's theory of literature, which divorced the literary text from its historical and cultural context. Similarly, as a classical scholar with a broad knowledge of Greek literature in addition to New Testament Greek, Lewis could see that the biblical critics' concentration on a brief corpus prevented them from developing "a wide and deep and genial experience of literature in general" (154).

For instance, Otto Pfleiderer in 1902 described the Gospel of John as "a transparent allegory of religious and dogmatic ideas" (*Interpretation* 315). Lewis quotes a derivative of this work which calls John "a 'spiritual romance,' 'a poem not a history' to be judged by the same canons as Nathan's parable, the book of Jonah, *Paradise Lost* 'or, more exactly, *Pilgrim's Progress*'" (154). To Lewis, such a grand confusion of literary genres was ludicrous; a man with such an obvious lack of appreciation for literary art could not possibly analyze the New Testament in terms of literary forms. Lewis goes on to argue that much of John is "reportage . . . pretty close up to the facts" on the ground that the technique of literary realism simply did not exist in the ancient world (155).

Another example of the narrow, unliterary pedantry of the biblical scholars was Bultmann's statement that the early Church preserved the Christian message rather than information about Jesus, that the Gospels do not record Jesus's personality. Lewis demands, "Through what strange process has this learned German gone in order to make himself blind to what all men except him see? . . . If anything whatever is common to all believers, and even to many unbelievers, it is the sense that in the Gospels they have met a personality" (156). Jesus, says Lewis, is as real a personality as Falstaff. Only three people in all the world, he goes on, have the factuality of history and the vividness of fiction: Plato's Socrates, Boswell's Johnson, and the gospelers' Jesus. The only possible conclusion is that the biblical critics have gone to the text to support a thesis, not to enjoy a story.

There is an indirect shot at linguistic philosophy in the address, for, as Collingwood, his Magdalen College associate, points out, the verification principle is inherently antihistorical. The biblical critics, influenced by modernist suppositions, are subtly biased against accepting what the ancients have said. Although Lewis does not specifically state the relationship between verification and antihistoricism, he does point out that some historical testimonies which had been regarded as unlikely have actually been vindicated by archaeological studies, such as "the belief of the ancient Greeks that the Mycenaeans were their ancestors and spoke Greek" (162). A New Testament example cited by Neill is the account of the healing of the paralytic at the pool of Bethesda (John 5:1–9). For years expositors said that the five porticoes symbolized the five books of the Law, but this historical detail has now been confirmed by an archaeological find (*Interpretation* 318).

Lewis's conclusion is that the Jesus of the Gospels is basically historical, and Bultmann's call to eliminate the mythological, unhistorical elements simply cannot be carried out. We have no criteria for separating the historical from the unhistorical. The assumption of the demythologizers, "if miraculous, unhistorical," begs the question by simply accepting the verification principle. Likewise, the form critics' method of breaking the text into small pieces in order to deny the historicity of the whole is philologically invalid. The texts we have are the texts we have, and the unbiased philologist will be cautious in his reconstructions, inferences, and emendations. Nevertheless, Lewis also denies the belief that the Bible was dictated by God. He applauds the labors of the textual critics in dealing with disputed readings and agrees that "passages almost verbally identical cannot be independent." Speaking as a devout scholar, he says, "We are not fundamentalists" (163).

But having said this, Lewis is ready to accept the Gospel accounts as they stand. They are as close as we can get to the event. Furthermore, the more we treat them with the receptiveness we give to literary texts, the more accurate our perceptions are likely to be. If the older Lewis who addressed the seminarians had been writing *The Pilgrim's Regress,* the voice of God might have answered Wisdom's objections differently, saying, "Child, because all language is metaphorical, facts are reported as myths, and you have no way of knowing which myths are factual. My world is stranger than you suppose."

Till We Have Faces

"Modern Theology and Biblical Criticism" is a good introduction to *Till We Have Faces,* for in the novel Lewis sets up a situation parallel to that of the Gospels. He assumes that Psyche, like Jesus, is a historical figure. Just as Jesus performed miracles and arose from the dead, Psyche healed the sick and became the bride of a god. Jesus's life was recorded as history by people like Luke, "following the traditions handed down to us by the original eyewitnesses," and Psyche's life was recorded by her sister Orual. Jesus came to be seen as a resurrected god; a shrine was built for Psyche and she was worshiped as a goddess.

Till We Have Faces, like a science fiction story, is an extrapolation from what is known and accepted into what is speculated and imagined. Lewis knows the pagan myths that seem to foreshadow Jesus and accepts the Gospel accounts as fact. He calls the Incarnation "myth become fact." The speculation begins as Lewis asks where the pagan myths came from. The more sophisticated Greeks had developed the idea of euhemerism, the explanation that many of the gods were historical personages who became deified. If Bacchus and Apollo were real people whose stories became myths, then those myths were justified, authenticated, by the appearance on earth of Jesus Christ, the real wine-god and sun-god, the myth become fact. That is what Lewis depicts in *Till We Have Faces.* The story of Psyche, a real person, becomes a myth which is to be authenticated by the Incarnation of the real God of Love. Lewis extrapolates from the principle of euhemerism to ask, "What would it have been like to be a witness when Psyche was experiencing the events that later became a myth?" People who are both imaginative and scientifically minded often wonder just what they would have seen if they had been present at Cana or Bethesda. Lewis poses the question in a less controversial form by using the Psyche story. In fact, the novel could be summarized as "Rum thing, all that stuff about the union of the Soul with Love. Rum thing. It almost looks as if it really happened once."

Although *Till We Have Faces* is subtitled "A Myth Retold," it is important not to jump over its historical realism in our eagerness to go myth hunting. R. J. Reilly, in a valuable study of the relationship between Lewis, Barfield, and others, has written, "The major obstacle that the reader encounters in the book is the temptation to accept the characters of the book as 'real' characters, people who have a life of their own on the story level. . . . The truth is that Orual and Psyche are not 'real' persons but rather adumbrations of real persons" (125–26).

On the contrary, if anything whatever is common to all readers of the novel, it is the sense that in Orual they have met a real person. The book is, as Lewis wrote to Professor Kilby, "A work of (supposed) historical imagination" (*Letters* 273), and Lewis was careful to give the story a realistic surface. Careless in the details of his Narnian stage setting, he was remarkably consistent in his description of Glome. As Van der Weele has said, Lewis chose "to demythologize" the original story (in Schakel, *Longing* 186). From the information he provides, we can locate Glome in time within two or three decades and on the map within two or three locations. The economic activity, the military organization, and the religious cults are all consistent with the supposed time and place. But just as the authenticity of the Gospels is mediated by the literary style of the four evangelists, so also it is the style, the narrative voice of Orual, that establishes the story as (supposed) historical fact. To fail to respond to her gutsy diction and feminist resentments is to repeat the fault of the biblical critic who saw the Gospel of John as a transparent allegory.

It is the business of history to record the unique, unrepeatable fact, and Lewis labors to display the uniqueness of the story of Psyche and Orual. Before finding universal, mythic significance in it, we must first respond to his effort to create the impression of history, of something that really happened. It was not easy.

In the preface to the first English edition of the novel, Lewis said that he had been haunted by his reinterpretation of the story of Psyche and Cupid all his life. The original story comes to us from *The Golden Ass* of Apuleius (b. 125 c.e.), an African who wrote in Latin. Lewis summarizes it in an appendix to *Till We Have Faces:* Psyche is such a beautiful girl that people worship her instead of Venus, but she has no suitors. An oracle instructs her father that she must be left on a mountain to be the prey of a dragon. But Venus's son, Cupid, falls in love with her and takes her to live with him in a beautiful palace. For fear of Venus, Cupid comes to Psyche only at night and forbids her to look at him. Her two sisters come to visit her and are consumed with envy because of her fine house. They tell her that her husband must be a monster and persuade her to betray him by hiding a lamp in the bedroom so that she can look at him while he sleeps and kill him. But as she gazes at his beauty, he awakens, rejects her for her lack of faith, and leaves her.

The salient point of Lewis's retelling of the story is the doubt about the factuality of what happens. Cupid's palace is only momentarily visible. Only one of the sisters, Orual, visits Psyche, so that she cannot verify her perceptions by comparing them with those of another person. It is the same problem of belief in unseen reality that Peter raises in *The Lion, the Witch, and the Wardrobe:* "Well, Sir, if things are real, they're there all the time." And the Professor replies, "Are they?" (45–46). Orual asks Bardia, a simple, god-fearing military officer, and the Fox, a Greek philosopher and her old tutor, whether to believe that Psyche's palace is really there. Bardia temporizes, "I don't well know what's *really,* when it comes to houses of gods" (135), while the Fox surmises that the "god" is nothing more than a mountain man, an outlaw. Orual chooses not to believe in the palace and persuades Psyche to test her god-husband. When the god rejects Psyche for her lack of faith, he also pronounces doom on Orual, who goes back to Glome to rule the kingdom after the death of her father, to live out her life as best she can. Toward the end of her reign she learns that Psyche has come to be worshiped as a goddess and that her own story has become part of the myth. In a Charles Williams–like process of substitution, Orual's sufferings have spared Psyche, and Psyche's beauty has been shared with her, so that both of them are worthy to stand before the god.

Convinced that it must have been possible, even reasonable, to doubt the existence of the palace, Lewis made several attempts to deal with his version of the story. He finally found the narrative viewpoint: the first-person account of Orual, Psyche's ugly sister; he found the conflict: Orual's struggle with belief and self-knowledge, a struggle which is bound up with her possessive love of Psyche; and incidentally, he found a reason for writing: to defend the validity of myth by an approach different from the science fiction of the Ransom trilogy and the children's fantasies of Narnia. In these earlier works, people from the world as we know it travel to places where myths are facts, or, more precisely, to places where our earthbound distinction between fact and myth is seen to be artificial. In *Till We Have Faces* the story of Psyche begins as history—something that really happened—and then is mythologized as she comes to be worshiped as a goddess. In the second part of the novel, Lewis goes on to demonstrate that the Psyche myth has worth beyond a mere story—that it is a fore-shadowing of the Christian Gospel.[6]

Lewis's change in the story allows him to show us, through Orual, what it would be like to live through the making of a myth. Orual's response to Psyche's "engodding" has much in common with that of the people in Jesus's hometown: "Is he not the carpenter's son? . . . Where then has he got all this from?" (Matt. 13:55, 56b). In living through Orual's struggle with belief, the reader experiences the mind-set that prevents moderns from believing in the historical-mythical Jesus.

Just as the Gospel writers locate the life of Jesus in time by referring to Augustus as emperor, Quirinius as governor of Syria, and Pontius Pilate as procurator of Judea, so Lewis locates the life of Psyche in time. Since Glome is so isolated from what we know of ancient history, our clues come through the Fox, the Greek slave who is Orual's teacher and later her friend and counselor. When Orual commissions the Fox to build up the royal library, the most recent work he buys is "some of the conversations of Socrates" (232), probably the Dialogues of Plato (428–348 B.C.E.). Thus Chad Walsh locates the time of the story between the death of Socrates (399 B.C.E.) and the birth of Christ.[7] But we can be more precise. The Fox is a Stoic (see Schakel *Reason* 39 and 189, n. 10), and Zeno, the founder of Stoic philosophy, began teaching in Athens in about 310 B.C.E. Whatever war resulted in the Fox's capture and enslavement could not have taken place before this date.

The latest date in which the story could be set is more difficult to determine. The Fox's capture must have taken place before the struggles of Pyrrhus against Rome (280–275 B.C.E.); otherwise Lewis would naturally have slipped in a reference to Rome.[8] Another possible speculation is that the Fox's knowledge of the Babylonian fertility goddess might have come from the history of Babylonia written by Berossus in 290 B.C.E., implying that he must have been captured after that. Finally, Euhemerus promulgated the view that the gods were historical personages in 300 B.C.E. The Fox does not use the euhemeristic explanation of the gods to combat what he regards as Orual's superstition. Holding the opinions he did ("Lies of poets, child, lies of poets"), wouldn't he have used it if he had known about it? Furthermore, Arnom, the "new" priest, who has "learned from the Fox" how to talk philosophically about the gods, explicates Ungit in terms of nature myth instead of euhemerism (*Faces* 270–71), which looks like a minutely accurate historical detail.

But given the way information was transmitted in the ancient world, it would be perfectly plausible that the Fox would not have heard of either Euhemerus or Berossus before he went to the war that resulted in his capture. As for the struggles with Rome, the Fox could have been one of the many Greeks who did not recognize the historical importance of them (see Boardman et al. 405). The most cautious conclusion is that the Fox's capture could not have been earlier than 310 or much later than 280 B.C.E.

Geographic details in *Till We Have Faces* also suggest a fairly specific location for Glome. There are mountains and a sea—"what we call the sea (though it is not to be compared with the Great Sea of the Greeks)" (95). The Grey Mountain is northeast of Glome, rising out of high, hilly country, and on the way to it Orual gets a gleam of the sea. It is beyond the empire carved out by Alexander, since Orual does not mention any past conquests of Glome from outsiders. It is beyond the areas colonized by Greeks, since Orual says that the new statue of Ungit came "not indeed from the Greeklands themselves, but from lands where men had learned of the Greeks" (234). Orual emphasizes Glome's isolation when she says, "Traders, perhaps twenty kingdoms away" learned that books could be sold in Glome (231). It is north of Greece, since the King speaks of the Greeklands as "down" (9) and since there are freezing temperatures in the winter (5). The climate supports figs (230), which grow in a variety of places, but also pears (9), which grow best in a somewhat northerly climate. There are lions (181), which suggest Africa and southwestern Asia now, but they were found even in Greece in ancient times (8) and may have been found farther north. However, what Orual calls a lion could be the much smaller mountain lion rather than the large cats of the genus *Panthera*.[9]

The small sea east of Glome must be either the Black or the Caspian; it could not be the Aral, which is surrounded by lowlands and is perhaps too far west. One clue is that Orual receives "an embassy from the Great King who lives to the South and East" (254). If she is speaking of a ruler with headquarters at Byzantium (not Alexander, since the time is undoubtedly the Hellenistic Age), then that would place Glome somewhere in the Balkans, perhaps not too far from the Danube. This area is consistent with the silver mines mentioned in the book.[10] But if the Great King's headquarters were in Persia, or even in India, a more likely location for Glome is in the Caucasus Mountains, looking east to the Caspian Sea. This location is closer to the outposts of the seventh-century Assyrian empire, which would account for the fact that Ungit resembled the Babylonian rather than the Greek Aphrodite (8).

In trying to interpret the geography, we must remember that Lewis would have depended on his reading of Herodotus, the *Anabasis*, or even Ptolemy, rather than what is known about that part of the world today. Since the Scythians (variously described as living north or west of the Black Sea and west of the Caspian) were described as wild, uncivilized people, he may have visualized Glome within their territory. He would not have hesitated to create details needed in the story, such as the hot spring and the silver mines, and it is unlikely that he did detailed map work in creating the novel. Steeped in Greek literature, philosophy, and history, he simply used his broad knowledge of ancient times to create a realistic setting. It is for literary critics—"clever undergraduate[s] . . . [and] dull American don[s]" (*Christian Reflections* 157)—to put together the clues in this way.

The accuracy and historical realism must be emphasized, however, because readers have typically come to the work expecting a fantasy and thus "gone and left out the whole point" (*Voyage* 119). The story of Psyche is, from our point of view, a myth, and, as Howard has said, "We don't want our myths taking place in 1929, or even 1066."[11] Lewis's book, however, is not the story of Psyche; it is the story of Orual and of Orual's experience of the myth—quite a different thing.

Although Lewis may not have worked as hard to plant the time and place clues as a person with a modern education must work to elucidate them, they do fit together plausibly, even on a level outside the story. The earliest account we have of Psyche is that of Apuleius himself, although it is thought that he used folk tales. If Psyche had been a historical person, it is plausible that she would have lived in the Hellenistic Age. Her story could not have been known earlier; if it had, surely it would have appeared in the work of at least one poet of the Greek Golden Age.

The feeling of historicity owes less, however, to the accurate clues of time and place than it does to Orual's language about it. Her initial description of Glome is observationally precise and objective:

> The city of Glome stands on the left hand of the river Shennit to
> a traveler who is coming up from the southeast, not more than a
> day's journey above Ringal.... The city is built about as far back
> from the river as a woman can walk in the third of an hour....
> About as far beyond the ford of the Shennit as our city is on this
> side of it, you come to the holy house of Ungit. (4)

Orual measures distances, not in modern units such as the English mile
or the Continental meter, but with the measures available to her. A day's
journey for someone walking and carrying a burden would be sixteen or
seventeen miles. A woman can walk a mile in a third of an hour. She measures time in hours, which can be judged by the movement of the sun, but
has no names for smaller units. Thus she commands her maids to wake her
two hours before sunrise, but it seemed "only a heartbeat later" (78). Similarly, the fight with Argan took a sixth of an hour (215), and the sound of
the god's voice lasted no more than two heartbeats (171).

Because she uses body movements and sensations to measure times
and distances, Orual's seemingly objective description involves the reader
through kinesthetic images. Before we know it, we are committed to
accepting her story as factual. We are prepared to believe that when she
is confronted with the marvelous palace and the god's voice she will
measure whatever there is to be measured. There are two slips in the
diction: "minute" (101) and "mile" (248), but these are not sufficient to
break the spell. The language about time and space in *Till We Have Faces*
resoundingly vindicates Barfield's theory about the way poetic diction
causes a shift in consciousness, for the diction expands our awareness of
what it would be like to depend on our bodies for measurement.

Like the measurements, the descriptions of Ungit and her worship
present a realistic historical surface, but it is the voice of Orual that draws
us into the experience of history.[12] We participate in her shock, disbelief,
and disgust at the worship of Ungit.

As the Fox tells Orual, Ungit is Aphrodite with many of the characteristics of the Babylonian Ishtar, called Baalath or Astarte by the Phoenicians,
Artemis at Perga in Pamphylia, and Derceto at Ascalon. In every case she
was the fertility goddess, worshiped almost everywhere by cult prostitution
(Frazer 5:34–37). Orual is disgusted by "Ungit's girls," partly because of
their sexual activity but largely because of the waste of their lives.

During the Hellenistic Age Greek deities and forms of worship became syncretized with Eastern ones. Aphrodite became fused with the Great Mother Goddess Cybele, worshiped under different names all over Asia (Frazer 5:36). She was also identified with the Egyptian goddess Isis, who was the mother of the dying and reviving god Horus, and sometimes with Hera, the goddess of marriage, or Diana, the goddess of childbirth. One center of the Great Mother cult was Mount Ida in the Troad; later the worship of Aphrodite replaced it. She also became identified with Venus, the morning star (Sales 2:110–11). Thus the Old Priest's statement that the gods "dazzle our eyes and flow in and out of one another like eddies on a river" (50) was historically true. It is a mark of Lewis's historical accuracy that the Fox's name for Orual was Maia, for Maia was one of the lesser goddesses who became syncretized with the Great Mother.[13] When Orual, in a climax of self-knowledge and repentance, cries, "Lord, I am Ungit" (279), her insight has historical as well as psychological truth.

Even the Greek Aphrodite was not as civilized as Homer makes her. She was the goddess of sex rather than romantic thrill, often associated with the darker side of love: rape, adultery, incest. In Corinth, Cyrus, and Eryx in Sicily she also was worshiped by cult prostitution. Orual's comment that the goddess might be "more beautiful in Greece than in Glome," but "equally terrible in each" (8), is correct.

The description of Ungit is a historically accurate description of Hellenistic syncretism, detailed enough to show that she is the Great Mother as well as Aphrodite. Orual describes Ungit as "a black stone without head or hands or face" (4). Conical stones used as images of the goddess were found at Byblus, Perga, and Golgi in Cyprus, and cones made of clay at Lagash and Nippur in Babylonia (Frazer 5:35). One of the shrines of the Great Mother in the Hellenistic Age was at Pessinus in Phrygia, where there was a small meteorite as a sacred symbol of her. In 204 B.C.E., at the behest of an oracle, it was moved from Pessinus to Rome in order to bring victory to the Romans.

The dove is Aphrodite's bird; the pigeon, a kind of dove, is sacred to Ungit. Ungit's house is egg-shaped, a symbol of fertility. The priest wears a bird mask and has to fight his way out of the temple to accomplish the birth of the new year, just as a bird fights its way out of the egg. Ungit is like the Great Mother in that the pig is important to her, but it is "an abomination" (*Faces* 207), cursed rather than sacred.

Other more general details are adopted from what we know of non-Christian religions throughout Europe and Asia Minor. Ungit's house is made with large columns like Stonehenge, but with brick filling the spaces between them. Stonehenge is thought to have been built in about 1848 B.C.E. and to have been connected with sun worship; when Orual says of the temple stones, "These are very ancient, and no one knows who set them up or brought them into that place, or how" (94), her words suggest a comparison with Stonehenge. The implication is that a more enlightened sun worship in earlier Glome was replaced with worship of the chthonic goddess and the light blocked out with the brick. In the story, the darkness becomes a symbol of the difficulty of using rational language when talking about deity.

But the historical accuracies of the description of Ungit are effective primarily because we experience them through Orual's disaffection for the goddess, especially her hatred of "the Ungit smell." Orual is one of those unfortunate individuals who has a keen sense of smell and an aversion to bad odors. One of her earliest memories is of sliding on ice composed of "the stale of the beasts" (6). She fears Hades because it is said that suicides "lie wallowing in filth there" (17). She describes Glome's difficulties in olefactory terms: her father's war "left a stench and a disaffection behind it" (29), and in the drought the Shennit became "the corpse of a river and stank" (40).

So also her earliest memory of Ungit is her fear of Ungit's priest because of "the holiness of the smell that hung about him—a temple-smell of blood . . . and burnt fat and singed hair and wine and stale incense" (11). Almost her last memory is the holy smell of the new year's rite:

> There had been censing and slaughtering, and pouring of wine and pouring of blood, and dancing and feasting and towsing of girls, and burning of fat, all night long. There was as much taint of sweat and foul air as (in a mortal's house) would have set the laziest slut to opening windows, scouring and sweeping. (269)

Since Ungit is a goddess of sex and fertility, it is not surprising that Orual associates the holy smell with sex. When she is trying to shame Psyche into leaving her husband, Orual compares Psyche's life to that of "Ungit's girls," who live with "blood and incense and muttering and the reek of burnt fat" (125). Later on, she declares that her virginity is better than Psyche's "sty" (163). But after her confrontation with Bardia's wife she realizes that it was her love for Bardia, not the lust she falsely attributed to Psyche, that "stank." She describes her illicit love as a plant that put forth an "overpowering smell" but had a shallow root (267).

She also associates the holy smell with her lack of freedom. She calls Ungit's house "an imprisoning, smothering sort of place" and contrasts it with the fresh, sweet air of the morning (269). On the first trip up to the Grey Mountain she is glad to pass the house of Ungit and leave it behind "because I felt as if the air were sweeter as we got away from all that holiness" (94). Freedom implies free thought, and it is fitting that the holy smell represents the irrational, not only to Orual but to the Fox, who exclaims, "When shall I have washed the nurse and the grandam and the priest and the soothsayer out of your soul?" (143). Finally, when Arnom, the new priest, begins to "talk like a philosopher about the gods," he also begins to have the temple washed after sacrifices so that "it smelled cleaner and less holy" (234).

Orual lives, as she herself says, in a "god-haunted, plague-breeding, decaying, tyrannous world" (97). It is the world that Christianity will replace, as the bloodless Eucharist, memorial of Christ's death once and for all, replaces the continual temple sacrifices. It is notable that Psyche, who in a sense belongs to the new order, brings good smells into Orual's life. At their first meeting on the mountain, Orual speaks of "the honey-sweetness, warm, breathing perfections of her" (124). When Psyche is deified, her temple does not smell, for she is "one of those small peaceful gods who are content with flowers and fruit for sacrifice" (240). The replacement of the pagan gods with Christ is mythic, but Lewis presents it on the sensory level of historical realism, drawing the reader into Orual's experience.

Other characteristics of Orual's narrative voice contribute to the historical depth and credibility of the story. Her language reveals her as more intelligent than most of the people around her, proud with the touchiness of the aristocracy, but practical and down to earth. She is not "a lover, a lunatic, or a poet," and still less a mystic; yet she loves Psyche with her whole being, she sees the god's palace (if only momentarily), and she labors to say exactly what she means.

Three features of her style are especially effective in helping to establish the story as history. First, she uses semiobsolete, dialectal, and marginally standard words, especially words that apply to both humans and animals.

This feature reflects the primitiveness of her society. Second, she uses functional shift in a way that gives an Elizabethan flavor to her speech, suggesting that her kingdom, like Elizabeth's, is in a time of change and that her personality is something like that of the Virgin Queen. Finally, she uses the schemes of classical rhetoric such as amplification, isocolon, and antithesis. This feature is historically plausible, since she would have learned rhetoric from the Fox. It also associates her style with the rhetorical elaboration of the Hellenistic Age.[14]

A few examples will suffice to illustrate the primitive effect produced by Orual's diction. Some semiobsolete words that she uses are "victuals" (193) for food, "worm" (72) in the sense of a dragon or reptile, and "bodkin" (53) in the sense of a small dagger. She uses dialectal words, especially words associated with Scotland and Northern England, in preference to standard words. For example, she calls her glimpse of the god's house a "ferly" (134, 142). She does not use the Latinate "vision" or "miracle," or even the native English word "wonder," but "ferly," listed by the *Oxford English Dictionary* as primarily Scottish. In addition to semi-obsolete and dialectal words, she uses marginally standard expressions, such as "Batta *shore* me" (5) instead of "sheared."

The most interesting feature of her diction, however, is her use of words that can apply to both humans and animals in preference to words that apply only to humans. For example, Psyche calls what will happen to her "to *wed* a god" (71) and "to be *married* to the god" (72), both human terms, but Orual calls it "to be *mated*" (72), a word equally applicable to humans and animals. Another interesting word is "drench." Orual speaks of the "*drenching* of horses and cattle" (232), a technical term which means to force a large dose of medicine mixed with liquid down the throat of an animal. Later she applies the term to herself, saying that the gods "drenched me with seeings" (276). Although in context Orual seems to be using the word in its more common meaning of to soak or saturate, her visions were also medicinal to her soul.

Orual's use of rough, dialectal words is highlighted by alliteration, which we associate with a less literate culture (since it facilitates memorization) and proverbial folk wisdom. Orual may actually be quoting a proverb when she warns herself, "Don't mar what you've learnt you can't make" (138), and she creates one when she says, "Weakness, and work, are two comforts the gods have not taken from us" (82). Alliteration also marks Orual's times of stress. When her mother died and her hair was cut she reports, "Lank and dull and little it lay on the floor beside Redival's rings of gold" (19). The turning point of her life is marked by a complex pattern of three alliterating sounds: "[The god's voice] was un*m*oved and *s*weet; like a *b*ird *s*inging on the *b*ranch a*b*ove a hanged *m*an" (173).

If Orual's primitive diction and use of alliteration convey the primitiveness of her society, so also the use of functional shift makes the reader aware of the resemblance between her situation and that of the first Queen Elizabeth. Historically, functional shift—using, for example, a noun for a verb or a verb for a noun—became an important source of new words in English during the Elizabethan period. Shakespeare is cited as the originator of many such locutions. Some examples of Orual's use of functional shift include "How quickly we learn to *queen* or *king* it" (194), "I'd *queen* it with the best of them" (201), and her speech to Bardia's wife, "Oh, dear Lady, *un-queen* me a little, I beseech you" (259). When she visits the temple of Psyche she asks, "How was she *godded?*" (241), substituting a functional shift of an Anglo-Saxon word for the Latinate "deified." It both sounds Elizabethan and also supports Orual's character as a user of plain speech.

The subliminal resemblance between Glome and Elizabethan England has far-reaching implications. Like Elizabeth, Orual is the daughter of a king who is unable to provide a male heir to the throne. Like Elizabeth, she manages her kingdom so as to bring order, economic progress, and increased support of learning and art to the country. Orual also reflects Elizabeth's techniques in her handling of religion, for she increases her power by making it possible for the priest to support her. She accepts the existence of the gods but is not really a believer; the rituals annoy her, and she cuts them out of her practical life as much as possible. Like Elizabeth, she tolerates as much variation of religious observance as possible. The temple of Ungit with its carved Hellenistic Aphrodite in front of the shapeless stone Aphrodite can be seen as an analogue of the Elizabethan Compromise. Thus a relatively small detail of style, an occasional use of functional shift, contributes to the historical realism of the novel. Orual is more believable as a historical figure because she reminds the reader of Queen Elizabeth, another well-known historical figure.

Combined with her harsh words and functional shift is Orual's use of the civilized tricks of classical rhetoric. The critics who see in her sentence structure an effort by Lewis to indicate that she is writing awkwardly and painfully in Greek as a second language have perhaps allowed the rough diction to influence their perception. On the word level, her language is gritty and harsh; on the sentence and phrase level, it is carefully crafted. The most frequent rhetorical figure she uses is the amplification of a sentence through naming a series of related items such as "cat's fur, dog's muzzle, hog's tusks" (147), "eloquence and figures and poetry" (235), or "mother and wife and child and friend" (304). Most frequently the amplification comes through piling up synonyms, as in "the meaning, the pitch, the central knot" (234) or "clear, hard, limited, and simple" (302) or "his trull, his drab, his whore, his slut" (148). In one sentence there is a list of similes: "still as ice, heavy as lead, cold as earth" (157), which becomes memorable through interchanging the usual adjectives (cold as ice, still as earth). This use of amplification contributes to the Elizabethan sound of the language, for the Elizabethans admired "coppie," or plenteousness.

It is a mark of Lewis's craftsmanship that despite the richness of texture achieved through amplification, the style seems sparse and plain overall. The sentences are so patterned that no word seems superfluous, especially in Orual's use of isocolon, parallelism, and antithesis. Isocolon occurs when sentences and clauses are matched in length and grammatical structure:

> Nothing that's beautiful hides its face.
> Nothing that's honest hides its name. (160)

On the phrase level there are many grammatically parallel structures, as in "my dark witch-shape and my tapping stick" (280). Many of the isocolons and parallelisms also express antithesis:

> We'd rather you drank their blood than stole their hearts.
> We'd rather they were ours and dead than yours and made immortal. (291)

The frequent use of antithesis is perhaps a measure of the ambiguity of Orual's experience, her inescapable frustration. Her lifelong enmity toward the gods is expressed in an extended antithesis:

> Now, instantly, I knew I was facing them—I with no strength and they with all; I visible to them, they invisible to me; I easily wounded

(already so wounded that all my life had been but a hiding and staunching of the wound), they invulnerable; I one, they many. (245)

All these means of heightening the style and thereby building up the historical reality—the smell imagery, the diction, the classical figures of rhetoric—go unnoticed in a first reading. We are too involved with Orual's struggle with the gods, too much under the spell of her voice to consider *how* the effect is achieved. Lewis's biographers tell us that he wrote quickly, fluently, with little or no revision.[15] But *Till We Have Faces* is a book about a person writing a book, and Lewis's fluency was not transferred to Orual. Her struggle with the gods was a struggle with language. In some ways it is analogous with the early twentieth-century struggle over language that is present in most of Lewis's fiction.

The essence of Orual's problem was first displayed in the confrontation between the Old Priest and the King over the need to make the Great Offering. The Old Priest sets up a dichotomy between the holy wisdom and Greek wisdom. Holy wisdom consists of statements that are illogical and self-contradictory but nevertheless provide understanding of how to sacrifice to the gods: "the Brute is, in a mystery, Ungit herself or Ungit's son, the god of the Mountain; or both" (48). The Fox calls this nonsense: "A shadow is to be an animal which is also a goddess which is also a god, and loving is to be eating—a child of six would talk more sense" (49). What the Fox says is Greek wisdom, pointing out the old Priest's violation of the Greek logic's Law of Contradiction. But the old Priest taunts that Greek wisdom has no effect on the gods, since "it brings no rain and grows no corn," and no effect on men, since "it does not even give them boldness to die" (50). In I. A. Richards's terminology, the Fox's language is referential language; it has no aesthetic appeal and does not "adjust attitudes."

Orual moves back and forth between these two language systems, finding them both inadequate. Concerning the description of the rebirth ritual in the temple, she says, "But of course, like all these sacred matters, it is and it is not" (268). But she recognizes that the Fox's language of Greek wisdom is also inadequate. He dismisses the myths as "lies of poets, lies of poets," but he loves them better than the abstract formulations of principle that he considers closer to the truth. He is like the biblical critics who would demythologize the Gospel by removing the dramatic, poetic miracles in order to concentrate on the principles of virtue but then find themselves loving the stories.

In portraying Orual's vacillation between the two language systems, Lewis is dealing with a thoroughly modern problem, one which some historians of thought attribute to the rise of literacy. Once books became cheap and plentiful, it was possible to compare what one saw in the environment with what was printed in the book. The book eliminated the slipperiness of the information. Readers could see whether a certain flower really did have five petals, or whether a person's tongue developed a white coating during a certain illness. They came to expect that religious information would have the same fixity. The existence of the Bible as a printed book led to the assumption that it contained facts which could be verified, could be used as the premises in a logical argument, and could be compared to objects in the environment. In *Till We Have Faces* the Old Priest denies the validity of this expectation: "They demand to see such things clearly, as if the gods were no more than letters written in a book" (50). But Lewis believed that myths were polysemic, and that the Christian Gospel relates a myth become fact.

The extent to which Lewis participated in what we may call "the literacy assumption" is debatable. Because he professed himself to be a thoroughgoing supernaturalist, many readers of Lewis have attributed to him more literalism in his approach to the Scriptures than he actually held. After all, in "Modern Theology and Biblical Criticism" he does say, "We are not Fundamentalists." Moreover, in tracing Orual's perplexity, Lewis seems to be saying that literacy, whether of a hand-copied book or of more modern information technology, does not produce the basic problem. Orual lives in a primitive society, but she and her companions, Bardia and the Fox, are not more credulous concerning miracles, myths, and the supernatural than twentieth-century people are. Orual's inability to decide whether the palace was really there was a deficiency in her heart, not her hardware. Lewis has carefully established the historical context of the story so that we may accept the story of Psyche as a unique, unrepeatable happening, but the attitudes and conclusions from which Orual must choose are analogous to the ones facing modern people.

Her choice is more complex than simply deciding between the world-views of the Fox and Bardia. Because the Fox is a Stoic, his worldview excludes the supernatural and the hard-to-explain. He believes that everything happens in accordance with the laws of Nature and that Nature is a seamless web. When Orual points out the objective improvement in

Glome's situation since the sacrifice of Psyche—that the rains have come, the disease has run its course, and that Glome's rival kingdom has ceased to be a threat because of civil war—the Fox replies that the apparent cause-effect relationship is mere chance. But then Orual reminds him, "How often, Grandfather, you have told me there's no such thing as chance." He blames the apparent contradiction on language, "an old trick of the tongue," and reaffirms his belief that all events have been determined from the beginning (84–85).

When Orual asks whether the Universe might have two tiers, whether "there might be things that are real though we can't see them" (141), the Fox replies that moral attributes such as Justice are real. He is unable to stomach the idea that there might be gods with enough personality to have the kind of freedom a human being has and to use this freedom to tamper with the deterministic web of Nature. The Divine Nature (his word for the reality behind the myths) could not possibly love a human being—"You might as well say the universe itched or the Nature of Things sometimes tippled in the wine cellar" (143).

Despite his belief in determinism, however, he insists that human beings have free will in choosing their response to the things that happen to them, as Psyche was able to choose to die bravely even in her outward helplessness. He never deals with the problem of how the moral freedom that he values so much can exist in the seamless web of Nature. In the Fox's noble futility Lewis dramatizes his own conviction that those who deny the supernatural (like Bultmann) constantly walk a tightrope between their philosophic beliefs and the way a person naturally has to think in order to get through a day. In "Modern Theology" Lewis tells the seminarians that if he believed as they do and had to deal with "a parishioner in great anguish or under fierce temptation . . . I'd find my forehead getting red and damp and my collar getting tight" (153). Lewis portrays the Fox's disbelief as a subtle dishonesty similar to that of the seminarians and simultaneously shows that his actions are better than his principles.

Like the Fox, Bardia has developed a way of getting through his days without resolving the contradictions between his own values and what he has been told about the gods. As a military man, his life is based on loyalty, and he refuses to criticize the object of his loyalty. When the King orders him to kill the temple guards he replies, "I'm for the King of Glome and the gods of Glome while I live. But if the King and the gods fall out, you great ones must settle it between you" (53). While faithfully observing the taboos and offering the appointed sacrifices, he respects and fears the gods because they are powerful, never asking why men should serve beings who are so cruel. He is quite certain that Psyche is sane, but when asked if the palace is *really* there, he hedges: "I don't well know what's *really*, when it comes to the houses of gods" (135). His agnostic brand of supernaturalism in the final analysis renders the gods simply irrelevant to himself. He is neutral: he refuses the attempt to reduce the gods to ordinary language, he makes no complaint against them, and he does not appear in Orual's visions of the hereafter. Orual sees "Batta and the King my father and the Fox and Argan [the king she killed]" (289), but not Bardia.

Caught between the polite, sophisticated disbelief of the Fox and the plain, superstitious disbelief of Bardia, Orual struggles to make sense of her experience. When she meets Psyche on the mountain, she feels "a sickening discord, a rasping together of two worlds, like the two bits of broken bone" (120). It is not the relatively simple choice of the scientific versus the religious explanation of the data. The Fox's "scientific" explanation is that Psyche has mated with a mountain man, who forbids her to see him to maintain her illusion that she is married to a god. Bardia's "religious" explanation is that Psyche has indeed been married to a god, who forbids her to see him because his appearance is horrible. Orual says that she can not choose one explanation over the other because, linguistically speaking, they belong to different universes of discourse: "each was well-rooted in its own soil" (151). Lewis is showing us that the stratagem of separating factual from nonfactual discourse, referential from emotive language, and Gospel history from mythological truth is an oversimplification.

As Orual deals with her experience, she falls into this same trap of oversimplification. In a syllogism that ironically recalls Lewis's argument for the deity of Christ in *Mere Christianity*, Orual argues that Psyche's husband is "either a monster . . . or a salt villain" (160). But an either-or syllogism is invalid unless its two terms really exhaust all the possibilities. In *Mere Christianity*, Lewis sets up an argument based on three possibilities: Christ was either insane or a charlatan or really the Son of God. Orual's argument leaves out the third possibility, that Psyche's husband might really be a god.[16] Not until years later—when it is too late—does she form the argument correctly: "the bride of a god, or mad, or a . . . villain's spoil" (249).

In setting up Orual's syllogism, Lewis is using a technique of characterization common in medieval literature but unfamiliar to many modern readers—the technique of allowing the character to make elementary mistakes in formal logic. Orual not only sets up the syllogism incorrectly, but she also makes a wrong decision based on the false conclusion. She decides to force Psyche to test her husband, even though she has good evidence that neither Bardia nor the Fox would do such a thing. Bardia would be prevented from it by his unquestioning piety, the Fox by his ethical principles. Orual's situation is analogous to that of Eomer in *The Lord of the Rings*. Eomer says, "It is hard to be sure of anything among so many marvels. The world is all grown strange. . . . How shall a man judge what to do in such times?" Aragorn replies, "As he ever has judged. Good and ill have not changed since yesteryear" (2:40–41). Even though Orual's faulty logic leads to a false conclusion, the perception of unchanging "good and ill" should have prevented her from carrying it out. Her either-or syllogism is nothing more than window dressing for the unloving, jealous way she has already decided to act, for she has decided to ignore the evidence that it would be best to let Psyche continue in her obvious happiness.

Lewis traces Orual's self-deception very carefully. First she rejects the unknown and fears the loss of control. As she says, "The whole world (Psyche with it) [is] slipping out of my hands." The loss of control leads to insecurity, and she responds with a fury like one of her father's tantrums. Then, influenced by Psyche's certainty, she is tempted to believe in the god-husband. But if she believes in him, she will lose Psyche to the gods, and though the thought occurs that Psyche belongs with the gods, her self-centered love will not accept it. Jealously, she listens to Psyche "saying *he* every moment, no other name but *he*, the way young wives talk" (122), and hardens her heart against Psyche's husband. She hates him so much she can smell it: "Faugh! it's like living in the house of Ungit. Everything's dark about the gods . . . I think I can smell the very—" (124). Her hate is reinforced by her fastidious attitude toward sex. She says, "You like it! Oh, Psyche!" Throughout this passage, Orual is responding, not to sensory perceptions alone, but to her fears and angers.

Then comes the rain. Orual's sensory perception is that Psyche is getting wet, but Psyche insists that she is sitting in her house, that she is dry. Orual must decide whether to believe her own perception or to admit the possibility that Psyche's experience is somehow real. Clearly she cannot verify either perception, but suddenly she does not need verification: "I saw in a flash that I must choose one opinion or the other; and in the same flash knew which I had chosen" (126). In the twilight of the next morning, Orual actually sees Psyche's palace for a moment and realizes that she must renounce her previous decision that it was illusory. She hesitates to punish her pride in that way, and as she considers whether the palace is real, it vanishes from her sight.

In telling the Fox what she found, Orual does not say that she *seemed* to see the palace and that it was in an unknown architectural style, one that she could not have imagined for herself. Like a scientist who automatically discounts an experimental result that seems wildly out of line with the others, Orual gives the Fox only the items of evidence that she thinks he will accept, admitting, "Already he was making me ashamed of half the things I had been thinking" (142). But the Fox had accepted Psyche's healing touch as a possibility. Did he not deserve to be trusted with the momentary evidence for the existence of the palace, even though it was contrary to his usual rationalism and skepticism? Again Orual's pride, her fear of being laughed at as a superstitious barbarian, keeps her silent.

But it is not just fear of being laughed at that keeps Orual silent. Bardia would never laugh at her, and yet she leaves out the part about seeing the palace when she tells her experience to him. Without that piece of evidence, he can only conclude that Psyche's husband is monstrous. When Orual reasons that Psyche's husband is not a god, because Bardia and the Fox, with their different premises, have come to the same conclusion about him, she is using their conclusions to bolster her own; but theirs are based on incomplete data, an incompleteness for which she is responsible. It is a subtle way of begging the question, an action which Lewis attributes to both the language philosophers and the biblical critics. Orual has chosen her opinion "in a flash," and neither logic nor evidence will change it. Furthermore, her seemingly objective perceptions are actually controlled by her beliefs. Her first, uncontaminated view of Psyche's valley is of an earthly paradise. It is "a new world," "bright as a gem," with air that becomes "warmer and sweeter every minute" as she and Bardia descend into it.[17] Later, after she has chosen not to believe, it becomes for her "the desolate valley." It looks hideous, she feels the cold, and instead of its greenness she notices the red and black of sunset behind the mountain's saddle (128).

Back at Glome in her own room, she compounds the self-deception by attributing the evidence in favor of Psyche's husband to her own wishful thinking: "Only my desperate wishes could have made it seem possible" (151). This is the logical fallacy that Lewis called "Bulverism"—discounting a conclusion by attributing it to an outside motivation. But she is also concealing from herself that her *first* wish was for Psyche's story not to be true, because she did not want to lose Psyche to the god and because of her reluctance to change her mind. As she says, "If this is all true, I've been wrong all my life" (115).

When Psyche obeys her and offends the god, Orual sees the storm, the upheaval of the ground, and the god himself. He even speaks to her. Yet she is able to choose to ignore the evidence: "Often, though I had seen a god myself, I was near to believing that there are no such things" (244). Her mental control is like the woman Lewis tells about who had seen a ghost but did not believe in the afterlife. He concludes, "Seeing is not believing" (*Miracles* 3). Thus Orual struggles with a historical but unverifiable fact. Her choice is not based on the claims of rationality, or science, versus the claims of faith; it is a choice contaminated by self-centeredness and the desire for control. The character expressed in her language—objective, tough-minded, rational, Elizabeth-like—is vulnerable to her selfish love of Psyche, and her choice is fundamentally self-defense. Orual implies that she guessed, and guessed wrong, because the gods misled her out of malice, but the careful reader sees that she could have chosen rightly.

In the first part of the novel, Lewis has narrated Orual's experience with great historical and psychological realism in order to demonstrate the process by which a fact might become a myth. The climax of this part occurs when Orual learns that her history has become a myth, that the priest of Psyche knows about it, even though it took place on the mountain, and only she and Psyche were there. Then she finds that the priest's myth makes the choice of the elder sisters quite clear, whereas she believes that her choice was not clear at all, and she blames the gods for lying about her. However, the priest's version of the story is not a lie. Orual's version may be more *factual* than the priest's, but his version is closer to the *truth*. She really was jealous of Psyche, and her choice really did stem from her determination to prevent Psyche from being happy apart from her. If this relationship between factual detail and truth can be imagined in a pagan myth, the same relationship might exist in the story of Jesus, which Lewis regards as myth become fact. Just as the slight error in the priest's story does not destroy it as evidence, the discrepancies of detail among the four Gospels do not provide reasons for doubting the historicity of Jesus. Just as Orual based her argument on two possibilities rather than three, the demythologizers of the New Testament choose to leave out the third possibility.

In the second part of the novel Lewis dramatizes his view of myth as an adjunct to Christian belief. According to some students of the subject, the purpose of myth is to explain the rituals of a community. The priest of Psyche believes that the myth he tells is of that sort. In the spring and summer Psyche is a goddess. At harvest time, when the sun is beginning to shine for fewer hours, the lamp is brought into the temple. Then she is veiled and the winter commemoration of her wandering and weeping begins. The purpose of the story is to justify the custom. As the priest tells Orual, "The sacred story is about the sacred things—the things we do in the temple" (246); in the terminology of A. J. Ayer, it is nonfactual language which may nevertheless have aesthetic value. The demythologizing biblical critics explain passages in the Gospels in this way, but in *Till We Have Faces* Lewis presents the possibility that "the sacred story . . . about the sacred things" could also be historically accurate.

A different purpose of myth, the quasi-scientific explanation of environmental phenomena, is presented in Arnom's elucidation of Ungit. Arnom, the new priest, explains the actions of the gods as natural events when he says that Ungit is a symbol for the earth and her son a symbol for the air and the sky, because "mists and exhalations" arise from the earth; but her son is also her husband, because "the sky by its showers makes the earth fruitful." The explanation is couched in story form, Arnom suggests, "to hide it from the vulgar" (270–71). Orual does not find his elucidation either enlightening or helpful. She thinks, "It's very strange that our fathers should first think it worth telling us that rain falls out of the sky, and then, for fear such a notable secret should get out (why not hold their tongues?) wrap it up in a filthy tale so that no one could understand the telling" (271).[18] Stated in that way, the justification of myth seems believable only if we assume that primitive people were stupid as well as lacking in technology. A major purpose of *Till We Have Faces* is to deny this superficial view of myth, a view which also is involved in the demythologizing of the Gospels.

A third purpose of myth, the one Lewis espouses, is to foreshadow the coming of Christ and to build up metaphors and mental pictures through which pagans can understand the significance of the Incarnation when they hear of it. In the second part of the story, he portrays the dissemination of the Psyche myth as an event brought about by God— the God of Christian revelation. As Orual speculates, the gods must have put the story into someone's mind "in a dream, or an oracle, or however they do such things" (243). The myth of Psyche and Cupid is available to depict the relationship of the soul and Christ because, as Lewis said in *The Pilgrim's Regress,* "the Landlord succeeded in getting a lot of messages through" (153).

The second part of the novel validates the message by showing how the gods act to prepare Orual's heart for the coming of the God of Love. In the story, of course, he is still Eros, the son of Aphrodite (or Ungit), but in the process he becomes more and more identified with Christ.

The process begins when Orual labors over her book, for the writing changes her heart by forcing her to be more objective. (Perhaps we may say that she reflects upon "the extreme improbability—by historical standards—of [her] own life.") When the book is completed, she has a chance interview with Tarin, her sister Redival's former lover. His very different memory of what happened chips a piece from her self-centeredness by suggesting that she had contributed to Redival's loneliness. The next interview, with Bardia's widow Ansit, is more than a chip; Ansit's accusation that Orual loved Bardia selfishly cracks her stony heart down the middle. In despair, Orual asks Arnom the priest, "Who is Ungit?" (270), but he is unable to answer her.

In a series of visions she begins to learn the mythic significance of her historical experience. In the first vision she meets her dead father who forces her to see her face in the mirror, causing her to cry out in repentance, "I am Ungit" (276). In other visions she experiences the tasks of Psyche, such as gathering the golden fleece and bringing water from Hades to Ungit-Aphrodite. Brought before the court of the gods and required to read her book, she realizes that her complaint against the gods is self-answering: "To have heard myself making it was to be answered" (294). The Fox takes her to a chamber where there are living pictures on the walls, and she sees her own contribution to the tasks of Psyche—that she and Psyche have borne each other's pain as they lived their separate lives. The Fox tells her that she is Everyone: "All, even Psyche, are born into the house of Ungit. And all must get free from her" (301). Her life is now seen as the enactment of a myth. Finally Orual understands that she has been delivered from the ugliness of Ungit by performing Psyche's tasks. She comes to complete self-knowledge and is able to meet Psyche face to face, cleansed and forgiven.

In *The Pilgrim's Regress,* the wise hermit, History, says that God revealed Himself to the pagans by sending dreams and visions among them. Orual's life story was apparently communicated to others such as Psyche's priest "in a dream, or an oracle," and its significance is communicated to her by visions that have the flavor of myth (as contrasted with the history of the first part of the book). The history of Psyche, Orual and the god-husband has become a myth, one which will acquire a deeper meaning after Christ becomes Incarnate—after the myth-become-fact validates the pagan myths. As the Fox tells Orual, "This age of ours will one day be the distant past. And the Divine Nature can change the past. Nothing yet is in its true form" (305).

Orual's final vision, a meeting with the Divine Bridegroom, is an encounter with the grace of Christ, even though Lewis tactfully avoids describing the god. He is careful to remember, as some critics are not, that *Till We Have Faces* is a work of "(supposed) historical imagination." It is impossible for Orual to see the Divine Bridegroom as the historical Jesus, and it would be anticlimactic for her to see him as the Eros of a Greek sculptor. "For what you see and hear depends a good deal on where you are standing" (*Nephew* 125), and Orual is unable to stand in a later historical period. Nevertheless, the Divine Goodness is not limited to the revelation to "the Shepherd People"; Orual has received grace, so that, although she thinks it "strange," she "dared" to look up at him (*Faces* 308).

This encounter with the god is artistically contrasted with Orual's experience of the god on the mountain. She did see him there, but her categories of perception were so completely destroyed that she could not judge the god's size or exact location: "Its face was far above me, yet memory does not show the shape as a giant's. And I do not know whether it stood, or seemed to stand, on the far side of the water or in the water itself" (172). On the mountain, the god looked down on her with "passionless and measureless rejection" (173). His words "You also shall be Psyche" constitute a judicial sentence. In the final vision, Orual perceives the god's compassion and acceptance, and when he says "You also are Psyche," it is equivalent to a "Well done, thou good and faithful servant."

The god Orual saw on the mountain is to the god of the vision as the Old Law of judgment is to the New Law of grace (in Christian theology, which is perhaps an oversimplified view of the Hebrew god). As the Fox promised, the past is being changed. The myth of Psyche is becoming part of the total tissue of the pagan worldview, part of the myth that became fact at the Incarnation of Christ.

Lewis regarded *Till We Have Faces* as perhaps his best work of fiction. It has missed the acclaim it deserves: some readers expect the kind of fantasy they enjoyed in his earlier works and refuse to be drawn into the gritty realism of the first part of the book, while others expect every work of Lewis's to be a forthright defense of Christianity and refuse to accept the fact-become-myth of the second part. The cure for such disappointment is to realize that Lewis is doing better and more difficult things than his readers demand of him. First, this novel vindicates the classical literature he loved so much by giving it a place within the Christian explanation of the universe. In additon, it counters the trend of biblical scholars, who were placing more and more of the Gospel materials into the category of the nonfactual, by showing how the myth of Psyche could be based on historical fact. The one who saw it refused to believe, but her refusal was based on question-begging and self-centeredness. Furthermore, the novel places in perspective the language philosophers' concentration on verifiable fact by showing that the priest's story, which had some error in detail, was closer to reality than the ostensibly exact account of Orual. Finally, it expands the concept of revelation for those who can say with Justin Martyr, "Whatever things [including myths] have been well said by all men belong to us Christians."

POSTSCRIPT

Let us now praise famous men, and our fathers in their generations.
. . . leaders of the people in their deliberations and in understanding
of learning for the people, wise in their words of instruction; those
who . . . set forth verses in writing . . . —all those were honored in
their generations, and were the glory of their times.

—Ecclesiasticus 44:1–7

C s. LEWIS in his generation defended the meaningfulness of language and its reference to a meaningful universe as the very basis
◆ of a truly human life. He wrote essays and works of fiction,
instructed students at Oxford, and counseled people from all over the
world. Although he has perhaps not been honored as much as he deserved,
in his own way he was the glory of his time.

Lewis's fiction witnessed to the ability of man, the spiritual animal, to
experience transcendent reality through language. Instead of ignoring the
contemporary scene to live in the past, as he is often accused of doing,
he used the wisdom of the past to confront the problems of the early
twentieth century, especially the distrust of language. He fought the low
view of language, which would make of the eternal Logos a mechanical
operation of word associations created by conditioning. Against this view
he asserted the "psycho-physical parallelism" of the universe—that the
metaphorical structure of language, the structure of the human mind,
and the nature of the universe are related to each other. His use of
archetypal metaphors in his first work of fiction, *The Pilgrim's Regress*,
was based on this assertion. He also fought the reductionism of the low
view of language by portraying John, or Everyman, with a hunger for joy
and reality that the Spirit of the Age could not satisfy.

The low view of language leads to a denial of traditional evaluations of ethical principles, and Lewis confronted it again in the Ransom trilogy. As a whole the trilogy presented a critique of science and other kinds of learning practiced apart from the moral and spiritual law of the universe. By outdoing his Wellsian models in *Out of the Silent Planet* and *Perelandra,* Lewis showed us that lowly genre fiction can be morally passionate, stylistically skillful, and in some ways more interesting than morally neutral "serious" literature. In *That Hideous Strength* he tried, without complete success, to push science fiction to its limits by combining it with elements of the realistic novel. Each of the three novels focuses on a particular branch of science—cosmology in *Out of the Silent Planet,* biology in *Perelandra,* and the so-called social sciences in *That Hideous Strength.*

Each of the three confronts particular fallacies of the Spirit of the Age. In *Out of the Silent Planet,* the medieval cosmology denies the terrible silence of infinite space and the right of human beings to defy death through space travel. By depicting a social structure founded on joy and play, Lewis confronted both the grim economics of Wellsian social planners and the self-conscious snobbery of the Vigilant School of literary criticism. In *Perelandra,* he confronted modernist misinterpretations of the theory of evolution, especially the idea that there is no design in the universe. His joy in biological variety is unusual; no other science fiction writer has created an imaginary world with more vividly conceived animals and plants. Finally, in *That Hideous Strength* he confronted the modern reverence for science, the fallacy of attempting to apply the scientific method to human beings, and the danger of social control. He shows how the attempt to reduce language, the moral law, and the human personality to mere phenomena leads to Babel. Taken as a whole, the three books dramatize Lewis's conviction that a human being is not primarily a bundle of impulses and desires, and language is not hopelessly divided between referential language that refers to facts and emotive language that refers to nonexistent values, as the Ogden and Richards approach asserted.

At first glance, the Chronicles of Narnia might seem to represent a retreat from the struggle with modern problems. In them Lewis turned to another usually underrated genre, fantasy for children, taking his youthful protagonists to a medieval world where there is no New Criticism and no science—not even medieval science. The new genre, however, was in no way a retreat. By writing the seven stories, Lewis took on the task he had described many years before in *The Abolition of Man*—to train young

people, through pleasure, in making the right aesthetic and ethical responses. He does this, not as a Controller or Conditioner, but as "a Roman
father. . . giving the boy the best he had, giving of his spirit to humanize
him as he had given of his body to beget him" (*Abolition* 31–32). In the
Chronicles Lewis gave children the best he knew, the heroism and narrative
technique of Spenser's *Faerie Queene* and also the classical culture that so
enriched his own life. He did not give them Christian dogmas to be
memorized, but an opportunity to experience the civilizing and matur-
ational effect of imaginative cognition.

Finally, in *Till We Have Faces*, Lewis showed how the language philosophers' cool objectivity and insistence on verifiable fact might, like Orual's,
be contaminated by self-interest. Subtly and indirectly, he explored the
nature of history in relation to fact and myth, showing that the demythologizers' denial of historicity to the Gospel story may be similarly
contaminated. He also reasserted the "psycho-physical parallelism" of the
universe by finding validity in the myth-making capacities of paganism.
Just as the Chronicles offer to children a training of the stock responses
in an experience of reading that is like living, *Till We Have Faces* offers
to adults an imaginative reliving of the experience of conversion—of
discovering one's inner ugliness and need of grace. His last work of fiction
is thus a completion of the first, for *The Pilgrim's Regress* also offered an
experience of conversion. First and last and in between, Lewis's fiction
"proclaimed prophecies" and combined pleasure with his "wise words of
instruction."

Today I. A. Richards's New Criticism, or Formalism as it is now called,
is no longer new and exciting. But a new generation of literati goes much
farther in promoting a low view of language. Where the formalists denied
that literary art referred to objective values or had any significance outside
itself and its ability to adjust attitudes, present-day deconstructionists are
denying that literary works have any stability of meaning at all. Where
King and Ketley said that a value statement is "only saying something
about [one's] own feelings," a deconstructionist like de Man denies that
it is possible to say "something." The new "meaning of meaning" states
that grammar and logic produce an illusion of coherence, but each verbal
construct can be deconstructed, thus depriving it of any objective, agreed-
upon meaning, whether referential *or* emotive.

Like Lewis's early twentieth century, the threshold of the twenty-first
century where we stand is the best of times and the worst of times, a

time that needs successors to Lewis. In his fiction Lewis preserves the possibility of meaning in literature and the traditional values of Western culture. His stories present in simplified form the images of classical and northern mythology as well as the philosophical beauties of Plato, Dante, Spenser, and Milton—the great writers who, in accordance with today's literary fashion, are dismissed as "dead white males." Lewis followed the classical and medieval tradition of telling old stories in new forms—as Chaucer put it, "getting new corn out of old fields." He also followed the time-honored tradition of expressing high thoughts in a lowly medium. As the New Testament was written in koiné rather than classical Greek, as Jerome translated the Bible into Vulgar rather than classical Latin, as Dante and Chaucer chose to write in their native tongues instead of Latin, so Lewis chose to write science fiction and fantasy instead of the new forms of the novel being developed by artists of the high culture such as Joyce and Woolf.

We need a new generation of writers and intellectuals who are willing to confront the issues of their own time as Lewis did, who are willing to spend their story-making talents in bringing joy and merriment and good sense to fiction, often in nonprint forms, since the number of people who read for pleasure grows steadily smaller. Such successors are not easy to find, and those who exist usually lack Lewis's broad education in the classics, his deep perception of myth and dream, and especially his easy, lucid style. But one can always reread Lewis.

NOTES

1. See Robert E. Longacre's review for an evaluation of Urban's *Language and Reality* from a linguist's point of view.

2. John Wain says Lewis's "chief allegiances" were to the Edwardian age, that Lewis "noticed the 1920s only to draw away from them in hostile dissent," and that "he disliked modern literature because it reflected modern life" (71).

3. See Roy Harris's Preface to *Linguistic Thought in England, 1914–1945.*

4. Qtd. in Ogden and Richards 18n.

5. Lewis and Barfield met at Oxford, just as Ogden and Richards met at Cambridge. After he wrote *Poetic Diction* and *History in English Words* (1926), financial need forced Barfield to leave Oxford and become a solicitor. Ogden is best known for his invention of Basic English, fictionalized as Newspeak in George Orwell's *Nineteen Eighty-Four.* He translated Wittgenstein's *Tractatus Logico-Philosophicus* in 1922 and was well acquainted with Russell's thought (Wolf 86–87, 93–94). I. A. Richards developed the low view of language into the New Criticism, sometimes called Formalism, that dominated English studies during Lewis's career.

6. They use the term "engram" (literally, "scratching"), coined by Semon, to explain how this comes about. Physical stimuli leave "residual traces" on the brain that contribute to the individual's present response to a similar stimulus. See Wolf's critique of the engram theory, 97–99.

7. Here they anticipate the Chomskyan definition of metaphor in terms of the violation of selectional restrictions.

8. One can only speculate that they had never conversed with country folk, or even Cockneys.

9. The first edition of *Poetic Diction* implicitly refutes *The Meaning of Meaning,* although Barfield notices it only with a passing remark that the authors have written "a long and clever book on Meaning" without grasping its essential characteristic, the relationship of meaning to metaphor (134). In the preface to the second edition, he asserts that his theory of poetry is a refutation of *The Meaning of Meaning* and linguistic analysis in general— that it is, in fact, "not merely a theory of poetic diction, but a theory of poetry: and not merely a theory of poetry, but a theory of knowledge" (14). Although I used all three editions in the preparation of this manuscript, all page references are to the third edition.

10. Basic English is the model for Orwell's Newspeak in *Nineteen Eighty-Four,* the basic premise of which is that the reduction of vocabulary leads to the destruction of thought.

11. Barfield's insight is a remarkable anticipation of Thomas Kuhn's "paradigm shift" in *The Structure of Scientific Revolutions.*

12. See the Afterword (1972) to Barfield's *Poetic Diction,* 218, 221.

13. Barfield's epigram harmonizes with J. R. R. Tolkien's tart comment in 1938 that mythology is no more a disease of language than thinking is a disease of the mind. Incidentally, Tolkien adds another epigram to the nosegay: "The incarnate mind, the tongue and the tale are in our world coeval" ("On Fairy-Stories" 21–22).

14. The unspellable title of the essay is suggested by a passage in *Poetic Diction* in which Barfield imagines what would happen if Shelley's line "My soul is an enchanted boat" in *Prometheus Unbound* should give rise to a new word, "chambote." The original meaning of the word would be "the concept 'soul' as enriched by Shelley's imagination" (66), and it would exist in accordance with Barfield's assertion that our concepts of the world are "reflected" in words. Barfield then goes on to speculate about what might happen as the metaphorical nature of the original word was forgotten. In *Studies in Words* (1960), Lewis returned to "chambote" to spell out exactly what Shelley's imagination would add to the concept "soul" (217). Barfield's complaint (in 1985) that scholars are inaccurate when they attribute "to Lewis ideas or opinions they find in Barfield" (*C. S. Lewis* 111) must be balanced against this verbal resemblance.

It is interesting to note that Ogden and Richards create a word, "wousin," to stand for "the group of phenomena involved or connected in the transit of a negro over a rail-fence with a melon under his arm while the moon is just passing behind a cloud" and use it to make the point that there is no necessary relationship between the symbol and its referent, that "the primitive idea that Words and Things are related by some magic bond" is false (46–47).

15. Between the publication of *The Meaning of Meaning* in 1923 and Lewis's essay in 1939, others had augmented the thought of Ogden and Richards by asserting that even though such words are metaphorical in origin, they are now dead as metaphor. Composition textbooks began to include exercises of classifying metaphors as Living, Dead, or Dying (no longer felt as figurative but not yet arbitrary). Students were told that the use of dying metaphors would lead to solecisms and mental confusion and were marked down for them.

16. This is indeed an archetype rather than an influence, since according to Carpenter (57), Lewis apparently read *The Hobbit* in early 1933, after he had written *The Pilgrim's Regress.*

17. For example, Dante uses this metaphor in *The Inferno,* Canto 31, in which one of the giants is Nimrod, the builder of the tower of Babel.

18. Identified by Haigh, "Fiction" 42.

19. Richards cites it approvingly in *Principles* 73.

20. Noel glosses *Eschropolis* as obscenity (8).

21. Christopher cites an unpublished letter in which Lewis identifies Victoriana with Edith Sitwell (*C. S. Lewis* 11).

22. *Science and Poetry* 79. Since this work was not published until 1935, it is not a direct source for Lewis's satire.

23. *Principles of Literary Criticism* (2nd ed.) 292. Again, this can not be a direct source of Lewis's satire.

24. Barfield made this explicit statement against linguistic analysis in the preface to the second edition of *Poetic Diction* (1952), so it is not a direct influence on Lewis's characterization of the Three Pale Men.

25. Patrick 112–13; see also Carnell 129–30.

26. A classical and medieval form, allegorical and philosophical, which artistically alternates prose with verse.

2. THE CONTEXT OF LITERARY CRITICISM AND GENRE

1. In Lewis, *Selected Literary Essays.*

2. CSL to Joy Davidman, Dec. 22, 1953, Wade Collection, The Marion E. Wade Center, Wheaton College, Wheaton, Illinois.

3. John G. Cawelti, in his study of genre fiction, attributes this attitude to the fact that "our age places a particularly high value on innovation and originality" and therefore "automatically relegate[s] [genre fiction] to an inferior artistic status" (qtd. in Aldiss 445). Lewis as a scholar in medieval and renaissance literature and Tolkien as a philologist did not overvalue "innovation and originality."

4. All but three of these essays are reprinted in *Selected Literary Essays.* See Walter Hooper, "A Bibliography of the Writings of C. S. Lewis" in Como 250–88.

5. See Robert B. Meyers for a recent analysis of *An Experiment in Criticism.*

6. Of course, *An Experiment in Criticism* was not Lewis's first attack on Richards's system. In "Christianity and Culture" (1940) he wrote: "This great atheist critic found in a good poetical taste the means of attaining psychological adjustments which improved a man's power of effective and satisfactory living all round, while bad taste resulted in a corresponding loss. Since this theory of value was a purely psychological one, this amounted to giving poetry a kind of soteriological function; it held the keys of the only heaven that Dr. Richards believed in" (*Christian Reflections* 12).

7. F. R. Leavis in *The Great Tradition* (1948) was the prime exponent of realist fiction. According to Haigh, he was the master of the Vigilant school of critics that Lewis combated in *An Experiment in Criticism.* The headnote of *The Great Tradition* was a quotation from D. H. Lawrence: "One has to be so terribly religious, to be an artist" (Haigh, in *Word and Study* 184). Since my topic is Lewis's combat with the low view of language and Richards's criticism is explicitly related to *The Meaning of Meaning,* I naturally focus on Richards rather than Leavis.

8. Lewis appears to have contradicted this viewpoint earlier in *The Allegory of Love* in praising Spenser's *Faerie Queene* for its contribution to mental health (see chapter 4). The difference is in motive; he expects readers to go to *The Faerie Queene* for pleasure and to gain mental health as a by-product.

9. Lewis dramatizes this fear in his treatment of the dwarfs in *The Last Battle.*

10. Brian W. Aldiss, in *Trillion Year Spree,* a history of science fiction, discusses Kafka's *The Castle,* on one line calling it "a sort of *haute* SF" and on another "manifestly . . . not SF." He also says it does not "fit into the symbolist camp" (181, 180).

11. Aldiss notes that it has always been impossible to draw a line between science fiction and fantasy (155). Lewis praises *Fantasy and Science Fiction* as "the best of the American magazines" because it does not rule out either one (*On Stories* 63).

12. Michael Bell calls Joyce's use of myth ironic because heroic Greece is juxtaposed with unheroic Dublin. Science fiction, in contrast, gives weight to ancient myths by retelling them in new settings. Edens, Isles of Circe, golden fleeces and metamorphoses occur over and over. Robert Heinlein's "Universe" retells Plato's myth of the cave, and James Tiptree, Jr.'s "Houston, Houston, Do You Read?" takes us to the country of the Amazons.

13. See Bleiler's more comprehensive classification in *Science-Fiction: The Early Years* (1990).

14. But cf. Wollheim (51–52), who regards only *Silent Planet* as belonging to the science fiction genre.

15. Although Lewis cited David Lindsay's *Voyage to Arcturus* as an influence on his science fiction, the resemblance to *First Men in the Moon* is much closer. Concerning Lindsay, see Glover 33, 74–76.

16. Aldiss remarks, "But questions of categorization arise again in the nineteen-eighties, when many novels announced on publishers' lists as SF are undisguised fantasy, and SF which does not affront our sense of veracity is harder to find than at any time since the twenties" (155).

17. See Hillegas, *The Future as Nightmare* (1967) 135, and Filmer 43–54. I am personally indebted to Boenig's treatment of the resemblances.

18. Hillegas, citing Nicholson, notes that the idea of the hollow moon comes from Kepler's *Somnium* (51).

19. See Lewis's *Studies in Words* (ch. 5) on the relationship between freedom of action and magnanimity or generosity.

20. See Myers, "What Lewis Really Did to *The Time Machine* and *The First Men in the Moon*" *Mythlore* 49 (Spring 1987): 47–50, 62.

21. Chad Walsh summarizes Ransom's reeducation as follows: "[Ransom] now *knows* the truths he once believed as an heroic act of faith. Never again will he listen to the Enemy's chatter about 'cold, dead space.' Never again will he blaspheme against the meaningfulness of God's universe" (in Schakel, *Longing* 70–71). He emphasizes Ransom's education in bravery rather than the broader issues of economics and aesthetics. Glover quotes a 1951 letter in which Lewis complains that "No one else sees that the first book is Ransom's *enfances* [sic]: if they notice a change at all, they complain that in the later ones he 'loses the warm humanity of the first etc.'" (78).

22. Aldiss emphasizes the gap between the low-brow American SF magazines "devoted to gosh-wowery" and the more high-brow productions of British novelists Aldous Huxley and Olaf Stapledon (176–77). Lewis, with his unarguable learning and unselfconscious choice of reading, deemphasizes this gap.

23. See Robert Houston Smith 92. He quotes from *That Hideous Strength* as follows: "For this was the language spoken before the Fall and beyond the Moon and the meanings were not given to the syllables by chance, or skill, or long tradition, but truly inherent in them as the shape of the great Sun is inherent in the little waterdrop" (229). See also the use of True Speech as symbol in Ursula K. Le Guin's Earthsea Trilogy.

24. *Silent Planet* 137; the "Beyond" is from the final sentence of George Bernard Shaw's *Back to Methuselah* (Christopher, *C. S. Lewis* 92).

25. Weston's grandiose "It is not by tribal taboos and copy-book maxims that [Life] has pursued her relentless march" (136) is remarkably similar to a line from the *Soldier's Pocket Book for Field Service*, quoted by Odgen and Richards, to the effect that traditional maxims of morality are nothing more than "pretty sentence[s] . . . for a child's copy-book" (*Meaning* 17).

26. "The floor [of Ransom's room] was so small that the bed and a table beside it occupied the whole width of it" (22). Compare the calculation in Heinlein's "Misfit," in which an asteroid a hundred miles in diameter has a horizon less than a third of a mile away (*Revolt in 2100* 179–80).

27. Heinlein's work provides a useful standard for what constituted science fiction in the 1940s and 1950s; no one has ever said his work was not science fiction, and he maintained a high level of factual accuracy. But even he could not foresee the personal computer. Some examples of the intrusive references to slide rules in his juvenile novels are *Space Cadet:* "I see you type, use a slide rule and differential calculator" (70); *Red Planet:* "Frank got out his slide rule" (73); *Between Planets:* Don made a small pile of "indispensable clothing, a few capsules of microfilm, [and] his slide rule" (11); *The Rolling Stones:* Hazel threatens her genius grandson, "No, don't start whimpering—or I'll take your slide rule away from you for a week" (29).

28. In fact, the difference between the area of the floor and the area of the ceiling would be so great that a wall and the floor would form a perceptibly obtuse angle.

29. In the *Cosmographia*, *"Oyarses"* means "governor." See Dronke's introduction to his edition of Bernardus (41–42) and Wetherbee's introduction to his translation (44).

30. See Collings 101–02, 107n1.

31. Linguist Suzette Hadin Elgin's science fiction novel, *Native Tongue*, is based on the speculation that all anthropomorphic extraterrestrials would have languages structurally similar to human languages. Her speculation is based on the linguistic theories of Noam Chomsky, which of course did not exist when Lewis was writing *Out of the Silent Planet*. His assumption that the Martian language would be intelligible is derived from his Christian belief that God created an intelligible universe. See Collings 107.

32. Samarin played a tape of glossolalia for a group of linguists and a group of medical doctors. The linguists first thought they were hearing "some Malayo-Polynesian language" but then "began to feel uncomfortable about their first appraisal." Among the doctors, "a few" called it "a made-up language" and "not a language" because "it just sounds monotonous" (104–05). Both groups were responding to the lack of linguistic patterning.

33. From the pen of Lewis himself come the acknowledgment of this literary debt: "*Voyage to Arcturus* is not the parody of *Perelandra* but its father" (Jan. 4, 1947, to Ruth Pitter; qtd. in Glover 33). In the same letter he says that "other planets in fiction are . . . good for . . . *spiritual* adventures" and that he is combining the fantasy of "the Novalis, G. MacDonald, James Stephens sort" and the science fiction of "the H. G. Wells, Jules Verne sort." Because my topic is Lewis's confrontation with the language philosophy of his time, I focus on the science fiction aspect.

34. In *The C. S. Lewis Hoax* (1988) Kathryn Lindskoog alleges that *The Dark Tower* was written as a literary hoax. Reviews of her book include Lyle W. Dorsett, *The Christian Century* 106.6 (Feb. 22, 1989): 208–09; David Bratman, *Mythlore* 15.3 (Spring 1989): 46–48; Nancy Jane Tyson, *Extrapolation* 31 (Fall 1990): 284–86; Brian Murray, *Modern Fiction Studies* 36 (Winter 1990): 618–19.

35. See Hannay for a careful comparison between *Perelandra* and Lewis's reading of *Paradise Lost*.

36. What Darwin really said was that random variations occur; if they have survival value within that specific environment, they will be preserved. See Rachels 71ff.

37. As an antivivisectionist, Lewis would have approved of the phraseology of the 1979 American *Book of Common Prayer*: "You formed us in your own image . . . so that . . . we might rule and serve all your creatures" (373).

38. *Fortnightly Review*, n.s. 50 (July 1891): 106–11; qtd. in Huntington 3, among other places.

39. Hannay, explicating *Perelandra* in relation to *Paradise Lost*, points out the issue of control: "The Green Lady is therefore tempted to stay on the Fixed Land . . . so that she can depend on her own will rather than the will of Maleldil" (86). The issue of control is implicit, but not explicit, in both Genesis ("the knowledge of good and evil") and Milton, where the emphasis seems to be on the serpent's acquisition of Reason and rhetorically skillful speech. See *Paradise Lost* 9:600, 670–78, 745–49.

40. Although the mountain is a natural phenomenon, it is like technology in that it provides a basis for the augmentation of man's unaided powers; indeed, all technology makes use of natural phenomena.

41. As Hannay points out, he also corrects some of the Miltonic details that are likely to be misunderstood by modern readers, especially in making the Un-man petty and disgusting instead of powerful and attractive, like Milton's Satan (73–74).

42. Heinlein uses this premise to depict Venus as an enormous swamp in his 1941 story "Logic of Empire," his 1947 *Saturday Evening Post* story "The Green Hills of Earth," and his 1951 young adult novel *Between Planets*.

43. Darwin himself said that both pain and pleasure are motivators in natural selection, but pleasure is more common. He believed, therefore, that the world contains more happiness than misery (Rachels 106).

44. The use of heartbeats to measure time in a nontechnological society is also a feature of Orual's narration in *Till We Have Faces*.

45. Bergson was not a Darwinian evolutionist, since he believed that evolutionary changes are not produced by random variation, but by the *elan vital,* a "'current of consciousness' that permeates living bodies" (Rachels 72).

3. THE CONTEXT OF LANGUAGE CONTROL

1. In *The Abolition of Man* Lewis also refers briefly to an earlier book, E. G. Biaggini's *The Reading and Writing of English* (1936), calling it "Orbilius."

2. Lewis's own literary theory on this point is ambiguous. In *An Experiment in Criticism* he said that a person who goes to literature for mental health is not serious about loving literature, but in *English Literature in the Sixteenth Century* he praises Spenser's poetry for training the reader's stock responses—another way of saying "the understanding of how to live."

3. For example, in *Miracles* Lewis says, "The description we have to give of thought as an evolutionary phenomenon always makes a tacit exception in favour of the thinking which we ourselves perform at that moment" (23).

4. It would be interesting, but beyond the scope of this book, to explore the relationship between dividing language into referential and emotive categories and experiencing the "dissociation of sensibility" which T. S. Eliot made famous.

5. The existence of this relationship in Lewis's mind, though never explicitly stated in *The Abolition of Man,* is supported by Aslan's remark in *The Magician's Nephew:* "Jokes as well as justice come in with speech" (119).

6. King and Ketley do not specifically define the reasoning process in this way, but their masters, Ogden and Richards, do.

7. G. E. Moore, in *Principia Ethica* (1903), called the drawing of ethical conclusions from physical facts the "naturalistic fallacy" and used the principle (derived from Hume) to refute Spencer's social Darwinism. See Rachels 66–67. Darwin himself believed that associationist psychology (apparently an earlier version of the engram theory) would explain how complex human mental operations arose without postulating what Greta Jones calls a "mysterious psychical origin" (14–15).

8. Vera Brittain, in *England's Hour* (1942), mentions the development of the chemical industry and the tank in addition to the airplane and the radio. She mourns the perverted use of the airplane, "which could have been used for the unification of the world and the saving of life" (225), and the radio, "which might have increased knowledge and brought distant peoples into friendly contact" (226). Her point is similar to Lewis's in that she attributes the destruction to "spiritual maladjustment," but she calls for a "scientific" study of moral values, while Lewis asserts that "ought" can never be derived from science's description of what "is."

9. According to Jones, the post–World War I "eugenics movement felt a mixture of apprehension and admiration at the progress of eugenics in Germany" (168). German eugenics was, of course, discountenanced in 1954 when the extent of its activity became

known. It is also worth remembering that not until the Lambeth Conference of 1930 did the Anglican Communion become "grudgingly permissive" toward contraception (Church of England 13).

10. The fear of being trapped in a closed circle of thought limitations appears in many twentieth-century science fiction works. E. M. Forster's "The Machine Stops" (1909) is a forerunner and a classic example of life in a closed environment. Robert A. Heinlein's "Universe" (1941; see *Orphans of the Sky*) depicts a spaceship whose inhabitants think there is nothing outside the hull. Gary K. Wolfe deals with the closed universe under two rubrics, "Icon of the Spaceship" and "Icon of the City."

11. In the 1952 preface to *Poetic Diction,* Barfield explains that Goethe "gave more attention to botany, zoology and scientific method than he did to poetry" and "grasp[ed] the reality of nature by participation"—in other words, he made his discoveries by imaginative insight rather than external analysis. Barfield also refers to "thinkers and experimentalists"— Steiner and his followers—who have "made notable advances in agriculture, medicine and elsewhere" by applying Goethe's method. This discussion in the preface is an expansion of the point Barfield makes in the original text that scientific knowledge is metaphorical and poetic in nature (138–40).

12. Cited by Glover 105, 219n and Griffin 218.

13. Robson qtd. by Glover 109; Glover himself praises the novel for its "unity and effectiveness of technique" (114). Carnell cites unfavorable opinions from Anne Fremantle, Theodore Spencer, and Dabney Hart but calls it his favorite of the trilogy despite its occasional "floundering bathos" (103–05).

14. Michael Collings, while agreeing that Lewis attacks scientism, suggests that "the presence of science itself—both in its abused state as 'scientism' and in its proper state as knowledge derived from observation—unites *That Hideous Strength*" ("Science and Scientism" 138).

15. Hart lists the Williams-like features of the novel as follows: "the realistic contemporary setting, the carefully drawn emotional and spiritual conflicts of an intellectual young husband and wife, the physical immanence of supernatural forces, the domesticated bear and the severed head, the prophetic dreams" (127). The significance given to the name "Logres" could be added to the list.

16. Or, as Christopher calls it, "olla podrida" (*C. S. Lewis* 98).

17. Purtill 94–96; Glover 118; Gregory Wolfe 70; Christopher, *C. S. Lewis* 98–102.

18. See Christopher on Lewis's use of Bracton in *English Literature in the Sixteenth Century* (*C. S. Lewis* 26–30).

19. "Poetic Diction and Legal Fiction" was not published until 1947 (in *Essays Presented to Charles Williams,* edited by Lewis), too late to be claimed as a direct influence on *Abolition* and *Strength.* Barfield does discuss Bacon in his 1926 study *History in English Words* (134–35), but his point seems more clearly stated in the essay. My citations to it are from Barfield's *The Rediscovery of Meaning and Other Essays.*

20. It is also a symbol of the Church, the protector and celebrator of human nature.

21. Manuel 47, cited in Patterson 7.

22. Thomas Aquinas's use of Aristotle in his synthesis of philosophy and Christian revelation, popularly believed to be the essence of medievalism, came later.

23. Patterson traces the history of bowling to at least the thirteenth century and concludes, "This bowling green . . . is England" (11).

24. Patterson suggests that Nathaniel Fox is a substitute for Rupert Brooke (17–18).

25. To trace all the resonances of the allusion to Versailles is beyond the scope of this book. I discuss it more fully in "Law and Disorder: Two Settings in *That Hideous Strength.*"

26. Hunt and Willis, eds., *The Genius of the Place*, 7.

27. Is there, perhaps, a reflection here of the scorn Lewis expressed toward King and Ketley for their prissy, middle-class remarks about cleanliness and good plumbing? See *Abolition* 41n.

28. Patterson discusses this passage in detail, showing that all the references are closely related to the story. She gives evidence that both the St. Anne's garden and the garden of Peter Rabbit are old-fashioned British cottage gardens. She also gives evidence that the "rose" of *The Romance of the Rose* is a Tudor rose, just as Jane's maiden name is Tudor, and states that it "forms the basis of the special iconography of the 'heraldic rose.'" It is also the rose at the center of Arthur's Round Table as depicted at Winchester Cathedral. She connects the reference to Klingsor's garden in *Parzifal* with the Arthurian motif of Lewis's novel, observing that Klingsor is a doublet for the Fisher-King, one of the names of Ransom. She points out that "the garden on the top of some Mesopotamian ziggurat" gave rise not only to the idea of Paradise, but also to the tower of Babel (21–23).

29. Of course, she does not fully experience the unified consciousness of ancient man— Barfield would regard that as impossible—but she does approach it.

30. *The Letters of C. S. Lewis to Arthur Greeves* 501. George Sayer, in *Jack: C. S. Lewis and his Times*, suggests that "the delightful Fellowship of St. Anne's . . . may be based on a group of young women who joined together before the war as fans of Williams, calling themselves 'the Household' or 'the Companions of the Coinheritance' [sic] and pledging themselves to follow his wishes" (178).

31. "Distributivism" (*Strength* 19) may have been suggested to Lewis by G. K. Chesterton's Distributism.

32. Glover makes this point more strongly. Even though he cites the letter to Father Peter Milward in which Lewis denies that the book is antiscience, Glover says it "presents . . . a condemnation of modern experimental science in nearly all its aspects: sociological, psychological, medical, and clinical" (109).

33. Filostrato is an illustration of Barfield's parable about the motor car of the universe in the preface to the second (1952) edition of *Poetic Diction*. One group of passengers is trying to discover the principles of internal combustion, while another group pushes and pulls levers to find out what will happen. Filostrato belongs to the second group. Even the goal of clearing organic life from the planet interests him more as a technique than as an expression of a principle.

34. Ironically, H. G. Wells agrees with Lewis on this point; in 1906 he read a paper to this effect, "The So-Called Science of Sociology" (Hillegas, *Future* 57).

35. The first letter (July 4, 1955, to Peter Milward) is cited by Glover (77). The second, also in the Wade Collection, is to Joseph M. Canfield, Feb. 28, 1955. Collings is one of the few critics who discusses MacPhee as a scientist. See his "Science and Scientism" 132.

36. The same might be said of Lewis's treatment of contraception and wifely submission.

4. THE CONTEXT OF CHRISTIAN HUMANISM

1. Secular humanism is described as the opposite of Christian humanism by T. F. McMahon: while Christian humanism is "eschatological and incarnational," secular humanism "postulates nature as the self-sufficing totality of being; appraising man's ordination toward eternal life as a degradation of his nature, it tends to emphasize current human values to the exclusion of man's relation to God and His divine providence."

2. See *Surprised by Joy* 213. Concerning Lewis's conversion, Carnell notes that "his thinking for the most part was shaped by older writers whose ideas have lived on in works well known to students of literature" (68).

3. The development of his attitudes toward the Christian value of literature is usefully summarized in Carter's "Sub-Creation and Lewis's Theory of Literature" in Edwards 129–37.

4. The Clark Lectures, which became the basis of *English Literature in the Sixteenth Century Excluding Drama*, were delivered the year after the Riddell Lectures, which comprised the first version of *Abolition*. The introductory chapter, entitled "New Learning and New Ignorance," at first seems antihumanist, for it expresses distaste for renaissance scholarship in Greek and Latin. But what Lewis disliked about the renaissance humanists was their concern with purity of style to the detriment of content and their overserious misunderstanding of the ancients. Oddly enough, he seems to have disliked them for the same reason he disliked the New Critics—their approach to literature lessened the sense of freedom and recreation that were so important to him.

5. Huttar, in "A Lifelong Love Affair," documents Lewis's dislike of the "Prufrock" image by citing a letter to Kathryn Farrer (Feb. 9, 1954, Wade Collection), "A Confession" in *Poems* (1), and *A Preface to "Paradise Lost"* (56).

6. The idea of writing a children's story for oneself is not an uncommon one. Arthur Ransome, quoting Stevenson, says, "You just indulge the pleasure of your heart. You write not for children but for yourself" (Crouch 17).

7. Stephen Medcalf designates this time as an "intermediate period" in which Lewis was concerned with "the strengthening of his persona" as a defender of Western culture. He wrote the Chronicles between 1948 and 1954, delivered the Cambridge inaugural address in 1954, and gave his Cambridge lectures on *The Faerie Queene* thereafter. Medcalf believes Lewis's reevaluation of himself may have been motivated by G. E. M. Anscombe's attack, using the categories and methods of linguistic philosophy, on Lewis's theological work *Miracles* (Schakel and Huttar 114–29).

8. Wilson implies that Lewis was fooling himself in describing "his conversion to Christianity as a cerebral and intellectual affair" (252). He may be influenced by the modernist assumption that religious conversion is per se a matter of emotion rather than intellect; in a letter to Rhona M. Bodle (Dec. 31, 1947) Lewis describes his own conversion as "gradual and intellectual" in contrast to St. Paul's, which was "sharp and catastrophic."

9. Glover suggests that two of Lewis's motives for writing were "the spiritual exercise [which he] now identified with the creative act of fiction writing" and "perhaps" the "psychological insistence" of his pictures, nightmares, and dreams (134).

10. It is sometimes argued that *Surprised by Joy* is almost as much a fictional construct as the works professing to be fiction. Wilson calls it "really a glorious sort of comic novel" (252). Nevertheless, Lewis was working in a nonfiction form, and I believe he was telling the truth as it appeared to him.

11. Schakel makes this point when he says, "Lewis seems to have intended that [the Chronicles] awaken in a child a love for Aslan and for goodness" (*Reading* 134).

12. In *English Literature in the Sixteenth Century* Lewis even says that "Richards' conception of the poem as a health-giving adjustment of impulses" applies to *The Faerie Queene* (393). His admiration for Spenser on this ground seemingly contradicts what he says against using literature for this purpose in *An Experiment in Criticism,* but in the latter he is exaggerating in order to make his point against the Vigilant critics and to maintain the all-important sense of play in literature.

13. As Hart notes, "*The Faerie Queene,* virtually unknown to modern readers, was for Lewis the touchstone for imaginative literature" (54).

14. For Tolkien's reaction to Spenser, Green and Hooper quote Lewis's diary (88). For his dislike of syncretism, see Carpenter 224. But cf. Christopher's detailed discussion of Tolkien's reaction in "J. R. R. Tolkien, Narnian Exile."

15. See Myers, "The Compleat Anglican," for comments on the Anglican approach to conversion as a process more than a life-changing moment in time.

16. Critics have connected the seven Chronicles with the Seven Virtues, the Seven Deadly Sins, and the Seven Sacraments. King and Hulan agree that gluttony is the central theme in *The Lion, the Witch, and the Wardrobe* and sloth in *The Silver Chair*, but they disagree on the others. Trupia relates the first three Chronicles to the theological virtues of love, faith, and hope, in that order, and the last four to the four cardinal virtues. He finds temperance, the opposite of gluttony, in *The Magician's Nephew* and fortitude, the opposite of sloth, in *The Last Battle*. Pietrusz partially follows my analysis ("The Compleat Anglican") in relating *Prince Caspian* to confirmation, *The Voyage of the Dawn Treader* to baptism (but not eucharist), and *The Horse and His Boy* to matrimony. It is a function of Lewis's excellent polysemy that all these readings "work" to an extent, but none, including my own, is definitive.

17. It is important to read the Chronicles either in the order of composition or the order of publication. (The only difference in these two orders is the reversal of *The Horse and His Boy* and *The Silver Chair*. The latter was written second but published first in order to keep the three Caspian stories together.) Early critics recommended reading the Creation story, *The Magician's Nephew*, first. In 1979 Schakel argued strongly that reading *Nephew* first spoils the tone of both it and *Lion* (*Reading* 143n6). See also Myers, "The Compleat Anglican" 184 and Ford, *Companion* (3rd ed.) xxxiv–xxxv. In a letter to a child Lewis says the chronological order is better than the order of publication (*Letters to Children* 68–69). Perhaps this opinion is a good example of what he said elsewhere about how authors are not necessarily the best interpreters of their own work (*Letters* 273).

18. My debt to Peter J. Schakel's *Reading with the Heart: The Way into Narnia* in my analysis of the Chronicles is immense. It is notable, however, that the training of feeling according to Spenserian (medieval-renaissance) didacticism does not involve the sharp distinction between emotion and cognition that is natural to modern people. Lewis is, I believe, working to recreate the state of mind obtained before the "dissociation of sensibility."

19. At the time of writing, Lewis apparently did not know that there would ever be a second chronicle, much less a seventh (see Ford xxxii). The way this detail foreshadows what will happen later is simply one more evidence of the creative power Lewis exercised in these stories.

20. Spenser 6.5.28; Lewis, *Spenser's Images* 88.

21. Schakel, *Reading* 140n; see also Green and Hooper 241.

22. Edmund is *restored* to kingship in that four thrones have been prepared for the children. As the White Witch says, "Four thrones in Cair Paravel. How if only three were filled? That would not fulfil the prophecy" (131).

23. The whole relationship between rhetoric and moral behavior, just hinted at here, is treated at length in *The Horse and His Boy*.

24. There is no doubt that Lewis himself found the panoply of classical gods deeply moving. In *Surprised by Joy*, after two chapters detailing his unhappiness at boarding school, he begins the next chapter by exclaiming, "Lies, lies! This was really a period of ecstasy. It consisted chiefly of moments when you were too happy to speak, when the gods and heroes rioted through your head, when satyrs danced and Maenads roared on the mountains" (118).

25. The reference to the Virgin Mary as *maris stella*, star of the sea, is an extension of this imagery, although Lewis as a thoroughgoing Protestant made no use of it. Because his

artistic purpose required that Reepicheep be the only animal aboard, he also made no use of the traditional identification of the Church with Noah's Ark.

26. I use the term that was current in Lewis's day rather than the term "Eucharist," which is more frequently used by Anglicans today.

27. Although technically people may shop around for a congregation that suits them, in *The Screwtape Letters* Lewis praises the commitment to the geographic parish (see ch. 16).

28. Lewis, ed., *George MacDonald Anthology* 21. There is also a resemblance to the description of the Lady Alice Quadrangle buildings as "humble, almost domestic" and belonging to "a sweet, Protestant world" (*That Hideous Strength* 20).

29. The contribution of this episode to the creation of people with chests is that it validates the experience of night fears, a validation heightened by the revision that Lewis made between the British and American editions. See Ford 149–51.

30. See Medcalf 109–10 for a comparison of the imagery in *Voyage* with a passage in *Surprised by Joy*. It is also reminiscent of a passage in *Mere Christianity:* "In one sense, the road back to God is a road of moral effort, of trying harder and harder. But in another sense . . . all this trying leads up to the vital moment at which you turn to God and say, 'You must do this. I can't'" (128).

31. It has some undeniable resemblances to the sacrament: the table is Aslan's Table, it holds the stone knife as a memorial of his passion, and it feeds the adventurers' real hunger (Schakel, *Reading* 62). But it also has some dissimilarities: the fear and doubt—not faith—with which the travelers approach the table, their inability to discern whether the magic is good or bad, and (the most important dissimilarity) the fact that Aslan is not present. Also, as a feast set only for "those who come so far" it is a poor image of a sacrament "generally necessary to salvation."

32. *The Annotated Book of Common Prayer* (Church of England) 434; see also the 1928 *Book of Common Prayer* (American) 580.

33. *Abolition* 14. The closed universe is not wholly a product of a low view of language. Other elements are the alienation from Nature caused by the rise of technology and the Cartesian notion that man is a machine, as amenable to control as other machines are.

34. *Surprised by Joy* 133–35; see also Green and Hooper 254.

35. In his lectures on Spenser, Lewis remarks that the dancing girls seen by Calidore are compared with the celestial dance of the stars (*Spenser's Images* 91; *The Faerie Queene* 6.10.13). It is noteworthy that Lewis, like Spenser, mentions the thumping of the feet (*Chair* 91).

36. Glover praises the scene highly: "It works both as a powerful statement of Lewis's belief in the validity of language as an expression of truth, and of imaginative literature as a moving and credible picture of that same truth" (169).

37. "For the wise men of old the cardinal problem had been how to conform the soul to reality, and the solution had been knowledge, self-discipline, and virtue" (*Abolition* 88).

38. See Cox's excellent discussion in "Epistemological Release in *The Silver Chair*."

39. Glover discusses the theme of *Horse* as "courage in the face of adversity" (157). However, courage is nothing more than the testing point of all other virtues, and thus is an element in all the Chronicles.

40. On his first adventure, Calidore, the hero of the Book of Courtesy, comes to a place where Briana, the lady of the castle, causes the hair of ladies and the beards of knights to be shaved off. She, "then [sic] which a prouder lady liveth none," is making a mantle of hair to win the love of the knight Crudor or Cruelty (6.1.14–15).

41. "The whole book is full of sweet images of humility" (*Allegory* 352).

42. In Book 6, canto 2, Spenser depicts a knight venting his displaced anger, perhaps a model for Rabadash.

43. King and Ketley are traditional enough to acknowledge the relationship between verbal expression and character in the introduction to *The Control of Language* (xiv), but they do not believe the traditional virtues are desirable.

44. There is an elaborated address when Edmund begins to tell Susan of their great danger: "My dear sister and very good Lady" (63), which can be explained as an expression of gentleness, since Edmund knows that what he is about to say will upset Susan very much.

45. Only one instance of this word is cited in the *Oxford English Dictionary.*

46. The only Narnian to use this old distinction is Queen Susan, who says to Shasta, thinking he is Corin, "Oh Corin, Corin, how could you? And thou and I such close friends ever since thy mother died" (58). She uses the "you" of polite address in her reproach and then switches to the "thou" of intimacy.

47. Lewis comments on the comparative plainness of Spenser's Book 6, denying that it is an indication that Spenser is "losing grip on the original conception of his poem" (*Allegory* 353). The same denial might be made about Lewis's miniature *Faerie Queene.*

48. The original quotation is as follows: "Now I take it that when we understand a thing analytically and then dominate and use it for our own convenience we reduce it to the level of 'Nature' in the sense that we suspend our judgements of value about it, ignore its final cause (if any), and treat it in terms of quantity" (*Abolition* 81).

49. *The Discarded Image* 35. Lewis's discussion of "the Lady 'Natura'" here and his essay on the word in *Studies in Words* both illuminate the tone of the creation of Narnia.

50. A full discussion of the identification of the Wood Between the Worlds in Lewis's story with Silva (as far as I know, an identification made here for the first time, although Silva has been seen as the origin of the trackless woods through which knights ride in romances) is beyond the scope of this work. See Lewis's discussion of *Bernardu's Cosmographia*, which he refers to as *De Mundi Universitate sive Megacosmus et Microcosmus*, in *Allegory* 90–98.

51. Letter to Rhona M. Bodle, June 24, 1949, Wade Collection, Wheaton College, Wheaton, Illinois.

52. The passage in which Lewis speaks of turning away from a scene to see it reflected in a mirror, "deeper, more wonderful, more like places in a story" (170) may seem like an error to many readers. After all, people are used to thinking of the reflection as less real than the object which caused it. But Lewis meant what he said; he was thinking of the celestial mirror of Urania, the muse of cosmic knowledge, in the *Cosmographia* of Bernardus Silvestris. Bernardus explains that the mirror is more real than what it reflects because it contains "ideas and exemplars, not born in time and destined not to pass away in time" (115).

5. THE CONTEXT OF MYTH AND HISTORY

1. On Lewis's use of his own life in the novel, see Christopher, "Archetypal Patterns in *Till We Have Faces*" 202–04.

2. Gellner paraphrases the verification principle as follows: "assertions not testable in certain approved ways, are not testable in those approved ways" (38).

3. Apr. 22, 1954, Wade Collection, Wheaton College, Wheaton, Illinois.

4. My account of the arguments about the life of Jesus is based on Neill's *The Interpretation of the New Testament, 1861–1961*. Parenthetical page numbers (on pp. 183–85) are from Neill unless otherwise indicated. Elsewhere cited as *Interpretation*.

5. See *Letters to Arthur Greeves* 425–28 and Carpenter 42–44.

6. In "Myth Became Fact" Lewis says, "We must not be ashamed of the mythical radiance resting on our theology. We must not be nervous about 'parallels' and 'Pagan Christs': they *ought* to be there—it would be a stumbling block if they weren't" (*God in the Dock* 67).

7. Walsh, *Literary Legacy* 162; see also Schakel, *Reason* 38 and 189n10.

8. As a general reference for this section I used Boardman, Griffin, and Murray, *Oxford History of the Classical World* (1986).

9. See Walker, *Mammals of the World* 1274–79. The maps I found most useful came from Breasted, et al. *European History Atlas* 10 and Shepherd, *Historical Atlas* 2–3, 12, 19.

10. Concerning silver, see Thomson 56 and passim for discussion of the Scythians.

11. Thomas Howard, "Myth: A Flight to Reality," in *The Christian Imagination: Essays on Literature and the Arts,* ed. Leland Ryken (Grand Rapids, MI: Baker Book House, 1981), 203; cited by Schakel in *Reason and Imagination in C. S. Lewis* 185n1.

12. Leopold characterizes the features of Lewis's nonfiction style as follows: "lucidity of argument; vividness of illustration; an immoderate use of quotation . . .; and a defiant old-fashionedness" (in Edwards 110). His discussion provides a baseline for judging the degree to which Lewis submerges his own voice so that Orual's can emerge. As subsequent analysis will show, the old-fashionedness is eminently appropriate for Orual.

13. See Schakel, *Reason* 188n4.

14. The impression of Schakel, who finds her language "slightly stiff, artificial" (*Reason* 7), is, as we shall see, borne out by close analysis.

15. According to Sayer, *Till We Have Faces* was written with some collaboration by Joy Davidman (later Joy Lewis), and three-quarters of it was finished during April 1954 (220).

16. I am indebted to Joe R. Christopher for pointing out that what I had thought of as a dilemma is really a "trilemma" (personal communication). Lewis uses the same form of argument in *The Lion, the Witch, and the Wardrobe* when Professor Kirke tells the older children that since Lucy is not mad and does not tell lies, she must be telling the truth—additional evidence, if any were needed, that Lewis did not talk down to his audience in his children's stories.

17. Although the depths of Psyche's valley are not quite as dramatic, the description of the place is reminiscent of the description of Adonis's valley in Frazer's *Golden Bough*:

> The hamlet stands among groves of noble walnut-trees on the brink of the glen. A little way off the river rushes from a cavern at the foot of a mighty amphitheatre of towering cliffs to plunge in a series of cascades into the awful depths of the glen. The deeper it descends, the ranker and denser grows the vegetation, which, sprouting from the crannies and fissures of the rocks, spreads a green veil over the roaring or murmuring stream in the tremendous chasm below. There is something delicious, almost intoxicating, in the freshness of these tumbling waters, in the sweetness and purity of the mountain air, in the vivid green of the vegetation. (5:28)

I am indebted to Thomas M. Myers for pointing out this passage.

18. Schakel points out that "Orual's words echo those used by Owen Barfield . . . to reply to the naturalistic theory of myths" (*Reason* 73).

WORKS CITED

Adey, Lionel. *C. S. Lewis's "Great War" with Owen Barfield*. English Literary Studies Monograph Series, No. 14. Victoria, BC: U of Victoria P, 1978.

Aldiss, Brian W. *Trillion Year Spree: The History of Science Fiction*. New York: Avon, 1988.

The Annotated Book of Common Prayer . . . of the Church of England. 2nd ed. Ed. John Henry Blunt. London: Longmans, 1892.

Augustine of Hippo. *The Confessions of St. Augustine*. Trans. Edward B. Pusey. New York: Random House, 1949.

———. *On Christian Doctrine*. Trans. D. W. Robertson, Jr. New York: Liberal Arts Press, 1958.

Ayer, A. J. *Language, Truth and Logic*. 1936. New York: Dover, n.d.

Barfield, Owen. *History in English Words*. London: Methuen, 1926.

———. *Owen Barfield on C. S. Lewis*. Ed. G. B. Tennyson. Middletown, CT: Wesleyan UP 1989.

———. *Poetic Diction*. 1928. 2nd ed. London: Faber and Faber, Ltd., 1952.

———. *Poetic Diction*. 1928. 3rd ed. Middletown, CT: Wesleyan UP, 1973.

———. *The Rediscovery of Meaning and Other Essays*. Middletown, CT: Wesleyan UP, 1977.

Bell, Michael, ed. *The Context of English Literature: 1900–1930*. New York: Holmes and Meier, 1980.

Bleiler, Everett F. *Science-Fiction: The Early Years*. Kent, OH: Kent State UP, 1990.

Boardman, John, Jasper Griffin, and Oswyn Murray. *Oxford History of the Classical World*. Oxford: Oxford UP, 1986.

Boenig, Robert E. "Lewis' Time Machine and His Trip to the Moon." *Mythlore* 2.7 (n.d.): 6–9.

Boethius. *The Consolation of Philosophy*. Trans. V. E. Watts. 1969. New York: Viking Penguin, 1984.

The Book of Common Prayer . . . According to the Use of the Episcopal Church. 1928.

The Book of Common Prayer . . . According to the Use of the Episcopal Church. 1979.

Bracton, Henry de. *De Legibus et Consuetudinibus Angliae* [*On the Laws and Customs of England*]. Ed. George E. Woodbine. Trans. and rev. Samuel E. Thorne. Cambridge: Harvard UP, 1968.

Breasted, James Henry, Carl F. Hath, and Samuel Bannister Harding. *European History Atlas*. 7th ed. Chicago: Denoyer-Geppert, 1947.

Brittain, Vera. *England's Hour*. New York: Macmillan, 1941.

Carnell, Corbin Scott. *Bright Shadow of Reality: C. S. Lewis and the Feeling Intellect*. Grand Rapids, MI: Eerdmans, 1974.

Carpenter, Humphrey. *The Inklings: C. S. Lewis, J. R. R. Tolkien, Charles Williams and their Friends*. London: George Allen and Unwin, 1978.

Carter, Margaret L. "Sub-Creation and Lewis' Theory of Literature." Edwards 129–37.

Chaucer, Geoffrey. *The Riverside Chaucer*. Ed. Larry D. Benson. Dallas: Houghton Mifflin, 1987.

Christopher, Joe R. "Archetypal Patterns in *Till We Have Faces*." Schakel, *Longing* 193–212.

———. *C. S. Lewis*. Twayne's English Author Series, No. 442. Boston: Twayne, 1987.

———. "J. R. R. Tolkien, Narnian Exile." *Mythlore* 55 and 56 (Autumn and Winter 1988): 37–45, 17–23.

Church of England Moral Welfare Council. *The Family in Contemporary Society*. London: SPCK, 1958.

Collings, Michael R. "Jesperson [sic] on Toast": Language Acquisition in C. S. Lewis." *Forms of the Fantastic: Selected Essays from the 3rd International Conference on the Fantastic in Literature and Film*. Ed. Jan Hokenson and Howard Pearce. New York: Greenwood Press, 1982.

———. "Science and Scientism in C. S. Lewis's *That Hideous Strength*." *Hard Science Fiction*. Ed. George E. Slusser and Eric S. Rabkin. Carbondale: Southern Illinois UP, 1986.

Como, James T., ed. "*C. S. Lewis at the Breakfast Table" and Other Reminiscences*. New York: Macmillan, 1979.

Conquest, Robert. "Science Fiction and Literature." Rose 30–45.

Covington, Michael A. "C. S. Lewis as a Student of Words." Schakel and Huttar 29–41.

Cox, John D. "Epistemological Release in *The Silver Chair*." Schakel, *Longing* 159–68.

Crouch, Marcus. *The Nesbit Tradition: The Children's Novel in England 1945–1970*. Totowa, NJ: Rowman and Littlefield, 1972.

Curtius, Ernst Robert. *European Literature and the Latin Middle Ages*. Trans. Willard R. Trask. New York: Harper and Row, 1953.

Dante Alighieri. *The Divine Comedy*. Rev. ed. 3 vols. Ed. John D. Sinclair. London: The Bodley Head, 1948.

Edwards, Bruce L., ed. *The Taste of the Pineapple*. Bowling Green, OH: Bowling Green State U Popular P, 1988.

Elgin, Suzette Haden. *Native Tongue*. New York: Daw Books, 1984.

Eliot, T. S. *The Complete Poems and Plays: 1909–1950*. 1934. New York: Harcourt, Brace, 1952.

Espey, John J. *Ezra Pound's "Mauberley": A Study in Composition.* Berkeley: U of California P, 1955.

Evans, B. Ifor. *English Literature Between the Wars.* London: Methuen, 1948.

Filmer, Kath. "*Out of the Silent Planet:* Reconstructing Wells with a Few Shots at Shaw." *Inklings Jahrbuch* 6 (1988): 43–54.

Flieger, Verlyn. "Language and Experience in *Out of the Silent Planet.*" Schakel and Huttar 42–57.

Ford, Paul F. *Companion to Narnia.* 1980. New York: Macmillan, 1986.

Forster, E. M. "The Machine Stops." *Science Fiction: The Science Fiction Research Association Anthology.* Ed. Patricia S. Warrick, Martin H. Greenberg, and Charles G. Waugh. New York: Harper and Row, 1988.

Frazer, Sir James George. *The Golden Bough.* 3rd ed. New York: Macmillan, 1951.

Fussell, Paul. *The Great War and Modern Memory.* New York: Oxford UP, 1975.

Gellner, Ernest. *Legitimation of Belief.* Cambridge: Cambridge UP, 1974.

Glover, Donald E. *C. S. Lewis: The Art of Enchantment.* Athens: Ohio UP, 1981.

Green, Roger Lancelyn, and Walter Hooper. *C. S. Lewis: A Biography.* 1974. New York: Harvest, 1976.

Griffin, William. *Clive Staples Lewis: A Dramatic Life.* San Francisco: Harper and Row, 1986.

Haigh, John D. "C. S. Lewis and the Tradition of Visionary Romance." Schakel and Huttar 182–98.

———. "The Fiction of C. S. Lewis," Ph.D. diss., University of Leeds, 1962.

Haldane, J. B. S. "Auld Hornie, F. R. S." Hillegas, ed. 15–25.

———. *Daedalus: or Science and the Future.* New York: E. P. Dutton, 1924.

Hannay, Margaret P. "A Preface to *Perelandra.*" Schakel, *Longing* 73–90.

Harris, Roy, ed. *Linguistic Thought in England, 1914–1945.* New York: Routledge, 1988.

Hart, Dabney Adams. *Through the Open Door: A New Look at C. S. Lewis.* University: U of Alabama P, 1984.

Heinlein, Robert A. *Between Planets.* New York: Ace Books, 1951.

———. *Beyond This Horizon.* 1942. New York: Signet, 1960.

———. *The Green Hills of Earth.* New York: New American Library, 1951.

———. "Logic of Empire." *The Green Hills of Earth.* New York: Signet, 1951.

———. *Red Planet.* New York: Ace Books, 1949.

———. *Revolt in 2100.* 1940. New York: Signet, 1953.

———. *The Rolling Stones.* New York: Ace Books, 1952.

———. *Space Cadet.* 1948. New York: Ballantine Books, 1978.

———. *Starman Jones.* 1953. New York: Ballantine Books, 1975.

———. *Stranger in a Strange Land.* 1961. New York: Berkley Medallion Book, 1968.

———. *Time for the Stars.* 1956. New York: Ballantine Books, 1978.

———. "Universe." 1941. *Orphans of the Sky.* New York: Ace Books, 1987.

Highwater, James. *Myth and Sexuality.* New York: New American Library, 1990.

Hillegas, Mark R. *The Future as Nightmare: H. G. Wells and the Anti-Utopians.* New York: Oxford UP, 1967.

Hillegas, Mark R., ed. *Shadows of the Imagination: The Fantasies of C. S. Lewis, J. R. R. Tolkien, and Charles Williams*. Carbondale: Southern Illinois UP, 1969.

Hulan, David. "Narnia and the Seven Deadly Sins." Narnia Conference Proceedings. Maywood, CA: The Mythopoeic Society, 1970. 21–23.

Hunt, John Dixon, and Peter Willis, eds. *The Genius of the Place: The English Landscape Garden 1620–1820*. New York: Harper, 1975.

Huntington, John. *The Logic of Fantasy: H. G. Wells and Science Fiction*. New York: Columbia UP, 1967.

Huttar, Charles A. "C. S. Lewis's Narnia and the 'Grand Design.'" Schakel, *Longing* 119–35.

———. "A Lifelong Love Affair with Language: C. S. Lewis's Poetry." Schakel and Huttar 86–108.

Hutton, Richard Holt. "Review in *Spectator*, 13 July 1895." *H. G. Wells: The Critical Heritage*. Ed. Patrick Parrinder. London: Routledge and Kegan Paul, 1972.

Huxley, Aldous. *Brave New World*. 1932. New York: Harper, 1989.

Jones, Greta. *Social Darwinism and English Thought: The Interaction between Biological and Social Theory*. Sussex, NJ: Humanities Press, 1980.

Keefe, Carolyn. *C. S. Lewis: Speaker and Teacher*. Grand Rapids, MI: Zondervan, 1971.

King, Alec, and Martin Ketley. *The Control of Language: A Critical Appraisal to Reading and Writing*. London: Longman, Green, 1939.

King, Don. "Narnia and the Seven Deadly Sins." *Mythlore* 10.4 (Spring 1984): 14–19.

Kuhn, Thomas. *The Structure of Scientific Revolutions*. 2nd ed. Chicago: U of Chicago P, 1970.

Leavis, Q. D. *Fiction and the Reading Public*. New York: Russell and Russell, 1965.

Leech, Kenneth. *Soul Friend: The Practice of Christian Spirituality*. San Francisco: Harper and Row, 1977.

Leopold, Paul. "Fighting 'Verbicide' and Sounding Old-Fashioned: Some Notes on Lewis's Use of Words." Edwards 110–27.

Lessing, Doris. *Re: Colonized Planet 5, Shikasta*. New York: Knopf, 1979.

Lewis, C. S. *The Abolition of Man*. 1943. New York: Macmillan, 1947.

———. *The Allegory of Love: A Study in Medieval Tradition*. 1936. London: Oxford UP, 1958.

———. "Bluspels and Flalansferes." *Selected Literary Essays* 251–65.

———. *C. S. Lewis: Letters to Children*. Ed. Lyle W. Dorsett and Marjorie Lamp Mead. New York: Macmillan, 1989.

———. *Christian Reflections*. Ed. Walter Hooper. Grand Rapids, MI: Eerdmans, 1967.

———. *The Chronicles of Narnia*. 1950–56. New York: Collier-Macmillan, 1974.

———. "*De Descriptione Temporum*." *They Asked for a Paper*. London: Geoffrey Bles, 1962. (See also *Selected Literary Essays*.)

———. *The Discarded Image*. 1964. Cambridge: Cambridge UP, 1970.

———. *English Literature in the Sixteenth Century*. New York: Oxford UP, 1954.

———. *An Experiment in Criticism*. Cambridge: Cambridge UP, 1961.

———. *God in the Dock.* Ed. Walter Hooper. Grand Rapids, MI: Eerdmans, 1970.

———. "High and Low Brows." *Selected Literary Essays* 266–79.

———. "Learning in War-Time." *The Weight of Glory.* Grand Rapids, MI: Eerdmans, 1949.

———. *Letters of C. S. Lewis.* Ed. W. H. Lewis. 1966. New York: Harvest-Harcourt Brace Jovanovich, 1975.

———. *Letters of C. S. Lewis to Arthur Greeves.* Ed. Walter Hooper. New York: Collier-Macmillan, 1979.

———. *Mere Christianity.* New York: Macmillan, 1952.

———. *Miracles: A Preliminary Study.* 1947. New York: Collier-Macmillan, 1978.

———. "Modern Theology and Biblical Criticism." *Christian Reflections* 152–66.

———. "Notes on the Way: George Orwell." *Time and Tide* 36 (Jan. 8, 1955): 43–44.

———. *On Stories.* Ed. Walter Hooper. 1966. San Diego: Harcourt Brace Jovanovich, 1982.

———. *Out of the Silent Planet.* 1938. New York: Macmillan, 1965.

———. *Perelandra.* 1943. New York: Macmillan, 1965.

———. *The Pilgrim's Regress: An Allegorical Apology for Christianity, Reason, and Romanticism.* 1933. London: Geoffrey Bles, 1950.

———. *A Preface to "Paradise Lost".* 1942. London: Oxford UP, 1961.

———. *The Screwtape Letters.* 1942. New York: Macmillan, 1961.

———. *Selected Literary Essays.* Ed. Walter Hooper. Cambridge: Cambridge UP, 1969.

———. *Spenser's Images of Life.* Ed. Alastair Fowler. Cambridge: Cambridge UP, 1967.

———. *Studies in Words.* Cambridge: Cambridge UP, 1960.

———. *Surprised by Joy: The Shape of My Early Life.* New York: Harcourt, Brace, and World, 1955.

———. *That Hideous Strength.* 1945. New York: Macmillan, 1965.

———. *Till We Have Faces.* 1956. New York: Harcourt, Brace, and World, 1957.

———. *Vivisection.* London: The National Anti-Vivisection Society, [1948].

Lewis, C. S., ed. *George MacDonald Anthology.* 1946. London: Geoffrey Bles, 1970.

Lewis, W. H. *The Splendid Century: Some Aspects of French Life in the Reign of Louis XIV.* London: Eyre and Spottiswoode, 1953.

Lindsay, David. *A Voyage to Arcturus.* New York: Ballantine, 1973.

Lindskoog, Kathryn. *The C. S. Lewis Hoax.* Portland, OR: Multnoma Press, 1988.

Longacre, Robert E. "Review of *Language and Reality* and 'Four Articles on Metalinguistics.'" *Language* 32.2 (Apr.-June 1956): 298–308.

McMahon, T. F. "Secularism." *New Catholic Encyclopedia.* Vol. 13. New York: McGraw-Hill, 1967. 36–38.

Manlove, Colin N. *C. S. Lewis: His Literary Achievement.* New York: St. Martin's Press, 1987.

Medcalf, Stephen. "Language and Self-Consciousness: The Making and Breaking of C. S. Lewis' Personae." Schakel and Huttar 114–29.

Milton, John. *Complete Poems and Major Prose.* Ed. Merritt Y. Hughes. New York: Odyssey, 1957.

Montague, C. E. *Disenchantment.* 1922. London: MacGibbon and Kee, 1968.

Meyers, Robert B. "'. . . the Abstractions Proper to Them': C. S. Lewis and the Institutional Theory of Literature." Edwards 37–56.

Myers, Doris E. T. "C. S. Lewis's Passages: Chronological Age and Spiritual Development in Narnia." *Mythlore* 41 (Winter-Spring 1985): 52–56.

———. "The Compleat Anglican: Spiritual Style in the Chronicles of Narnia." *Anglican Theological Review* 66 (Apr. 1984): 148–60.

———. "Law and Disorder: Two Settings in *That Hideous Strength.*" *Mythlore* 71 (Winter 1993): 9–14.

———. "What Lewis Really Did to *The Time Machine* and *The First Men in the Moon.*" *Mythlore* 49 (Spring 1987): 47–50, 62.

Neill, Stephen. *Anglicanism.* 1958. Baltimore: Penguin Books, 1960.

———. *The Interpretation of the New Testament, 1861–1961: The First Lectures, 1962.* London: Oxford UP, 1964.

Noel, Henry. "A Guide to C. S. Lewis's *The Pilgrim's Regress.*" *Bulletin of the N.Y. C. S. Lewis Society* 2 (Feb. 1971): 4–15.

Ogden, C. K., and I. A. Richards. *The Meaning of Meaning.* 1923. 8th ed. New York: Harcourt, Brace, and World, 1946.

Orwell, George. *Animal Farm.* 1946. New York: Signet Classics, 1961.

———. *Nineteen Eighty-Four.* 1949. New York: Signet Classics, 1962.

Owen, Wilfred. "Dulce et Decorum Est." *Norton Introduction to Literature: Poetry.* Ed. J. Paul Hunter. New York: W. W. Norton, 1973.

Patrick, James. *The Magdalen Metaphysicals: Idealism and Orthodoxy at Oxford, 1901–1945.* N.p.: Mercer UP, 1985.

Patterson, Nancy-Lou. "The Unfathomable Feminine Principle: Images of Wholeness in *That Hideous Strength.*" *The Lamp-Post* 9 (July 1986): 3–39.

Pietrusz, Jim. "Rites of Passage: The Chronicles of Narnia and the Seven Sacraments." *Mythlore* 54 (Summer 1988): 61–63.

Pound, Ezra. "E. P. Ode Pour L'Election de son Sepulchre." Espey 119–22.

Purtill, Richard L. "*That Hideous Strength:* A Double Story." Schakel, *Longing* 91–102.

Rachels, James. *Created from Animals: The Moral Implications of Darwinism.* New York: Oxford UP, 1990.

Ramsaye, Terry. "Robert Paul and *The Time Machine.*" *The Definitive Time Machine: A Critical Edition of H. G. Wells's Scientific Romance.* Ed. Harry M. Geduld. Bloomington: Indiana UP, 1987.

Reilly, R. J. *Romantic Religion: A Study of Barfield, Lewis, Williams, and Tolkien.* Athens: U of Georgia P, 1971.

Richards, I. A. *Practical Criticism.* 1929. New York: Harvest-Harcourt, Brace and Co., n.d.

———. *Principles of Literary Criticism.* New York: Harcourt, Brace, 1924.

————. *Science and Poetry.* London: Kegan Paul, Trench, Trubner, 1935.

Roetter, Charles. *The Art of Psychological Warfare 1914–1945.* New York: Stein and Day, 1974.

Rose, Mark, ed. *Science Fiction: A Collection of Critical Essays.* Englewood Cliffs, NJ: Prentice-Hall, 1976.

Sales, W. M. "Aphrodite." *Encyclopedia Britannica.* 14th ed. Chicago: William Benton, 1970. 2:110–11.

Samarin, William J. *Tongues of Men and Angels: The Religious Language of Pentecostalism.* New York: Macmillan, 1972.

Sandquist, T. A. "Bracton, Henry de." *Dictionary of the Middle Ages.* American Council of Learned Societies. New York: Charles Scribner's Sons, 1983.

Sandys, George. *Ovid's Metamorphoses Englished, Mythologized, and Represented in Figures.* 1632. Ed. Karl K. Hulley and Stanley T. Vandersall. Lincoln: U of Nebraska P, 1970.

Sayer, George. *Jack: C. S. Lewis and His Times.* San Francisco: Harper and Row, 1988.

Sayers, Dorothy L. *Unnatural Death.* 1927. New York: Avon, 1931.

Schakel, Peter J. *Reason and Imagination in C. S. Lewis: A Study of "Till We Have Faces."* Grand Rapids, MI: Eerdmans, 1984.

————. *Reading with the Heart: The Way into Narnia.* Grand Rapids, MI: Eerdmans, 1979.

Schakel, Peter J., ed. *The Longing for a Form: Essays on the Fiction of C. S. Lewis.* Kent, OH: Kent State UP, 1977.

Schakel, Peter J., and Charles A. Huttar, eds. *Word and Story in C. S. Lewis.* Columbia: U of Missouri P, 1991.

Shepherd, William R. *Historical Atlas.* 9th ed. New York: Barnes and Noble, 1964.

Silvestris, Bernardus. *Cosmographia.* Ed. Peter Dronke. Leiden: E. J. Brill, 1978.

————. *Cosmographia.* Records of Western Civilization. Trans. Winthrop Wetherbee. New York: Columbia UP, 1973.

Smith, Lyle H. "C. S. Lewis and the Making of Metaphor." Schakel and Huttar 11–28.

Smith, Robert Houston. *Patches of Godlight: The Pattern of Thought of C. S. Lewis.* Athens: U of Georgia P, 1981.

Spenser, Edmund. *The Complete Poetical Works of Spenser.* Boston: Riverside Press–Houghton Mifflin, 1908.

Thomson, J. Oliver. *History of Ancient Geography.* New York: Biblo and Tannen, 1965.

Tiptree, James, Jr. "Houston, Houston, Do You Read?" *Science Fiction: The Science Fiction Research Association Anthology.* Ed. Patricia S. Warrick, Martin H. Greenberg, and Charles G. Waugh. New York: Harper and Row, 1988.

Tolkien, J. R. R. *The Lord of the Rings.* 2nd ed. 3 vols. Boston: Houghton Mifflin, 1966.

————. "On Fairy-Stories." *Essays Presented to Charles Williams.* Oxford: Oxford UP, 1947. Rpt. in *The Tolkien Reader.* New York: Ballantine Books, 1966.

Trupia, Robert C. "Learning Christian Behavior: The Way of Virtue in *The Chronicles of Narnia*." *The Lamp-Post* 11.4 (Nov. 1988): 3–8.

Urban, Wilbur M. *Language and Reality: The Philosophy of Language and the Principles of Symbolism*. London: George Allen and Unwin Ltd., 1939.

Van Der Weele, Steve J. "From Mt. Olympus to Glome: C. S. Lewis's Dislocation of Apuleius's 'Cupid and Psyche' in *Till We Have Faces*." Schakel, *Longing* 182–92.

Wain, John. "A Great Clerke." Como 68–76.

Walker, Ernest P., et al. *Mammals of the World*. Baltimore: Johns Hopkins Press, 1964.

Walsh, Chad. *The Literary Legacy of C. S. Lewis*. New York: Harcourt Brace Jovanovich, 1979.

———. "The Reeducation of the Fearful Pilgrim." Schakel, *Longing* 64–72.

Weinbaum, Stanley G. "A Martian Odyssey." *Science Fiction: The Science Fiction Research Association Anthology*. Ed. Patricia S. Warrick, Martin H. Greenberg, and Charles G. Waugh. New York: Harper and Row, 1988.

Wells, H. G. *The First Men in the Moon*. 1901. *The Complete Science Fiction Treasury of H. G. Wells*. New York: Wings Books, 1978.

———. *The Time Machine*. 1898. *The Complete Science Fiction Treasury of H. G. Wells*.

Williams, Charles. *Many Dimensions*. 1931. Grand Rapids, MI: Eerdmans, 1970.

———. *The Place of the Lion*. 1933. Grand Rapids, MI: Eerdmans, 1972.

Williams, John. *The Other Battleground: The Home Fronts: Britain, France and Germany 1914–18*. Chicago: Henry Regnery, 1972.

Wilson, A. N. *C. S. Lewis: A Biography*. New York: W. W. Norton, 1990.

Wolf, George. "C. K. Ogden." Harris 85–105.

Wolfe, Gary K. *The Known and the Unknown: The Iconography of Science Fiction*. Kent, Ohio: Kent State UP, 1979.

Wolfe, Gregory. "Essential Speech: Language and Myth in the Ransom Trilogy." Schakel and Huttar 58–75.

Wollheim, Donald A. *The Universe Makers: Science Fiction Today*. New York: Harper and Row, 1971.

INDEX

Abolition of Man, The, 48, 129, 135, 179, 215–16, 226n.4; Christianity and, 119, 165; *The Control of Language* and, 73–84, 116, 178; language and, xii, xiii, 112; *The Magician's Nephew* and, 167, 169; *The Silver Chair* and, 150, 152, 154; Taoism and, 87, 98; *That Hideous Strength* and, 99, 103, 104–05, 106, 110; *The Voyage of the Dawn Treader* and, 144–45
Adey, Lionel, 6, 11
Agnosticism, 69, 188, 206
Ahoshta, 157
Alcasan, 95, 103, 106, 108
Allegory, 150, 152, 157, 171–72, 191; in *The Last Battle,* 176, 180, 181; in *The Pilgrim's Regress,* 12–13, 15–16, 18, 19, 24, 25, 125, 182; in *Prince Caspian,* 136, 138–40; in *The Voyage of the Dawn Treader,* 141–42, 145, 147
Allegory of Love, The, 114, 118, 130, 157, 158, 172, 173; metaphor and, 11, 12; Spenser and, 121–22, 126
Animal Farm, 111, 177
Animals, 141, 177–78, 200. *See also specific character names*
Ansit, 211
Anthroposophy, 6
Anvard, 159
Apuleius, 191, 195
Aravis, 158, 162, 163; marriage and, 148–49, 157, 159, 160–61
Archenland, 157, 158, 164
Archetypal criticism, x
Archetypes, 10, 117, 121, 123; metaphor and, 12, 13, 14–16, 22–23, 214

Argan, 196, 206
Aristotle, 81
Arnold, Matthew, 115
Arnom, 199, 211
Art, 15
Artistic techniques, 28
Aslan, 126; in *The Horse and His Boy,* 158, 159, 160, 161, 164; in *The Last Battle,* 175, 176, 177, 178, 179–80, 181; in *The Lion, the Witch, and the Wardrobe,* 128, 129, 130, 131, 132, 136; in *The Magician's Nephew,* 168, 169, 170, 171, 172; in *Prince Caspian,* 127, 133, 134, 135, 139; in *The Silver Chair,* 152, 154, 155, 156; in *The Voyage of the Dawn Treader,* 141, 143, 144, 148
Aslan's Country, 176
Aslan's How, 133
Aslan's Mountain, 124, 150–51, 153, 155
Aslan's Table, 147
Aunt Letty, 174
Ayer, A. J., 10, 183, 184, 210

Babbitt, Irving, 19
Bacchus, 138–39, 140, 151, 156
Badger, 125
Bardia, 192, 199, 204, 205, 206, 208
Barfield, Owen, xii, 6, 28, 45, 183, 191; *The Abolition of Man* and, 73, 74, 77, 78, 80, 81, 84; language and, 4, 7–11, 19, 41, 50, 70, 196; metaphor and, 12, 13–14, 66, 67; *That Hideous Strength* and, 89, 90, 98, 100, 101, 103, 104
Barth, Karl, 184–85
Battle of Beruna, 128

Behavior, 17, 23, 150, 152, 173, 176; in *The Abolition of Man*, 73–84; in the Chronicles of Narnia, 123, 125, 127; culture and, 34, 119, 120; in *The Horse and His Boy*, 149, 156, 159, 160, 164; language and, xi, 2, 5, 72; in *Out of the Silent Planet*, 40; in *Prince Caspian*, 135; in *That Hideous Strength*, 85, 97, 110

Belbury, 85, 93, 102–03, 104, 109, 110; allegory and, 86, 87, 88, 98, 105–06; setting and, 94–97

Bell, Clive, 15

Bell, Michael, xi, 32, 33, 38

Bern, 143

Bernardus Silvestris, 54–55, 58, 171–72

Biology, 215

Bism, 151, 155, 180

Black Hole, 17

"Bluspels and Flalansferes," 10–11, 24, 70

Boethius, Anicius Manlius Severinus, 23, 146

Bottomley, Horatio, 2

Bracton, Henry de, 89

Bracton College, 85, 88, 90–91, 93, 107, 136, 180; as setting, 94–96, 97, 98

Bragdon Wood, 91, 92, 93, 94, 96, 110

Breakfast of the Lamb, 142–43

Bree, 157, 160

Bridges, Robert, 3

Brittain, Vera, x–xi, 223n.8

Broadcast talks, 187

Brothers Grimm, 117

Bulgy bears, 137

Bultmann, Rudolf, 184, 185, 186, 187, 188, 189, 205

"Bulverism," 18, 209

Bunyan, John, 11, 23

Calormenes, 162–65, 175, 179, 180

Cartesianism, 94–95

Caspian, 133, 134, 135, 137, 138, 150, 151, 176; in *The Voyage of the Dawn Treader*, 140, 141, 143, 144, 147, 148, 180

Chastity, 148–49

Chaucer, Geoffrey, xvi, 113, 146, 217

Children, 124, 125, 127, 134, 135; Lewis's attitude toward, 118–19, 123, 126, 153

Christian humanism, 150, 181, 225n.1; Lewis and, 113–21, 123, 165, 167

Christian Reflections, 115

Christianity, 30, 31, 124, 139, 161; history and, 183–89; humanism and, 113–21, 123; in *The Last Battle*, 126, 176, 179, 181; Lewis and, ix, xi, xii, xiii, xiv, 1, 78, 86, 165–67, 216; in *The Lion, the Witch, and the Wardrobe*, 125, 130, 131–32; in *The Magician's Nephew*, 168–69, 172; in *Perelandra*, 57–62, 65–69; in *The Pilgrim's Regress*, 11–15, 22, 23; in *The Silver Chair*, 149, 151, 153; in *That Hideous Strength*, 92, 100–101, 105, 106; in *Till We Have Faces*, 182, 190–91, 193, 199, 204, 210–11, 212–13; in *The Voyage of the Dawn Treader*, 141–43, 147–48. *See also* Religion, Christian humanism

"Christianity and Culture," 115, 220n.6

"Christianity and Literature," 115

Christopher, Joe R., x

Chronicles of Narnia, the, xii–xiii, 25, 127, 150, 166, 215–16; humanism in, 113–24; language and, 111; symbolism in, 125–26. *See also individual titles*

Claptrap, 17

Class, 59–60, 101, 118, 177

Clevers, 16, 24

"Cliche Came Out of Its Cage, A," 178

Cognitive Thinking, 7, 120, 126, 216

Coleridge, Samuel Taylor, 7, 75, 183

Collingwood, R. G., 183, 189

Communism, 20

Consciousness, 45, 65, 68, 78, 157, 196; in *That Hideous Strength*, 99–100, 110

Conservatism, 163–64

Consolation of Philosophy, The, 23

Context of English Literature: 1900–1930, The, xi

Control of Language, The, xii, 72, 98, 119, 136, 150; *The Abolition of Man* and, 73–84, 116; *The Last Battle* and, 177, 178, 181; *The Lion, the Witch, and the Wardrobe* and, 128, 131

Controllers, 140, 148, 216

Coriakin, 144

Corin, 158, 159

Cosmic Dance, 152

Cosmic Intelligence, 7, 8
Cosmographia, The, 54–55, 171–72
Courtesy, 156
Culture, 41, 74, 119, 120, 165, 188, 200;
    Christian humanism and, 113, 115;
    Lewis and, 216, 217; literary theory
    and, 27–38
Curry, 91, 96
Cynicism, 112

Dante, 11, 65–66, 113, 151, 181, 217,
    219n.17; *The Voyage of the Dawn
    Treader* and, 146, 147
Dark Island, 143
Deathwater Island, 143
"De Descriptione Temporum," xi, 15
De legibus et consuetudinibus Angliae, 89
Deconstructionism, 216
Denniston, 100, 102, 108
Devine, Dick, 40, 42, 43, 63, 171
Dibelius, Martin, 185, 188
Diction, 200–203. *See also* Language
Didacticism, 120, 121, 122, 123
Digory, 166, 167, 168, 171, 172, 173, 174.
    See also Professor Kirke
Dimble, 86, 100, 102, 103, 108, 109
Director, the, 97–98, 101, 109
Discarded Image, The, 92, 96, 114
Disenchantment, 3
Divine Bridegroom, 212
Donne, John, 99
Dr. Cornelius, 136
Drudge, 20, 21, 23
Dufflepuds, 140, 143, 144, 174
"Dulce et Decorum Est," 3–4
Dulce et decorum tradition, 80, 81, 93
Dwarfs, 175, 176, 177, 181
Dyson, Hugo, 186

Eddison, E. R., 85
Edward, 159
Eldila, 54
Eliot, George, 32
Eliot, T. S., 16, 19, 25, 99, 116
Emerson, Ralph Waldo, 10
Emeth, 180
England's Hour, x

*English Literature in the Sixteenth
    Century,* 120–24, 140
Eschatology, 57, 63, 71
Eschropolis, 16
Euhemerism, 190, 194
Evans, B. Ifor, 27, 28–29, 30
Everyman, 13, 214
Evolution, 56, 57, 59; in *Perelandra,* 60,
    61, 63, 67, 69, 70, 71, 215
Experiment House 148, 150, 155
Experiment in Criticism, An, xii, 30, 33–34

Faerie Queene, The, 129, 130, 141, 144,
    158, 170, 172, 220n.8; the Chronicles of
    Narnia and, xiii, 121–26, 150, 166, 216
Fairy, 102, 112
Fairy Hardcastle, 106
Fairy tale, the, 37, 117, 123
Fantasy, 30, 36, 38, 100, 101, 165, 217
Farsight the Eagle, 178
Father Christmas, 130, 131, 139
Feverstone, 91, 102, 106, 110
Filostrato, 102, 106, 108, 225n.33
First Men in the Moon, 127, 155; *Out of
    the Silent Planet* and, xii, 39–47, 52–
    54, 215
Five Children and It, 127
Fixed Land, 60–61, 68
Foerster, Norman, 19
Ford, Paul F., 117
Formalism. *See* New Criticism
Fox, the, 193, 194, 200, 203, 213; Orual
    and, 192, 196, 197, 199, 204, 205, 206,
    207, 208, 211, 212
Frank, 167, 173
Free will, 205
Friendship, 148
Frost, 79, 87, 95, 104, 106

Gender, 101–02
Genesis, 61–62, 68, 87, 165–69, 172
Genre fiction, 215, 220n.3; Lewis and,
    27–38
George, 179
Giants, 151
Ginger, 180
Glenstorm the Centaur, 137

Glimfeather the Owl, 153
Glome, 191, 192, 193, 194, 198, 201
Glossop, 107
Glover, Donald E., 117, 131
Glozelle, 137–38
Glugly, 16
Goethe, Johann Wolfgang, 84
Goldwater Island, 144
Great Dance, 57
Great Divorce, The, xiv
Great Offering, 203
Green, Richard Lancelyn, 188
"Green Book, The." See *Control of Language, The*
Green Lady, the, 58–59
Green Witch, the, 151, 153
Greeves, Arthur, 100
Griesbach, J. J., 184
Griffiths, Dom Bede, 183
Gumpus, 143

Haggard, Rider, 3
Haigh, John D., x
Haldane, J. B. S., 41, 44, 86, 106, 110
Halfways, Gus, 15, 16
Harfang, 153, 155
Hegel, Georg Wilhelm Friedrich, 106. *See also* Hegelianism
Hegelianism, 6–7
Heinlein, Robert A., 53, 54, 221n.27
Helen, 167
Henty, George Alfred, 3
Hermit of the Southern March, the, 157, 158, 160, 164
Herodotus, 195
Hesperides, 26
Hierarchy, 140, 142, 144, 180; in *The Magician's Nephew,* 169–70; in *Perelandra,* 59–61, 71; in *That Hideous Strength,* 97–98
"High and Low Brows," 28–29, 74
Hingest, William, 93, 102, 106–07, 108
History, 182–89; *Till We Have Faces* and, 190–91, 193–201, 203, 204, 206, 209–11, 213, 216
History in English Words, 8
History the Hermit, 19, 20, 23, 212
Hobbit, The, 14

"Hollow Men, The," 25
Horse and His Boy, The, xiii, 124, 148–49, 162; 161, 163; imagery in, 164–65; Spenser and, 158, 160, 161, 163; theme in, 156, 157, 159
Hrossa, 45–49, 65
"Hugh Selwyn Mauberley," 4
Hulme, T. E., 19
Humanism, 113–16, 118. *See also* Christian humanism
Humor, 22–23
Huttar, Charles A., 166, 170
Huxley, Aldous, 72, 79
Hwin, 157, 160, 163
Hyoi, 49, 55

Idealism, 2–3, 19
Imagery, 69, 136, 172, 216, 217; in *The Horse and His Boy,* 149, 154–55, 164–65; in *The Lion, the Witch, and the Wardrobe,* 128, 129–30; in *The Pilgrim's Regress,* 16, 25–26; in *Till We Have Faces,* 196, 203; in *The Voyage of the Dawn Treader,* 140, 141–43, 146, 147
Imagination, 7, 11, 37, 191, 216
Imperialism, 47
Ironwood, Grace, 97, 102
Island of Desire, 13, 19–20, 24, 132
Istra, xiii. *See also* Psyche

Jadis, 167, 168, 169, 170–71, 172–73, 174. *See also* White Witch, the
Jesus, xiii, 183–84, 187, 188–89, 190
Jewel the Unicorn, 176, 178, 180
Joy, xiii, 124, 126–27, 140, 151, 182; in *The Lion, the Witch, and the Wardrobe,* 129, 131; in *Prince Caspian,* 132, 136
Joyce, James, 32–33, 36, 220n.12
John, 214; in *The Pilgrim's Regress,* 12–25, 49, 132, 182, 186
John Bull, 2
Judaism, 20
Jules, Horace, 87, 110
Julian of Norwich, 161
Jung, Carl Gustav, 10, 25, 91, 117, 121

Kepler, Johannes, 167

Ketley, Martin, xii, 86, 87, 102, 105, 216; *The Control of Language* and, 72–84, 116, 119, 128, 131, 136

King, Alec, xii, 86, 87, 102, 105, 216; *The Control of Language* and, 72–84, 116, 119, 128, 131, 136

Kirkpatrick, W. T., 151

Knowledge, 22, 78, 159, 179; *The Abolition of Man* and, 83, 84; humanism and, 113–14; imagination and, 11, 216; language and, 7–8, 10; in *The Magician's Nephew*, 167, 169; in *Out of the Silent Planet*, 41, 43; in *Perelandra*, 68, 70; in *The Silver Chair*, 124, 149, 150, 151–56; in *That Hideous Strength*, 91, 103, 106, 107, 109; in *Till We Have Faces*, 192, 197, 212

Korzybski, Alfred, 72

Lady Alice Quadrangle, 92, 95, 97

Landlord, 13, 14, 17, 21, 23

Language, xiii–xiv, 1–3, 116, 214–15; *The Abolition of Man* and, 74–84; Barfield and, 4, 6–10, 196; behavior and, xi, 5, 72–73; the Chronicles of Narnia and, 112–13, 119, 120, 124; culture and, 27, 217; literary theory and, x–xii, 30, 216; *Out of the Silent Planet* and, 39, 40–41, 47, 50–51, 55, 56, 127; *Perelandra* and, 56, 63, 65–70; *The Pilgrim's Regress*, 11–26; *Prince Caspian* and, 137; in *The Silver Chair*, 149, 153; *That Hideous Strength* and, 85–98, 99–107, 110–11; in *Till We Have Faces*, 182–83, 198, 199–204, 206, 208, 209, 210, 213; in *The Voyage of the Dawn Treader*, 142

Language, high evaluation, 6, 8, 73, 91

Language, low evaluation, 1, 4, 72, 73, 77, 80, 88, 95

Laplace, Pierre-Simon, 58

Lasaraleen, 157–58, 162

Last Battle, The, xiii, 124, 127, 167, 180, 181, 182; animals in, 141, 177–78; mortality in, 175–76; Revelation and, 165–66, 174; symbolism in, 126, 179

Law, 89–90, 110, 136

Lawrence, D. H., 16

"Learning in Wartime," 114, 115

Leavis, Q. D., 29, 33

Lewis, C. S., 62, 65, 66, 68, 70, 212; Christian humanism and, 113–18; *The Control of Language* and, 73–84; genre fiction and, 27–38, 215; hierarchy and, 59–60, 61, 71; history and, 183–89, 209; *The Horse and His Boy* and, 149, 156–64; language and, xi–xiv, 1–6, 10, 16, 39–41, 55, 72, 85–93, 99–107, 110–11, 112, 119, 214; *The Last Battle* and, 174–81; *The Lion, the Witch, and the Wardrobe* and, 127–31; literary theory and, ix–x, 48, 50–51, 216; *The Magician's Nephew* and, 168–73; "Modern Theology and Biblical Criticism" and, 204, 205; morality and, 43, 120; mutability and, 165–67; *Out of the Silent Planet* and, 42, 44–45; *Perelandra* and, 56–58, 63–64; *Prince Caspian* and, 132–39; religious metaphor and, 11–15, 17–26, 67, 69, 210–11; science and, 52–54, 108–09; setting and, 94–98; sexuality and, x; *The Silver Chair* and, 148, 150–55; social science and, 46–47, 49; Spenser and, 121–25, 217; *Till We Have Faces* and, 182, 190–203, 206–08, 213; *The Voyage of the Dawn Treader* and, 140–47; Wordsworth and, 126

Lewis, W. H., 94

Linguistics, xiii–xiv, 2, 119, 189, 222nn.31, 32; Barfield and, 81; in *Out of the Silent Planet*, 40, 55; in *Perelandra*, 56–57, 63; in *The Pilgrim's Regress*, 18–19; *That Hideous Strength* and, 86, 90; *Till We Have Faces* and, 184, 187, 206. *See also* Language

Lion, the Witch, and the Wardrobe, The, 118, 124, 156, 168, 180, 192; Aslan in, 136; children in, 125, 127, 134, 135; Christianity and, 126, 131–32, 139, 148; imagery in, 128–30, 154; Joy and, xiii; nature in, 133, 138

Literary theory, xi–xiv, 75; culture and, 27–38; humanism and, 115–16, 118; Lewis and, ix–x, xv–xvi, 51, 215, 216; *Out of the Silent Planet* and, 39, 47–50, 54

Literature, 107–08, 120; humanism and, 112–18
Logical atomism, 2
Logical positivism, 2, 19, 106, 183
Lone Islands, 143
Lord of the Rings, The, 174, 187, 207
Lune, 158, 159, 161, 163, 164, 180

MacDonald, George, 112
MacPhee, 86, 97–98, 102, 107, 108, 109
Magician's Nephew, The, xiii, 26, 124, 125, 182, 212; Genesis and, 165–69
Malacandra, 54–55, 63
Maledil, 59, 67, 68, 70, 98, 100, 105
Manlove, C. N., 117, 118
Marriage, 101
Marshwiggles, 155
Marxism, 21
Mass Man, 144, 177
Master Parrot, 18
Meaning of Meaning, The, 29, 183; language and, 8, 30, 50, 72, 75, 77, 84, 98; Lewis and, xii, 4, 6, 68, 112–13, 177
Media, 2
Meldilorn, 25, 54–55
Merlin, 73, 84, 87, 88, 100, 109
Merlin's Well, 91, 93, 96
Metaphor, 31, 80, 154, 218n.7; language and, 5, 7–10, 74, 83, 214; in *The Pilgrim's Regress*, 11–26; in *Perelandra*, 66–70; in *That Hideous Strength*, 87, 89–90, 98, 99, 100; in *Till We Have Faces*, 210–11
Milton, John, 113, 170, 172, 181, 217; *Perelandra* and, 58–59, 61–62, 68
Miracles: A Preliminary Study, 138
Miraz, 133, 137–38, 141, 163
"Modern Theology and Biblical Criticism," 187, 190, 204, 205
Modernism, 115, 116, 119, 151, 193, 218n.2; literary theory and, 32–33, 35, 189; *Out of the Silent Planet* and, 41, 49, 51; in *Perelandra*, 65, 215; in *The Pilgrim's Regress*, 16, 18, 25–26; in *That Hideous Strength*, 38, 73, 98, 100, 110, 111; in *The Voyage of the Dawn Treader*, 145, 146
Montague, C. E., 3

Morality, xii–xiii, 21, 118, 126, 139, 205, 215; in art, 31–32, 35, 116, 120; in *The Horse and His Boy*, 124, 157, 159; language and, 75–80, 82; in *The Lion, the Witch, and the Wardrobe*, 129, 130; in *The Magician's Nephew*, 171, 172, 173; in *Out of the Silent Planet*, 39–43, 47, 53; in *Perelandra*, 56, 63, 65, 68–69; in *The Silver Chair*, 149, 150; in *That Hideous Strength*, 86, 89, 90, 91, 92, 101, 102, 103, 105, 107
More, Paul Elmer, 19
Morris, William, 3
Mortality, 175, 176
Mother Kirk, 13, 21–23
Mr. Angular, 19, 21–22, 25
Mr. Beaver, 129, 134
Mr. Britling Sees It Through, 3
Mr. Broad, 21, 22
Mr. Enlightenment, 16–17, 18, 25
Mr. Halfways, 15, 49
Mr. Humanist, 19
Mr. Neo-Classical, 19
Mr. Sensible, 20, 21, 23, 25
Mr. Tumnus, 129, 131, 134
Mr. Wisdom, 19–20, 23, 24
Mrs. Beaver, 125, 160
Müller, Max, 8, 10
Mutability, 165–67, 170, 175
Myth, 30, 36, 46, 111, 123, 138, 217, 220n.12; history and, 182–84, 186, 187, 189; language and, 10, 38; *The Last Battle*, 177; in *The Lion, the Witch, and the Wardrobe*, 129, 131; in *Perelandra*, 63–64; in *The Pilgrim's Regress*, 24; in *The Silver Chair*, 156; in *That Hideous Strength*, 88, 99, 101; in *Till We Have Faces*, xiii, 190–95, 197, 199, 201, 203–4, 206, 209–13, 216; in *The Voyage of the Dawn Treader*, 140; Spenser and, 122, 126
Mythopoeism, ix–x, xiv, 36–37, 70

Narnia, 164–65
National Institute of Coordinated Experiments (N.I.C.E.), 85, 86, 90, 95, 104, 106, 107, 110

Natural law, 78, 80, 81–82, 84, 94–95. *See also* Tao

Naturalism, 2

Nature, 10, 124–30; in *The Last Battle*, 178; in *The Magician's Nephew*, 167, 169–70, 171–72, 173; in *Prince Caspian*, 133–34, 135, 138, 140; in *The Silver Chair*, 151; in *Till We Have Faces*, 194, 204, 205

Nesbit, E., 127–28, 161–62, 174

New Criticism, xiii, 49, 99, 185, 215, 216; language and, 72, 74–75

New Testament, 115

Newton, Isaac, 91–92, 167

Newton Quadrangle, 91–92, 93–94, 95, 96

Nikabrik, 136, 137

Nineteen Eighty-Four, 111, 174

Nominalism, 1

Objective Room, 98, 104

Occult, 20

Ogden, C. K., xii, xiii, 41, 50–51, 177, 183; language and, 4–12, 15, 17, 18, 22, 30, 72–77, 79, 81, 84, 112; *That Hideous Strength* and, 86, 87, 90, 103, 215

Old Priest, 197, 203, 204

"On Science Fiction," 36–37, 63

"On Three Ways of Writing for Children," 118

Ornamental Pleasure Grounds, 94

Orual, 199–204; Psyche and, 190, 191, 192, 198, 207–09, 212; in *Till We Have Faces*, xiii, 182, 193–97, 205, 206, 210–11, 216

Orwell, George, 110–11, 174, 177

Out of the Silent Planet, 25, 30, 48–49, 55, 105, 171; *First Men in the Moon* and, xii, 39–47, 52–54, 215; language and, 38, 50–51, 56, 65, 82, 85, 127; *Perelandra* and, 58, 59, 63, 68, 71

Owen, Wilfred, 3

Oxford University, 114

Oyarsa, 40, 44, 45, 54, 55, 58; Weston and, 47, 50, 68, 82

Oyéresu, 87–88, 109

Paradise Lost, 58–59, 61, 123, 170, 188

Parliament of Owls, 155

Pattertwig the Squirrel, 136

Pendragon, 96, 99

Perception, 45, 48, 100, 182, 207–08

Perelandra, 25–26, 48, 105; evolution in, 56, 57, 59, 60, 61, 63, 67, 69, 70, 71; language and, 38, 65, 66, 68, 85; *The Time Machine* and, xii, 37, 58, 62, 64, 215

Perennial philosophy, 20

Pevensie, Edmund, 127–29, 132, 163; in *Prince Caspian*, 134, 135, 138, 139; in *The Voyage of the Dawn Treader*, 140, 141, 142, 144, 146, 148

Pevensie, Lucy, 128–29, 132, 133, 134, 135, 137, 139; in *The Voyage of the Dawn Treader*, 140, 141, 144–45, 148

Pevensie, Peter, 140, 142, 163, 181; in *The Lion, the Witch, and the Wardrobe*, 127–29, 130, 132, 192; in *Prince Caspian*, 133, 134, 135, 137, 138, 139

Pevensie, Susan, 134, 135, 137, 139, 158, 161, 163, 181; in *The Lion, the Witch, and the Wardrobe*, 127–29, 130

Pfifltriggi, 45, 48

Pfleiderer, Otto, 188

Phally, 16

Philology, 2, 58, 77, 122, 127, 184, 189; in *Out of the Silent Planet*, 40, 46, 49, 51, 54–56; in *That Hideous Strength*, 85, 89, 91, 107, 108

Philosophy, 20, 112–13, 116, 119, 122, 216, 217; in the Chronicles of Narnia, 127, 128; in *The Control of Language*, 76, 78; in *The Last Battle*, 176; in *Out of the Silent Planet*, 51, 53; in *Perelandra*, 56; in *The Pilgrim's Regress*, 186; in *Prince Caspian*, 136; in *The Screwtape Letters*, 144; in *That Hideous Strength*, 104; in *Till We Have Faces*, 195, 205

Pilgrim's Progress, The, 11, 23, 188

Pilgrim's Regress, The, 49, 52, 132, 179, 211, 212; allegory in, 114, 182; language and, xii, 1–2; metaphor in, 11–26, 186, 190, 214; *The Silver Chair* and, 151, 154; symbolism in, 80, 125

Plato, 78–79, 113, 168, 189, 193, 217. *See also* Platonism

Platonism, 7, 11, 92, 99, 151, 153, 180, 181; Lewis and, x, 19, 44, 50–51, 63, 68, 78,

Platonism (*continued*)
114, 120, 123, 171; Richards and, 30, 99, 103

Poetic Diction, xii, 4, 6, 7, 8, 218n.9; metaphor and, 12, 67, 70; *The Abolition of Man* and, 74, 77, 78, 80, 81, 84; *That Hideous Strength* and, 90, 98, 104

Poggin, 178

Pole, Jill, 149, 150, 152, 153, 154, 155, 175, 178

Polly, 166, 173

Popular culture: literary theory and, 27–38. *See also* Genre fiction

Pound, Ezra, 4

Practical Criticism, 30, 34, 50

Pragmatometer, 38

Preface to "Paradise Lost," A, 30, 61–62, 116, 120

Pre-Raphaelites, 16

Prince Caspian, 125, 126, 137, 148, 156, 163, 169; hierarchy in, 140, 143; Joy and, xiii, 127, 132, 136; nature and, 133–34, 135, 138–39

Principles of Literary Criticism, xii, 15, 16, 19, 68, 69, 77; culture and, 28, 30–31, 35, 36

Professor Kirke, 127–28, 132, 168. *See also* Digory

Propaganda, 77, 79, 82

Psittacism, 5, 18

Psyche, 193, 195, 204, 205, 206, 210, 211, 213; Orual and, 190, 191, 192, 198–99, 200, 201, 207–09, 212

Psychological realism, 88, 101, 209

Psychology, 17–18, 34, 110–11, 116, 150, 197

Ptolemy, 195

Puddleglum the Marshwiggle, 151, 152, 153, 154

Puzzle the Donkey, 125–26, 175, 176, 178, 179

Qoholeth, 181

Rabadash, 158, 159, 161, 162, 164

Ramandu's Island, 147

Ransom, 127, 171, 192, 215; in *Out of the Silent Planet*, 40–50, 52, 54–55; in *Perelandra*, 56–70, 91; in *That Hideous Strength*, 73, 85, 99–100, 108, 109

Realism, 6, 35–36, 123, 165, 188; in *That Hideous Strength*, 88, 100, 215; in *Till We Have Faces*, xiii, 191, 195, 196, 199, 201, 213

Reason, 1, 18, 22, 25

Redival, 211

Reilly, R. J., ix, 117, 191

Reepicheep the Mouse, 137 141, 145–46, 147

Rehabilitations and Other Essays, 10, 30

Religion, 30–32, 35, 126, 131, 137; in *The Last Battle*, 176, 177; Lewis and, ix, xi, xii, xiii, xiv, 1, 114, 122–23, 126; in *Out of the Silent Planet*, 41, 56; in *The Pilgrim's Regress*, 11–26; in *That Hideous Strength*, 92, 101, 105, 109; in *Till We Have Faces*, 197–98, 204, 206. *See also* Christianity

Republic, The, 78–79

Republic Quadrangle, 96

Revelation, 165–67, 174

Richards, I. A., xii, xiii, 128, 177, 216; culture and, 28, 30–36, 115, 116; language and, 4–12, 15–19, 22, 72–77, 79, 84, 112, 120, 203; *Out of the Silent Planet* and, 39, 41, 48, 50–51; *Perelandra* and, 68–69; *That Hideous Strength* and, 86, 87, 90, 215; *Till We Have Faces* and, 183, 185, 188

Riddell Memorial Lectures, 73, 94

Rilian, 150, 151, 152, 153, 55, 176, 180

Roads, 19–20

Romanticism, x, 15 16, 18, 19, 20, 44

Roonwit the Centaur, 178, 180

Rules, 19–20

Russell, Bertrand, 2

Sayers, Dorothy L., 28–29, 30

Schakel, Peter J., 117, 121, 131

Schmidt, K. L., 185

Schweitzer, Albert, 184

Science, 74, 82–84, 128, 144, 151, 215; in *Out of the Silent Planet*, 39, 41, 51–56; in *Perelandra*, 56, 60–61, 63–64, 68–

69; religion and, 183–84, 185, 188; in *That Hideous Strength*, 73, 85, 86, 87, 90, 104, 105–07, 108, 109, 110; *The Last Battle* and, 177, 179; *The Magician's Nephew* and, 167, 170, 171, 172, 173; *Till We Have Faces* and, 206, 208, 209, 210

Science and Poetry, 30, 31–32

Science fiction, 36, 37, 117, 190, 192, 217; development of, xii, 30, 38, 39, 47, 51, 53, 54, 55, 73; *That Hideous Strength* and, 88, 108, 215

Screwtape, 144

Screwtape Letters, The, xiii–iv, 144

Scrubb, Eustace, 149, 150, 152, 175, 178; in *The Voyage of the Dawn Treader*, 140, 141–46, 148

Secularism, 113

Sehnsucht, 123

Seroni, 45–47

Setting, 93–98, 141

Sexuality, 197, 198, 207

Shakespeare, William, 81, 133, 154, 163, 189, 201

Shasta-Cor, 149, 157, 158–59, 161, 162, 164

Shelley, Percy Bysshe, 7

Shepherd People, 20

Shift, 175, 176, 177, 179, 180

Sidney, Philip, 119–20, 150

Sigismund (Sigmund), 17–18

Silenus, 140, 151

Silver Chair, The, xiii, 26, 124, 148–49, 155, 165, 180; knowledge and, 150, 151, 152–54, 156

Silver Sea, 147

Sitz im Leben, 185, 187

Social Darwinism, 47

Social science, 46–47, 49, 83, 86, 215

"Sometimes Fairy Stories May Say Best What's to Be Said," 117

Sopespian, 137

Sorns, 48–49, 54

Spenser, Edmund, 113, 148–49, 170, 173, 180; *The Horse and His Boy* and, 157, 158, 160, 161, 163, 164, 165; Lewis and, xiii, 118, 121–26, 182, 216, 217; *The Lion, the Witch, and the Wardrobe* and, 128, 130, 131; *Prince Caspian* and, 133, 136, 138; *The Silver Chair* and, 150, 151, 155; *The Voyage of the Dawn Treader* and, 140, 141, 143, 146

Spenser's Images of Life, 123

Spirit of the Age, 14, 17, 18, 19, 22, 185, 214, 215

St. Anne's-on-the-Hill, 85–86, 87, 88, 93, 96–97, 102

Stapledon, Olaf, 41

Steiner, Rudolf, 6, 84

Stewards, 17, 21, 22

Stone Table, 131. *See also* Aslan's How

Straik, 106

Strauss, David Friedrich, 183–84

Structure, 56–57, 123, 140, 141

Studdock, Jane, 81, 84, 88, 93, 104, 108, 126; language and, 73, 85, 98–102, 105, 112; perception and, 96, 97, 145

Studdock, Mark, 79, 84, 85, 89, 93, 100, 103, 106; language and, 73, 88, 98–99, 102, 104–05, 110, 112; perception and, 95, 96, 97

Superbia, 19, 23

Surprised by Joy, x, 6, 7, 24–25, 177, 181, 182, 185, 186–87; the Chronicles of Narnia and, 119, 126–27; Lewis and, 182, 185; 186–87

Symbolism, 5, 92, 97, 116, 126, 146, 149; in *The Last Battle*, 177, 179; in *The Magician's Nephew*, 171, 173; in *The Pilgrim's Regress*, 12–15, 125; in *The Silver Chair*, 151–52; in *Till We Have Faces*, 198, 210; in *The Voyage of the Dawn Treader*, 144–45

Syncretism, 122

Tao, the, 78, 116, 139, 169, 171, 180, 181; *The Abolition of Man* and, 80–82, 83; *The Silver Chair* and, 150, 152; *That Hideous Strength* and, 87–90, 93, 98, 100, 101, 105, 109–111; *The Voyage of the Dawn Treader* and, 144, 145

Tarin, 211

Tash, 175, 177

Tashbaan, 164

Tautology, 103–04

Teaching, ix

Technology. *See* Science

Telmarines, 133, 134, 135, 139

Temptation, 61–62, 67–69, 70

Tennyson, Alfred Lord, 3

That Hideous Strength, 48, 79, 81, 108–09, 126, 136, 145; language and, xii, 38, 47, 73, 85–92, 99–107, 110–11, 112; Lewis and, 84, 116–17, 215; setting in, 93–98

Theism, 119, 184, 185

Theme, 156, 159, 162, 163; Spenser and, 157, 158, 160, 161, 164–65

Theology, 165

Theosophy, 20

Till We Have Faces, xiii, 182, 196, 205, 207; history and, 184–89, 197–98, 216; language and, 56, 183, 199–204, 206, 208, 209, 210; myth and, 190–95, 211–12, 213

Time Machine, The, 155; *Perelandra* and, xii, 37, 56–58, 60–61, 62–63, 64, 67, 71

Tinidril, 60, 62, 67–68, 70, 71, 105; Ransom and, 57, 59, 61, 64, 65, 66

Tirian, 175, 177, 178, 179

Tolkien, J. R. R., 14, 41, 121, 122, 136, 187; genre fiction and, 29–30; myth and, 186, 219n.13

Tone, 156

Tor, 60–62, 105

Tortured Planet, The, 85

Tractatus LogicoPhilosophicus, 2

Traditionalism, xi

Transcendentalism, 7

Trufflehunter the Badger, 137

Trumpkin the Dwarf, 133, 134, 137, 139, 150, 153

Ulf, Fenris, 130

Ulysses, 32–33, 36

Uncle Andrew, 165, 167, 168, 169, 171, 172–73, 174

Underland, 150, 155

Ungit, 196, 198, 201, 203, 210; Orual and, 197, 199, 207, 211

Unity, 136

Un-man, 63; Tinidril and, 57, 60, 61–62, 66, 68–70

Urban, Wilbur M., 1

Venus, 63–64, 87, 101

Verne, Jules, 37

Vertue, 22, 23

Victoriana, 16

"Vivisection," 170

Voyage of the Dawn Treader, The, 125, 144–45, 148, 165, 174, 180, 216; *The Faerie Queen* and, 121, 127, 163; imagery in, 141–43, 146–47; Joy and, xiii, 140

Waddington, C. H., 77

Wain, John, xi

Walsh, Chad, ix, 221n.21

"Waste Land, The," 16, 25

Well at the World's End, The, 3

Wells, H. G., xii, 3, 37, 85, 127, 155, 215; *Out of the Silent Planet* and, 39–47, 52–54; *Perelandra* and, 56–58, 60–61, 62–63, 64, 67, 71

Weston, 43, 47, 61, 63, 66, 82, 105, 171; language and, 50–51; Ransom and, 42, 46, 68, 69; science and, 40, 41

"What Christians Believe," 187

White Witch, the, 128, 129, 130, 131, 132, 134, 135, 168. *See also* Jadis

Williams, Charles, 85, 88, 89, 99, 100, 101, 192

Wither, 87, 96, 102, 103, 106

Wittgenstein, Ludwig, 2

Wood Between the Worlds, 171–72

Wordsworth, William, 126–27, 129, 134

World War I, x, xiii, 24–25, 167, 176, 177, 184; language and, xii, 1–4, 6, 17, 27

World War II, x–xi, xiii, 2, 82, 167, 174

Wrede, William, 187